WE WILL NOT BE STRANGERS

nights and longings and desires and thou...
So many ideas g... ... ...d a
read - memories, ...
philosophy - you ... ...
evoke all these, t... ... more
all my love - we ... ...re s...
not be strangers ... ...
for we give all, ...
now, so many ni... ...hen
continue to grow ... do
"outward" together, ...

It is late ... ...
at the crack of dawn - have a bit
work to cram in before I leave at 7...

I have so many things to tell you
always - the desire to share every
minute aspect of life with you.

I shall whisper them as I crawl in
bed thinking of you beside me, feel...
your warmth and vitality. Goodnight
husband. I love you.

WE WILL NOT BE STRANGERS

KOREAN WAR LETTERS BETWEEN A

M.A.S.H. SURGEON AND HIS WIFE

Edited by Dorothy G. Horwitz

Foreword by James I. Matray

University of Illinois Press
Urbana and Chicago

Library of Congress Cataloging-in-Publication Data
Horwitz, Dorothy G. (Dorothy Gotterer), 1928–
We will not be strangers : Korean War letters between a M.A.S.H. surgeon
and his wife / edited by Dorothy G. Horwitz ; foreword by James Matray.
p.   cm.
ISBN 0-252-02204-1 (alk. paper)
1. Horwitz, Dorothy G. (Dorothy Gotterer), 1928–   —Correspondence.
2. Horwitz, Mel—Correspondence.
3. Korean War, 1950–1953—Personal narratives, Americans.
4. Korean War, 1950–1953—Americans.
I. Horwitz, Mel. II. Title.
DS921.6.H68   1997
951.904'2—dc20   96-35654
                                        CIP

CONTENTS

Illustrations follow pages 2, 92, and 202

FOREWORD

James I. Matray

Dorothy and Melvin Horwitz were living the "American Dream" when the Korean War began in June 1950. Their grandparents had immigrated to the United States from Eastern Europe in the late nineteenth century seeking religious freedom, civil rights, and economic opportunity. Mine did too, although they would settle in Chicago rather than New York City. But Dorothy and Mel were not ordinary Americans. After finishing high school in wartime Brooklyn, both graduated from prestigious universities with the education needed to pursue upwardly mobile professional careers. Highly intelligent and deeply thoughtful, these two young people were careful and astute observers of domestic and international politics. They enjoyed reading a wide assortment of literature, enthusiastically seeking exposure to culture and the arts. But it was the writing talent of these two extraordinary people that helped them endure forced separation during the Korean War.

We Will Not Be Strangers records how two Jewish-Americans in their mid-twenties and married for barely one year reacted to the daily unpleasantness and frequent horror of war. Dorothy and Mel's wartime letters describe feelings and experiences that were typical for those fighting in Korea and their spouses waiting back home. Wars always bring the tragedies of death and destruction, but for different reasons. A large majority of Americans would agree that World War II was a "good war" because great sacrifices were necessary and justified to destroy the Axis powers. Other American wars rarely if ever have generated the same high level of popular unity and clarity of national purpose. While the Vietnam War may illustrate this point best, the "police action" fought in Korea was perhaps more unpopular and divisive than any earlier war in American history.

Swiftly and strangely forgotten, the Korean conflict caused more American deaths during three years than the Vietnam War, where U.S. soldiers died for more than a decade. Recent studies have demonstrated that the Korean conflict was a pivotal event in the Cold War. Dorothy and Mel's letters add to this literature a unique and illuminating perspective on the war before Vietnam.

Doctor Melvin Horwitz arrived at his M.A.S.H. (Mobile Army Surgical Hospital) unit in Korea during July 1952, after the war had reached a stalemate not only on the battlefield but also at the negotiating table. "The country is rugged, craggy mountains jutting up precipitously, smaller hills breaking up the valleys," Mel writes Dorothy in an early letter. "It is hellish country to fight in. It was difficult enough to drive through." Two years before Mel's arrival, Communist North Korea launched an invasion across the 38th parallel to reunite the peninsula. President Harry S. Truman committed U.S. ground troops to block the conquest of all Korea on June 30, 1950, after South Korea's army failed to stop North Korea's advance. Although two United Nations resolutions sanctioned U.S. intervention, the president did not ask Congress for a declaration of war, agreeing with a journalist's description of Korea as a "police action." During July, more U.S. troops and supplies flooded into Korea, but the Communist advance continued southward until U.N. forces under the command of General Douglas MacArthur had retreated to the Pusan Perimeter, a rectangular area in the southeast corner of the Korean peninsula.

Despite facing a seemingly desperate situation, MacArthur was confident that a battlefield victory was inevitable, boldly proposing a counteroffensive in coordination with an amphibious landing behind enemy lines to repel the invaders, preparatory to military conquest of North Korea. Truman and his advisors shared MacArthur's confidence, but a decision to cross the 38th parallel in pursuit of forcible reunification came only after a month of debate. Preventing renewed aggression required destroying North Korea's army, but State Department officials could not resist the temptation to win a propaganda victory in the Cold War. Military occupation of North Korea would permit the U.N. to supervise free elections for a government to rule a united Korea, presumably with close economic and political ties to the United States. American military leaders initially favored only reestablishing the prewar status quo, but reluctantly endorsed these new war aims in late July after defensive lines stabilized. When MacArthur staged the first U.N. counterattack on August 7, Truman already had decided to authorize the politically popular invasion of North Korea.

On September 15, 1950, MacArthur successfully implemented a brilliant counteroffensive, staging an amphibious landing at the port of Inchon on the west coast of Korea. U.N. forces liberated Seoul about thirty miles to the east and soon were poised for an advance across the 38th parallel. American leaders realized that extending hostilities northward risked Soviet or Chinese military intervention and perhaps a global war, but grossly underestimated the danger. Recently, Beijing and Moscow have released documents and personal accounts revealing that the Soviet Union and China were aware of North Korea's plan to conquer South Korea and gave consent for the invasion. After Inchon, Communist leaders viewed the impending U.N. advance into North Korea as a grave threat to China's national security. Beijing already was upset that Truman had deployed the U.S. Seventh Fleet into the Taiwan Strait after the outbreak of the Korean War, thus blocking elimination of the Nationalist redoubt on Taiwan. A month later, MacArthur visited the island and announced preparations to strengthen the military capabilities of Chiang Kai-shek's regime. Then, much to Truman's chagrin, the militantly anti-Communist general sent a message to the Veterans of Foreign Wars that seemed to threaten Beijing.

Communist leaders in China had tried to avoid war with the United States. On October 2, Foreign Minister Zhou Enlai warned India's ambassador that China would intervene if American forces crossed the 38th parallel. Administration officials thought the Chinese were bluffing. MacArthur told Truman during a personal meeting at Wake Island on October 15 that "if the Chinese tried to get down to Pyongyang [North Korea's capital] there would be the greatest slaughter." Even after the first clash between U.N. soldiers and Chinese "volunteers" later that month, the general remained supremely confident, despite his anger over Washington's refusal on November 8 to approve bombing in Manchuria because of British objections. On November 24, MacArthur launched his "Home by Christmas Offensive," placing American troops in the vanguard of the assault in violation of precautionary instructions. Two days later, China counterattacked in force, sending U.N. troops into a massive retreat. An atmosphere of supreme crisis gripped Washington as Truman declared a state of national emergency.

Chinese military intervention resulted in Truman's adoption of a "limited war" strategy in Korea to achieve the original goal of restoring the prewar status quo. MacArthur objected, arguing strenuously that escalation or evacuation were the only options. By March 1951, however, General Matthew B. Ridgway, as the newly appointed ground commander, had proven that the administration's "limited war" strategy was feasible, driving Chinese forces back into North Korea. Truman now planned to propose a cease-fire, but MacArthur scuttled this peace initiative when he issued a public ultimatum to the Chinese Communists with a humiliating demand for immediate surrender. This was the final act of insubordination, Truman later claimed, forcing his decision to recall MacArthur on April 11, thereby igniting a firestorm of public criticism. But recently declassified documents have revealed that Truman did not want the general in charge of atomic weapons he was preparing for use in Korea. Coming home to ticker-tape parades, MacArthur gave a televised speech to a joint session of Congress, declaring that there was "no substitute for victory." By then most Americans doubted the wisdom of continuing to fight "Mr. Truman's War."

Meanwhile, U.N. forces had repulsed two Chinese offensives, fashioning defensive positions along the Kansas-Wyoming line just north of the 38th parallel. A developing military stalemate now evidently persuaded the belligerents to seek an armistice. After Soviet U.N. Ambassador Jacob Malik publicly endorsed a cease-fire, armistice talks opened on July 10 at Kaesong. Nasty negotiations ensued, contributing to the Communists suspending talks for two months on the pretext of protesting alleged U.N. violation of the neutral zone. General Ridgway agreed to resume talks in October, after forcing movement of the negotiating site to Panmunjom. The delegates quickly agreed that the demilitarized zone would follow the line of battle, but then haggled over inspection procedures to enforce the truce. Rapid approval of a postwar conference to discuss the withdrawal of foreign troops and reunification early in 1952 brought talk of peace, but then the negotiations became hopelessly deadlocked on the issue of repatriation of prisoners of war. Truman adopted an inflexible stance on the principle of nonforcible repatriation, while the Communists demanded return of all prisoners, as the Geneva Convention required.

Mutual abandonment of victory as a war aim and pursuit of an early cease-fire dramatically altered the character of the Korean War. During the first year of fighting, the conflict was dynamic and volatile, with rapid shifts on the battlefield and excessive optimism causing tragic miscalculations. In sharp contrast, the second year resembled World War I, with a static battlefront and armies relying on barbed wire, trenches, artillery, and mortars. Both sides emphasized achievement and maintenance of defense in depth, increasing troop levels and stockpiling equipment behind the front line. At Panmunjom, the Communists waged a propaganda campaign to turn world opinion against the Americans, charging that the United States was practicing bacteriological warfare in Korea and brutally mistreating Communist prisoners of war. To force acceptance of a truce on American terms, the United States resorted to expanded air operations against North Korea. During the summer of 1952, massive U.S. bombing raids smashed the Suiho hydroelectric plant and destroyed the city of Pyongyang.

July 1952 marked both the start of a third year of fighting in the Korean War and the beginning of the nine months of wartime correspondence between Dorthy and Mel Horwitz contained in this volume. Readers will find that the letters provide an abundance of details about everyday activities, expressions of affection, and confessions about personal foibles and fears. But they also include much information that enhances our understanding of the broader significance of the Korean War. "Exchanging accounts of our work, concerns, hopes, and loneliness," Dorothy recalls, "we moved from determined optimism to restless frustration." Those Americans, Koreans, and Chinese who had reason to be interested in the Korean War ironically experienced an identical emotional transformation during the conflict's first two years. Mel does not mention it directly, but when the Communists rejected a U.N. proposal to end the deadlock at Panmunjom early in October 1952, the truce talks adjourned for a period of more than six months.

Silence at Panmunjom came as fighting continued for a third year in a conflict that had become a monotonous war of position and attrition. Military stalemate reduced warfare almost exclusively to routine patrols, probing operations, and occasional forays against enemy positions. Mel Horwitz records how a constant stream of wounded American soldiers arrived at his M.A.S.H. units, many with horrific injuries. "I was just walking through the admitting ward looking at a pt. [patient] brought in by helicopter," he writes Dorothy. "More horror. Both arms and legs gone—both eyes injured. I wonder if we are doing good by saving people like that." Soon he would confess that "I've had enough surgery. Enough cutting out blasted bodies, torn muscles and shattered bones, arms and legs. An amputation is no longer surgery to me." War's carnage has repelled other doctors, but death and destruction in Korea seemed without purpose. "Back and forth," Mel laments in another letter. "Lose a hill. Win one. It doesn't solve anything. Even if we pushed them back to the Yalu, we'd still have to sit there as we do now here."

Mel could have served in any war and grumbled about comrades who " 'desire to stay continuously drunk' and the constant talk of women and fornication." Soldiers throughout history could agree that "after a while we can think of nothing except our families and all we want is to go home." Any other war would have created for Dorothy the "overwhelming desire to know exactly what he was doing." To be sure, Mel and Dorothy "acted like any young couple separated by events over which they had no control." What caused Dorothy to refer to Korea as "this crazy situation," however, was "the effect of being trapped in a war that we didn't believe in." These two political liberals doubted whether the war in Korea was a necessary "defense of our free institutions" against "Russia's aggressive intentions," attributing popular acceptance of this justification to McCarthyism. "Who is responsible for having you at one end of the world and me at the other?" Dorothy would ask, "and for all those poor guys whom you see? . . . Who got us into this damn mess?" Struggling to understand the Korean War, Mel would write that "I do not say that we should not fight aggression, but is that what we are doing here? Are we gaining anything? Have we exhausted every other possibility? God I hate this business. Destruction. Waste of men, lives, money, time. I hate to work in a rubber apron as blood and dirt spills over me."

Young American soldiers also wondered why they were fighting and dying in Korea. While "the Soviet soldier gets eight hours of political lectures a week," Mel explains, the "US soldier gets a few posters and movies. . . . No wonder it is difficult to find reasons for this police action in Korea. Although morale here is generally good, each man feels . . . he is serving a term. Among the wounded, there is never any regret about leaving Korea or the battle—just about leaving the other men in their units. There is no desire to fight the enemy or to crush them—just to survive." Accidents caused countless wounds. "One never knows," Mel admits, "whether it was self-inflicted or not." Wartime attitudes at home mirrored profound battlefield indifference. Dorothy recalls how "the *Vancouver Sun* had run the same Korean War dispatch on its front page three days in a row. Not one of its 500,000 readers responded to the 'error.' Mel and I were convinced that no one believed in this war." "I was glad to be leaving," Mel confesses in April 1953, "Yet the feeling was more one of relief." Korea taught the unlearned lesson before Vietnam that the United States must choose its wars carefully. Popular support requires clearly defined goals that advance and protect the nation's interests.

Angry American voters elected Dwight D. Eisenhower president in

November 1952 in large part because they expected him to end a very unpopular war in Korea. Mel and Dorothy voted for Adlai E. Stevenson, having decided that "Ike seems to be short-sighted and merely following the Republican line." Eisenhower would fulfill his campaign pledge to visit Korea in December, concluding that further ground assaults would be futile. Mel and Dorothy would have been appalled had they known of Eisenhower's decision early in 1953 to signal the Communists that the alternative to a truce was an expanded war, employing atomic weapons. These threats may have influenced Beijing, but some experts argue that because of rising economic distress the Chinese already had decided to make peace once Truman left office. Soviet leader Joseph Stalin's death on March 5 added to China's sense of political vulnerability and caused the Communist delegation to break the logjam at Panmunjom later that month. Shortly after the Communists accepted the U.N. proposal to exchange sick and wounded prisoners, Dorothy and Mel Horwitz were reunited in Japan, ending their exchange of letters.

Achievement of the Korean armistice came as a postscript to the Horwitz's wartime correspondence. Two months after the truce talks resumed in April 1953, the belligerents agreed to turn over prisoners refusing repatriation to a committee of neutral nations. On July 27, 1953, the signing of an armistice agreement ended the Korean War. Few Americans understood that the goal of U.S. policy in Korea since World War II had been the creation of a united nation with a government that reflected the U.S. model of political, economic, and social development. In pursuit of this aim, the United States paid a steadily increasing price, as it later did in Vietnam. Mel and Dorothy knew that to wage a war for the building of democracy was foolish, urging instead "world attempts to equalize the standard of living." During the Korean War, Congress approved the kind of costly rearmament program that Mel and Dorothy deplored. Perhaps worse, South Korea and Taiwan became American protectorates, even though, as Mel succinctly states, Syngman "Rhee is a tyrant and as fascistic as Chiang." Americans quickly forgot Korea because the experiences there were so painfully unpleasant. Readers will find that the letters between Dorothy and Mel Horwitz offer a poignant way and multiple reasons for remembering the Korean War.

WE WILL NOT BE STRANGERS

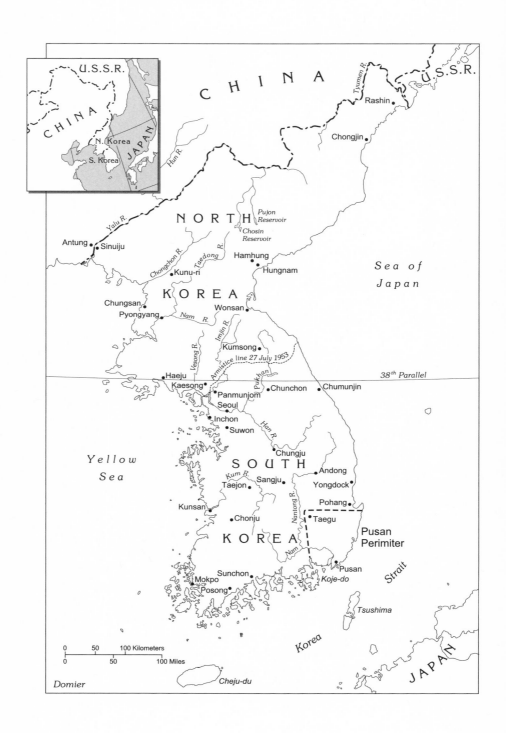

U.S.S.R.

CHINA

N. Korea

S. Korea

JAPAN

Tyumen R.

CHINA

U.S.S.R.

Rashin

Chongjin

NORTH

Pujon
Reservoir

Chosin
Reservoir

Yalu R.

Hun R.

Antung • Sinuiju

Chongchon R.

Taedong R.

Hamhung

Kunu-ri

Hungnam

*Sea of
Japan*

KOREA

Chungsan

Pyongyang

Wonsan

Nam R.

Vesong R.

Imjin R.

Kumsong

Armistice line 27 July 1953

Pukhan R.

38th Parallel

Haeju
Kaesong

Chunchon

Chumunjin

Panmunjom
Seoul

Inchon

Suwon

Han R.

*Yellow
Sea*

Chungju

SOUTH

Andong

Kum R.

Taejon

Sangju

Yongdock

Nantong R.

Pohang

Kunsan

Chonju

Taegu

Pusan
Perimiter

KOREA

Nam R.

Sunchon

Mokpo

Posong

Pusan

Koje-do

Strait

Tsushima

0   50   100 Kilometers

0   50   100 Miles

Korea

JAPAN

Domier

Cheju-du

INTRODUCTION

America's "forgotten war," the Korean War, lasted for three years. From 1950 to 1953 almost six million Americans served and over fifty-four thousand died. North and south of the 38th parallel altogether three million Koreans, mostly civilians, perished, along with five thousand allied troops and nine-hundred thousand Chinese. The war devastated Korea and brought wartime economic controls to the United States. "No one knows where to place it," said historian Bruce Cumings, "in the victory or lost column . . . the war and its memories drifted off into a void." In July 1995, forty-two years after the end of the war, the first national Korean War Memorial was dedicated in Washington, D.C., to honor the Americans who defended "a country they never knew and a people they never met."

During the conflict, American newspapers relegated grim fights and casualty rates to inside pages. Television was in its infancy. No nightly accounts of the battles appeared on the networks. People at home remained indifferent or calm in their conviction of a just cause, unless they had loved ones in uniform. Behind the front lines, at Mobile Army Surgical Hospitals (M.A.S.H.), surgeons debrided wounds and amputated limbs, working around the clock to save lives.

In blood-smeared apron and gloves, my husband Mel operated at one of these units in a dusty hospital tent. Adjusting to primitive conditions and army medicine, he vacillated between feeling useful and helpless, wanting to work, yet being repelled by the carnage. I lived in a comfortable Manhattan apartment with my recently widowed mother. At a Long Island junior high school, I taught Spanish and English in an atmosphere apathetic to the war and overcast by shadows of McCarthyism. Pursuing normalcy, I thrust myself into work, social rounds with family and friends, and the cultural life of the city.

Late in the nineteenth century, our grandparents had migrated with their families from Russia and Austria-Hungary to escape pogroms and economic deprivation. My maternal grandfather came to avoid serving in the Russian Army. That first generation of our ancestors to arrive in America settled in Manhattan and on Long Island. They worked as tailors or operated small dry goods stores or lunch places. Our parents were born on the Lower East Side of the city, except for Mel's mother, who at age eleven, had walked across Europe "following the crowds" of Russian immigrants. As soon as they had scraped together enough cash, our grandparents moved their families to the "country" in Brooklyn, where Mel and I were born and grew up.

We lived around the corner from each other in a quiet, middle-class Jewish neighborhood. We met at Midwood High School in 1941. On weekend nights, we jitterbugged and played Monopoly with friends in one another's homes. After high school, Mel enrolled at Columbia and I entered Bucknell. We didn't see each other for seven years. By that time Mel was in his surgical residency at Yale–New Haven Hospital, while I worked as an assistant buyer at Bloomingdale's. Mel's oldest friend had become engaged and passed on his "little black book" to Mel, who looked up that "skinny dark one from East 24th Street." One and a half years later, on July 1, 1951, we were married in a joyous ceremony at a New York hotel. Our celebration was short-lived. One week into our honeymoon, we learned that my father was to be operated on for a brain tumor. Returning home immediately, we spent the second week of our marriage with my mother and Mel's folks at a hotel adjacent to a Boston hospital. The following April, Dad died at the age of fifty-four.

Inspired by a cousin, a surgeon in Patchogue, Long Island, Mel had decided to be a doctor when he was still in elementary school. Skipping grades and completing his A.B. in less than three years, he entered Harvard Medical School at the age of nineteen. I majored in French literature because I loved French. My career goals, vaguely defined in the fields of language and dance, were obscured by a desire to get married.

Just as my father's death had jolted us into an awareness of our vulnerability, so the Korean War altered our neat blueprints for the future. Midway through his residency, even as we recited our vows, Mel was faced with the threat of a doctor-draft and induction into the army as an infantryman. Instead, along with all the other eligible M.D.'s we knew, he volunteered, was commissioned as a medical officer, and was sent to Korea.

Engagement, 1950. *(Photograph by Fred Marcus)*

All photographs by Melvin Horwitz unless otherwise noted.

First get-together of parents, 1950. Abe and Belle Gotterer (left), Hy and Rose Horwitz.

The brothers: Bert Horwitz (left), Gerry Gotterer. *(Photograph by Fred Marcus)*

July 1, 1951. Barbizon Plaza Hotel. New York City. *(Photograph by Fred Marcus)*

Public Relations Office, University of Connecticut, 1951. *(Photograph by University of Connecticut News Coordinator's Office)*

Writing letters was part of my growing up. My father had insisted that a night away from home required a letter to the folks. From summer camp, then a college dormitory, later a pension in Paris, I wrote to my parents every day. I didn't think it odd. I enjoyed recording my tame personal adventures, sharing with my parents what they conceived to be daring expeditions. Not until age twenty-three, when I left with Mel for a Canadian honeymoon, did Dad release me from this epistolary obligation.

The following year, while Mel was stationed in Korea, another letter-writing odyssey began. Across nine thousand miles, during nine months of separation, we each numbered six hundred airmail envelopes and between us scratched over one million words onto paper.

Exchanging accounts of our work, concerns, hopes, and loneliness, we moved from determined optimism to restless frustration. We shared everything, without holding back, so that we would not be "strangers when we meet." In a veritable Hit Parade of prose, we charted all the longings that encapsulated our fantasies—I'll See You in My Dreams . . . The Nearness of You . . . This Love of Ours . . . I'll Walk Alone . . . As Time Goes By . . . Goodnight Sweetheart—some World War II tunes, others older, others not yet written.

The letters became a way of life, a tireless need, an endless interlude. Detailing trivia as well as affections, we thought to re-create the reality of our lives apart. Between the I-love-you's, I-need-you's, I-miss-you's, I-want-you's, we recorded every quotidian ablution, bodily function, and physical sensation—showers, shaves, bowel movements, menstrual periods, menus, diets, masturbation, when we were hot and when we were cold, when we were tired and when we were sick. Humdrum routines assumed disproportionate significance. By examining the minutiae, we avoided exploring the emptiness, like looking through a screen but seeing only the wire mesh.

I listed daily phone calls, bills and insurance premiums, contributions, what phonograph records I bought. We commented on the radio music we heard. We critiqued the books we read and the movies we saw. I recounted for Mel concerts, plays, and social events that I attended in the city and my brief sorties into the countryside outside New York. Often we enclosed articles or letters from relatives and friends. He sent me photos, slides, and movies of his life in Korea. I sent him "pin-ups" of me.

Mel's passion for picture-taking not only added a dimension to his letters, but endeared him to the folks back home. We looked forward to hours spent in a darkened living room eyeballing a wobbly screen. Although other M.A.S.H. unit members also supported Kodak, none competed in volume with this photo-bug surgeon who spent every spare minute peering through a viewfinder (if he wasn't writing letters). When he was unable to obtain film and equipment in Korea or Japan, I mailed him the things he needed for his 8-mm movie camera and his two 35-mm still cameras.

Mostly, we talked, our words creating a scrim to shade the reality of separation. If dreaming didn't "make it so," at least "the dreams we dreamed" while asleep or awake were scripted onto paper. The rule was to tell all. Yet, at times, we vacillated between wanting to tell all and not wanting to write sorry-for-ourselves letters. So we wrote about that dilemma too.

Our two brothers were often the focus of our dialogues. Bert, seven years younger than Mel, was a freshman at Columbia, and Gerry, six years my junior, was in his first year at Harvard. Suddenly our kid brothers were grown up. It was their turn to sustain us with their compassion and good humor. Turning to them for consolation, we avoided burdening our anxious parents.

Several months after Mel's departure, one of his cousins, a journalist, proposed using Mel's letters for a series of feature articles on the M.A.S.H. I liked the idea. After getting Mel's okay, I started to whittle down his early letters to readable length. Because the task was more time-consuming than I had imagined, I changed my mind. Maybe some day, I said, I would do it for us, for our children.

Now, over four decades later, why do we seek to recapture this painful interval? Why do we choose to expose our naive longings, self-righteous pronouncements, awkward gropings toward maturity?

"I don't want to forget," Mel had said. "This is an historical document," a friend urged. The personal, she said, can be sociology or history, even in the absence of academic commentary. Today, I read these subjective chronicles as one more testimony to the gruesomeness of war and the loneliness of separation. They reflect who we were and, at times, who we are. Perhaps by sharing some of our private thoughts, the reader will remember this least-remembered war as more than a favorite TV sit-com. In response to the *M*A*S*H* show, Mel said, "It wasn't like that." Although he recognized the familiar setting of an emergency surgical hospital in Korea, he considered the characters to be exaggerated and almost every incident fictional. "But after all," he commented, "the producers' mission was to entertain."

Although I cut the letters to one-tenth their original length, minor changes to the text were made only for the sake of clarity. Parenthetical phrases are from the letters themselves. Bracketed notes are mine. Date-lines have been edited for consistency. Ellipses indicating omissions were left out so as not to interrupt the flow of the narrative. Several names were changed to protect privacy. The labels of the time, sometimes pejorative, were left intact—"Chinks," for example, along with the accepted use of "Negro." Beijing was still "Peiping," and jeans were "dungarees." A paper-back was a "pocket book," and we made "carbons," not photocopies. Our 78s were played on a "record player" or "victrola." Although not all these words are included in this collection, they were part of our vernacular and appeared in the original letters. I have added a list of abbreviations at the end of the book.

Erasing repetitious phrases and most of the deep purple prose was easy. Moving back and forth between past and present was not. The objectivity I sought often eluded me. I wanted to talk to the narrators, to give them the benefit of my experience, as though they were my children or grand-children. Fictionalizing would have been easier than editing, but the voices of those two naifs remain solidly in place.

Perhaps letters from the past are a suitable juncture for truth and fiction. As we look backward, we think we know who we were, but it no longer seems as important as who we are, especially when the years ahead span a considerably shorter interval than the years behind. Our past shaped us, as we now shape our past, coming as close as possible, we hope, to authenticity. We don't want to forget.

July

The winter and early spring of our first year of marriage, Mel and I commuted between New York and Connecticut. Balancing hospital visits to Dad with work schedules, we waited. We waited from July until April. Then, three days before Dad died, the letter arrived with its irrefutably precise message. Mel was to be inducted into the army within the month.

He was assigned for eight weeks of orientation to Fort Sam Houston in San Antonio, Texas. I was allowed to accompany him at my own expense. My mother bought us plane tickets. "Don't drive," she said. "Please spend the extra few days with me." After twenty-five years of marriage, she was to be alone.

During the next eight weeks, Mel and I savored every moment of our limited time together. At "Fort Sam" we rented a furnished apartment near the base. There we fed cardinals from the back porch, poured insecticide on the cockroaches, slept nude in front of a fan, and ate our first chili. On the army post, Mel learned how to march and where to pin his lieutenant's bar. The doctors wore their insignia randomly and took resolute pride in their lack of spit and polish. On the training fields, you could always distinguish their company from the "regulars." They were the straggliest marchers and the slowest to salute.

Part of the training included bivouacs, which Mel didn't mind except when he had to crawl under live gunfire. Prying ticks out of his sweaty back became routine for me upon his return from these forays. While he took lessons in soldiering, I worked as a clerk in the general's office. In my spare time, I read to the blind at the Lighthouse in downtown "San Antone" and learned to drive a rented stick-shift car.

On weekends we explored Texas. Hitting eighty miles an hour on long, straight roads, we drove to the little mountain town of Bandera and to Corpus Cristi, where we stayed in a small motel on the Gulf of Mexico. We roamed the still-pristine beaches of Padre Island and at night listened to the waves lap the sand. In Houston and Dallas we visited relatives who had migrated from the north and marveled at their southern accents.

Mel frequently invited people home from the base for beer and pretzels. That's how we met Jan and Ernie from San Francisco, and Esther and Gene from Brooklyn. Like Mel, the men were surgeons in training who had volunteered as medical officers rather than be drafted. Like me, their wives had shaped their lives around their husband's professional assignments. We had all married within the past few years. At the end of the eight weeks, we all went to say our good-byes at Camp Stoneman in Pittsburgh, California, the army port of embarcation in San Francisco.

The day after Mel left for the Far East, I flew from the cool of northern California into a steamy New York heat wave, the longest recorded in eighty years.

In Mom's upper-eastside apartment, the air conditioner was on the blink. Sweating in ninety-degree temperatures, we adapted to new routines. We filled the house with fresh flowers and alternated frenzied activity with intervals of relaxation. I sorted cartons that had been hastily packed in our tiny New Haven apartment. Mom began daily taxi rides downtown to work at A. Gotterer, Inc. This export firm was founded by my father in the early thirties and represented, among others, the Maiden Form Brassiere Company, as it was then known. Occasionally I pitched in at the office. Mom replaced her traditional furnishings with modern pieces. I tried to figure out how I could fit dance classes into my schedule. I talked on the phone a lot. Nights after dinner we read and sometimes watched television. We both wore high heels and dark red lipstick, in the fashion of the day. She preferred bright colors and went to the beauty parlor every week. My tailored clothes were subdued, and my severe, self-styled hairdo gave me a sense of control.

Neither of us liked confrontation, so we accomodated occasional differences without having to work too hard at it. Mother and daughter succeeded in comforting each other without talking things out. We rarely discussed our sorrow or loneliness. From Mom I learned the art of using optimism and activity to cover distress and doubt. Only with my father had she been argumentative.

Our primary source of news was the *New York Times,* where we inevitably turned first to the daily feature, "Official Reports of Fighting in

Korea." There we read accounts of marines being "cut to ribbons" by Chinese troops or "raked with withering machine-gun and artillery fire." I noted that enemy casualties were often included in the tactical summaries at the top of the page, while ours were listed inobtrusively at the bottom. Beijing continued to warn the U.N. Command that they would "have their heads broken" if they extended the fighting. The daily jockeying back and forth on the hills of Korea continued. Why we were there was rarely treated in the press except in an occasional glib comment about the "defense of our free institutions" or "Russia's aggressive intentions." As our bombers pounded Pyongyang, we read about stalled truce talks at Panmunjom and appeals for emergency blood. I gave silent thanks that Mel was at a M.A.S.H. and not directly in the line of fire.

As Mom and I adjusted to a life together, Mel and I shaped our lives apart. Although we had anticipated the separation, we couldn't have foreseen how the intensity of longing and frustration would pervade the habits of our daily lives. We had just grown accustomed to the comfort of being together.

There were moments when I had an overwhelming desire to know exactly what he was doing. Or I would stop in mid-sentence to allow a memory to invade my consciousness. I pushed my senses to their limit in order to remake or invoke images and textures that might connect us.

We were scared. Mel expressed his fear simply, explicitly. I kept mine mute, just as the grief over my father's death remained voiceless. Yet, my only defense against the pile-up of sadness was in my words to him, usually written before I went to sleep. That one-sided dialogue became a passionate ritual that not only eased my melancholy, but fulfilled my need to talk things over at the end of the day, the way "normal" couples might.

I wanted him beside me as I watched the first televised political conventions in history, where commentators were criticized for talking too much when "You can SEE what's happening!" At the Democratic Convention, I saw the presidential candidate, Adlai Stevenson, select as his running mate John Sparkman, a white supremacist from Alabama. Although I understood Stevenson's choice to be a wooing of southern "Dixiecrats," my own liberal Democrat loyalties were unsettled by what I considered a betrayal of political faith.

Opposing him on the Republican ticket was Dwight Eisenhower, with Senator Richard Nixon as his running mate. Ike promised to go to Korea if elected, although he had previously said that there was no "clean-cut" answer to bringing the Korean War to a successful conclusion. When he pledged a "total victory crusade," I had to remember that he was talking about the election campaign.

At the end of the month, for the first time, I saw the acronym "M.A.S.H" in print. The *Times* reported that a United Press man was treated at one of these units after his jeep overturned on a steep hill near the western front. Of equal significance to me was the news that in Canada our honeymoon lodge at Jasper National Park had burned to the ground. Although I saw no facile symbol in the ruin of these rustic cabins, the article recalled a week of hikes on wooded paths and picnics shared with the ubiquitous chipmunks.

Although we couldn't believe it at the time, we acted like any young couple separated by events over which they had no control. We deplored our fate and gave ourselves pep talks. We relived the past, imagined the future, and filled the present with words.

───────────────

JULY 10, 1952, 10:45 P.M.

My darling,

It seems impossible! A few hours ago you were wiping off my lipstick and now you are many miles from my side. I say it. I write it.

As I sit in our room at the Chancellor Hotel, I keep expecting you to come barging in. I can still see you clearly, fussing with your bags after you got out of the car. I'm glad that I drove back because it gave me something else to concentrate on besides what is inside of me.

I had clear sailing all the way into San Francisco, but something went wrong when I got to Post Street, and I drove around a few extra blocks before I found Turk. Guess what? I loved driving up and down the hills. Can't you just see me? Wheeeeee! However, because California drivers are madmen, I exercised all precautions. At intersections, it's just a question of who gets there first—I was very polite!

That particular drive from Pitt to S.F. is beautiful. It would have been so good to share it again with you this afternoon. I caught only glimpses of the magnificent hills and trees and just as we have always noticed, as soon as you travel in another direction, the views are different.

When I arrived here, I found Mom's telegram and in the box, a message to call her, which I did (collect). The folks asked how you were traveling. I said we didn't know.

No sooner did I hang up when Jan, Esther, and Gene called from downstairs to pick me up for dinner. It was Gene's treat, at an Indo-

Chinese restaurant in the neighborhood. I had an assorted Indo-Chinese plate. The won-ton was interesting, like crisp kreplach. The others had fried chicken. I wasn't hungry, but ate anyway, acting only on nervous energy tonight. As soon as I stopped to pause, I was completely fagged out.

Poor Gene. Alone with three sad females. Not that we let too much of that come to the surface. But every once in a while, Jan and I would stare off into space. Then Gene would explain that he shouldn't be there. I guess he felt left behind by his buddies. He didn't seem happy about his extra day. I can really understand it, almost as though he'd already left, or should have.

After dinner we split up, and I went to United, TWA, and American to get a flight out. The first available coach is on Tuesday. I couldn't make up my mind until I got back to the hotel. When I saw your message and realized that I had missed hearing your voice, even for a few minutes, I decided to get to NY as soon as possible so as not to miss your next call.

Sooo you can add $70 to that phone bill from Yokohama, because I'm taking a deluxe flight ($183) Saturday morning, TWA Constellation. It will bring me in about 11:40 P.M. I hope that your folks don't bother coming down at that hour. I wired Mom tonight to tell her.

I'm really exhausted and probably will have no trouble falling asleep, as long as I don't wake up in the middle of the night hoping to feel your wonderful backside rubbing against mine. Honey, we'll have to cook up some pretty good dreams to last us for however long they'll have to last.

You forgot the alarm clock. Guess the bugle will do. Still so much to say, but it will wait till morning. My throat feels scratchy—allergy, psychosomia, quelle maladie!

Oh my darling, I want to squeeze you. You know, the kind of squeeze that says that nothing can be said. We have so much more than so many. Although I can't reach out to bite a piece of you, goddammit, our love warms me through and I hope and wish for the day soon that I feel you crushing the breath from me and making my thighs all black and blue. But I'm beginning to feel sorry for us, and that will never do. Now to bed.

Goodnite my love. Sleep well. Write me all your thoughts and your love so that we may be together in the best possible way in this crazy situation.

I love you my darling.   Dorothy

Good morning, my darling,

I have the feeling that you're still at Camp Stoneman and I'll probably get a call late this afternoon telling me when you'll be "home." Where is home? I feel rested but restless. No hairy chest to snuggle up to. No gentle hand to feel for tears so quickly dissipated. I haven't cried, my darling, just a few silent trickles before I fell asleep. Crying does no good. I'll keep busy. You know me. I'll stick to that, except for a moment now and then . . . oh my love my love

I washed out a few things this morning, took a shower, had breakfast sent up, sewed on a suit button, took care of the suitcase for Railway Express, called the Post Office and learned that the best way of dealing with your lost stud box is to leave a forwarding address at the hotel.

Why don't we number our letters so we'll know which ones to open first and which may have gone astray?

As I lay in bed this morning, I wondered what part of the Pacific was under you, what you were thinking, whether you were snoring. I hope it's a good trip, my love, and the news, when you land, is good.

The chambermaid is coming in, so I'd better get out.

If I don't write this P.M. I will tonight so you'll know all I have done and thought today. I love you my darling.   Dorothy

Darling—

It's now 6 A.M. (whatever time it is called) and we're two hours from Honolulu. So much has happened in the last day that it is difficult for me to be sure that it has happened. I don't seem to be reacting. I hope that later my feelings may crystallize. I shall try to put them down for you—for us both—as soon as I can, lest I forget. I love you very much.

We parted in a hurry. Perhaps it was better that way. "Good-bye my love. See you soon. Take care of yourself." And away you drove. Then we went in, signed out, and waited 1½ hours for the bus that was supposed to come in five minutes. Rode about 30 miles to Travis Air Force Base, a field much like those you and I have taken off from during the past year, but loaded with bombers as well as transports. We checked our luggage and were told the plane would be late taking off—scheduled for

10:30 P.M. via DC-4 commercial aircraft, "The Flying Tiger Line." Had a nice steak dinner for $1.75, burped a few times, walked about the terminal (we were restricted to it), went to the PX (Post Exchange) and bought a few postcards. Mailed some to you and my folks.

Sat around waiting, listening to the loudspeaker blare forth its announcements. I looked at the people sitting around, mostly military, some civilians, like the people in any other terminal—but different. How, it's difficult to describe. There was an air of excitement, an anticipation of the unknown. At the time, I felt that all this had happened before. Once again I was waiting for a plane. The impact of why has not yet hit me. I can't really believe I am now 8,000 feet above the Pacific Ocean, 2,400 miles from San Francisco. I wish so much that we could be talking about it, as we have so often during the past two years [the period of our courtship and marriage]. I write TWO years. It doesn't seem long, but has almost shut out completely our meaning of what life was like before.

Finally we heard our flight announcement. Then, as in a Hollywood movie, we gathered into a group of about 50 and walked across the airfield in darkness, the stars and moon overhead, the shadowy planes standing quietly like giant birds sleeping. We boarded. Reclining seats, quite comfortable, perhaps a bit more crowded than usual. Two rows on one side, three on the other. One hostess and three crewmen. It's been exceptionally calm, except for a few bumps at the beginning. I dozed on and off during the night and am not too tired now, but would like to shower. As I dozed and awakened, I thought, where's Dorothy? She should be right here next to me.

The sunrise was magnificent. Now the clouds are breaking up so we can see the Pacific. It's frightening to think of trying to find an island in the middle of this very large ocean, not being able to stop at a gas station along the way to ask directions.

The hostess has just passed out "Ditching Procedures for a Water Landing" and is showing us how to put on Mae West jackets. Ernie and I look at each other and smile. My pulse rate rises and I WONDER— about things.

The sun is high and bright. The fellows are resting, playing cards, writing letters, reading. We were given a box lunch—or shall I say breakfast?—with two small containers of milk, three sandwiches, a chocolate bar, crackers, an apple, and a hard boiled egg. I had egg and milk and will get a hot meal in Honolulu. AM NOW ON A DIET.

Oh my love, I write of what I've seen and done. It's difficult to write of what I feel. How much I love you, you know. I hope and pray that we shall be together soon. Stay well. Drive carefully. Don't worry about dents in the fenders! I shall be thinking of you at every moment, remembering your smile and face and body and love. This past year has brought us close. I feel like a better person. I have meaning for my existence and I know you feel the same. The time must pass quickly. We shall make it so. My eyes swell. I feel good even though sad. Take care of yourself, my darling, my Dorothy. I shall write again soon.   Mel

JULY 11, 1952

My Darling,

3 P.M.—Wake Island Time, 6 hours earlier than San Francisco— again over the Pacific on another 2400 mile ride. We land at Wake about 2 A.M. I'm not sure which day as somewhere we gain or lose a day. From there, on to Tokyo, another 2000 miles.

We landed in Hawaii at 8:00 A.M. It was exciting to see the island from the air. (I hope these pictures and others I took come out. I've sent them directly to you, so please examine them and give me your cold critical opinion.)

Hawaii is beautiful. Most of the people at the airport were wearing orchid and gardenia leis. The countryside has hills very much like California, but the shrubbery is heavy and very green. We had a nice breakfast (gift of the Flying Tiger Lines) at the swanky International Airport restaurant. Then I shaved and showered (25 cents—towel provided). It felt good. I ALMOST had myself shaved by the barber. Most of the barbers in Hawaii and the Far East are WOMEN—not for me. I've seen how you handle a razor!

We were to have 8 hours in Hawaii and were sent by bus to Hickham Air Force Base to wait. An enterprising colonel and some pleasant USO [United Service Organizations, organized in 1941, providing recreational, welfare, and spiritual facilities for members of the armed services] women arranged a tour of Honolulu and other parts of the island. While waiting for it to start, I bought picture postcards and sent some to you and other people. (Save them, OK?) Also bought a large canvas toilet kit for $1.50, so now I'm all set. I resisted the temptation to send you flowers, monkey pod salad bowl (very nice but I think you would prefer myrtlewood), kerchief with a tiger on it, pornographic playing cards, et al.

The more I travel, the more I like it—present situation excepted, of course! My darling, we shall someday lie on the beach at Waikiki, get sunburned, and mutter in Hawaiian: It's a mechaya! [Yiddish, "super-pleasure"] It usually isn't money that prevents people from doing things, but time and inertia. We shall find the time. Another day comes to an end. Soon we'll know where I'm to be. I'm hoping and hoping it will be somewhere we can be together. I can't wait to hold you again close to me, to feel your warmth and to smell you.

I love you, MY WIFE, Dorothy. As I write it, I'm saying the words quietly and I feel better. This letter is my link with you and, as I write, I am closer to you—as each day passes, closer. Sleep well my darling.

Mel

P.S. Did you check with Mrs. Hurwitz downstairs at 9 East 96 [my mother's apartment building] to make sure she doesn't get any of your letters?

SATURDAY, JULY 12, 1952, 1:15 P.M. CALIF. TIME
EN ROUTE TO N.Y.

My darling—

The plane is freezing. I'm wrapped up in a blanket and my tweed coat. There's an empty seat beside me. My fountain pen leaked. Other-wise, things are smooth. We've been in the air for three hours and this is a ten-hour flight.

I spent my first day away from you mailing film and browsing in Paul Elder's bookstore. We've spent so many hours together poking around bookstores indulging our fancy to buy books. On my last day in San Francisco, I pampered my loneliness and bought *Quo Vadis* by Sienkiewicz, *Poems of William Carlos Williams,* Dorothy Canfield's *Deepening Stream,* Faulkner's *The Sound and the Fury,* and *My Life* by Isadora Duncan. Then I stuffed myself with strawberry waffles and whipped cream at Tiny's Waffle Shop next door to the hotel.

It was a grey ride to the airport, and I had to swallow hard a few times. On the way, I saw that blond girl, wife of the Air Corps Lieuten-ant with whom we had lunch at Stoneman. She was mailing a letter and didn't see me. I felt a kinship and sad at not being able to say a few words to her.

We took off on time. Until now the flight has been exceptionally smooth, as you can see by my writing. The sun is shining somewhere, and because of the cloud cover there's a glare when you look out the windows. Whoops! It's getting Coney Island-ish. I'm not frightened, but I sure would like to have you here to grin at each time I lose my stomach.

Incidental intelligence: South San Francisco is a completely separate city from San Francisco. The former got nationwide publicity recently when residents of a neighborhood barred a Chinese family from moving in.

Incidental intelligence: If you hold this paper up against the light, it's easier to read, especially when there is writing on both sides. The postage is the same as U.S. Air Mail, 6 cents per oz.

When I boarded the plane, I read yesterday's *New York Times* and am enclosing a clipping which might give you some insight into Ike's ideas, which didn't impress me. I'll send you pertinent material on the candidates and will check on your ballot when I get to NY.

It's warm and uncomfortable now. I'm anxious to get back only to get a call from you. Just a few words, to know where and how you are and to tell you that I love you.   Dorothy

SUNDAY, JULY 13, 1952, 6:00 P.M.

Konban-wa [Japanese, "good evening"] my darling—

After 36 hours in the air, 8 hours in Hawaii, and one hour on Wake Island, I am now sitting in the BOQ (Bachelor Officers' Quarters) having showered, s——, and shaved. I sent off a wire that you should get in about 24 hours. Imagine me, an old married man in a BOQ.

We arrived at Haneida Airport just outside Tokyo, then rode in an army bus 20 miles (1½ hours) to Camp Drake where I am now. My first time in a foreign country. Most striking is the numbers of people and the crowding. The Japanese use every inch of space for living or growing food. The entire area we drove through smells either of incense or feces, the latter used to fertilize the soil. Poverty abounds. The people are dressed in a curious mixture of Western clothes. Many of the children wear ragged baseball clothing. There are thousands of small shops, but I'm sure I'll do most of my trading at the PX.

As soon as we arrived, we stood in line to get processed, then changed all our currency into scrip and had our immunizations checked.

The Japanese around the Post are polite and cheerful. Some of them understood my Japanese. (I studied all the way over and can count to ten and ask where the bathroom is.)

I expect to be here for 3 to 4 days and will call as soon as I get my assignment. Your mail will not catch up with me for a while, but keep writing to APO 613 (Army Post Office) until I let you know differently. I hope my letters are getting to you.

(Several hours later) Had a bite at the officers' club and sat around listening to the band playing some good waltzes. They sounded like Guy Lombardo [bandleader noted for mellow ballroom dance music], but were all Japanese.

The evening has come and I'm to go to sleep—with you halfway round the world. My darling, I don't want to write letter after letter telling you how much I miss you. So I shall just say again and again how much I love you and how good it is to have our love to stabilize my thinking in this upside down world of ours.

I still walk and feel as though I am an onlooker in this camp of men who are truly here today and gone tomorrow, like the sea, always moving and changing. I'm tired and I shall sleep. Know that I am with you always darling in my thoughts and my dreams.   Mel

SUNDAY, JULY 13, 1952, 1:30 P.M., NEW YORK CITY

My darling,

Well, my love, now that I'm here I really have to decide what to do IMMEDIATELY. If I don't keep busy, I will get depressed. I suppose tomorrow (and tomorrow and tomorrow) I shall begin to study for the Spanish exam. If I set up some kind of schedule, it will be easier—I, I, I—how I hate writing in first person singular. It's been so long since "we" have written or spoken in "I's."

My darling, each time I think of something to tell you, I jot it down so that when I actually sit down to write I won't forget what I wanted you to share.

I would be happier on the west coast now, perhaps because you would be 3,000 miles closer. I'd rather be living alone, but I shall be unselfish and bide my time here, trying to make things as cheerful as possible for Mom. This morning she said that she was very proud of me, that I was very brave. She's quite a woman!

She showed me a letter from Great-Uncle Ephraim [formerly

Swetitsky, changed to Sweet by Ellis Island officials when he entered the United States] written from the tuberculosis sanatorium. He says that he is "drifting into the abyss of phlegmatism" but is "unyielding." He says "it is heartbreaking to watch young folks torn away from their families."

Dorothy love—

I'm sitting in the telephone room waiting for the call I placed about six hours ago to come through. I'm so anxious to speak to you, yet sad that I have to tell you unless something drastic happens, I shall be sent to Korea. I have been given verbal orders, but no official written ones yet. I'll call you tonight because I expect to be alerted tomorrow and leave shortly after that. What will happen these next few months, I don't know. We shall have to be apart, my darling, but as soon as we can, we shall be together again, no matter what we have to do.

I read *The Japanese Times* daily and watch the progress (if any) at the peace talks. I also read about rising anti-American feeling in Japan, though it isn't a strong movement.

I spent most of the day in Tokyo. Had to have my eyes reexamined because a form was lost from my folder. So I had an extra pair of glasses made. Met Ira Long from Tennessee, an ophthalmologist at Tokyo General Hospital who knew me from somewhere. Do you know him or where he could have gotten my name? Spent a pleasant few hours with him and was envious of his having been stationed in Tokyo.

Oh, I bought another camera, a bargain—$165 model for $80—a Retina II made in the American Zone of Germany. I still don't know enough Japanese to bargain with the merchants on the Ginza (the Broadway of Tokyo). The prices here are high, as the shopkeepers can get the money they ask from soldiers or tourists.

Item of interest: I have a very short crew haircut. It really doesn't look bad—perhaps it will stimulate growth. At any rate, it's easy to keep clean. Had one of the boys take a picture of me so you'll be able to see what I look like, in case I dispense with it by the time you come over. (See, I'm still optimistic.)

Since I'm not in a booth here, I won't be able to speak freely, but it won't matter who hears me tell you how much I love you and miss you. There are other people trying to call overseas, and the place is a madhouse. (I just called in again and the call will be delayed for 1 to 2 hours.)

(One hour later) The radio reception is poor and the call may be further delayed.

If it were not for this letter, I should feel very far from you. I haven't gotten any mail and don't expect it for a while, but it will be forwarded to me. I know you are thinking of me and love me, as I do you. Sleep well my darling.   Mel

TUESDAY, JULY 15, 1952, 10:45 P.M.

My darling—

Your call seems now like one split second in eternity. I waited so long for it, to hear your voice for a few moments and know that we were actually talking to each other across thousands of miles. Oh my love, the next months loom like an inescapable hell. As I write, I can't help thinking of the letters we wrote between New York and New Haven. That was "reasonable" frustration, because it ended a few times a week. Oh my darling Melvin, my heart is beating in my chest as my hands would beat against the wall. To know that it will be months before I see you, before we know the excitement and peace of each other's presence.

After your call and wandering about the house for a while, I sat down and studied Spanish for two solid hours. I've decided to do my best to pass that damn exam and if I don't, at least I will have tried. (We should play "Hearts and Flowers" at this point.) I would like to put my heart into teaching this Fall and I could do it at Valley Stream. However, really darling, what I don't know is appalling. It doesn't seem possible to substantially increase one's knowledge of a vocabulary and a culture in two weeks. The grammar is a cinch. Nuff sed! My next weeks will be well-occupied.

Spent the rest of the morning unpacking one of the crates and resting intermittently. It was hot and damp. My stomach was just about coming into its own. After a light lunch, I read the paper, got our records into a metal file, wrote to Blue Cross, and sent $60 to the bank. I asked for a statement. Do you want more checks?

At 3:00 P.M. the overseas operator called and said to expect "the call" at 5:00. Of course I couldn't do a thing from then on. I attempted the crossword puzzle (old reliable) but didn't get very far. So I had some food to quiet my growling stomach. Finally the moment arrived. How I hope for the impossible!

I wired Jan: "Boys probably going to Korea. We should receive mail soon giving details. Please write to me." Well, my love, now that I've studied, written to Uncle Ephraim, and spoken words of love to my dearest who is far from me this night, I shall try to relax in sleep. You are now in the bright sun of morning. How I miss you.   Dorothy

JULY 16, 1952, 8:00 A.M., JAPAN, CAMP DRAKE

Darling—

As usual, I didn't say half the things I wanted to, but it was good to hear your voice and to be close to you for a few minutes. Next time I call, we shall have to work it like a radio. First you talk, then I, with a momentary pause, as I think there is an operator who listens and flips a switch back and forth.

I was in the shower when the call finally came through. I went dashing through the barracks with a towel around my middle and soap in my ear. Oh my love. I guess there is no use feeling sorry for myself, or bemoaning my fate—our fate. I shall be flown to 8th Army Headquarters in Taegu, then reassigned to a permanent station somewhere in Korea. If it isn't one where I think I will have an opportunity to work, I shall squawk like hell.

I know you have been writing so I don't ask questions about what you've been doing. Keep busy. Don't work too hard and have fun over the summer. I keep wondering if you're going to study for that Spanish exam.

It's good to be married to you. Here there's a tendency to degenerate into a typical "army man"—no motivation in the army, only self-preservation. I can smile at the "desire to stay continuously drunk" and the constant talk of women and fornication. You and I wondered what trials might arise in this connection. I assure you our solution is preferable. I've lived at summer camp and in dormitories, but the tone, degeneracy, and steady stream of talk about sex is ten times as great here. When I feel bad, I think of you and relive the many hours we've had together. I imagine what you've been doing during the day, loving you all the time.

I shall write to your Mom today. Hope Gerry is enjoying his courses. I'm sure you keep them informed of my itinerary. Now I'll be off to mail this and wait for our orders out. Expect to be leaving tomorrow. I love you.   Mel

WEDNESDAY, JULY 16, 1952, AFTER MIDNIGHT

Melvin my love,

This has been a long, tiring day and I am even more exhausted when I think that you have another twelve hours of it to move through. What are you doing now? Is your tan wearing or increasing? Do your itches itch? Does your nose bother you? Are you learning things? How is your libido? Are you buckling your belt correctly? And so many other "important" questions.

Went to bed close to midnight and was up 15 minutes later to satisfy the gnawing in my stomach with some milk and cake. Fell asleep promptly after that.

Studied from 8:30 to 11:30 when your Mom called to find out what I was doing. When she heard I was studying she said that she would keep me company this afternoon. I told her to come with Pop tomorrow night when Bert is here for dinner.

Don [Oken, medical school roommate] and Paul [Merson, Mel's friend since childhood] phoned today and of course feel bad about your assignment. It's funny. Our close friends just don't seem to be able to find anything to say about it. I guess because there isn't much to say. The others will remark: "Well, it will work out for the best!" Best, hell! The only "best" is being with you and I'll bitch at times (to you darling) because you are feeling what I am feeling.

My love, the name Korea sounds ugly to my ears. I hope you can find satisfaction in work. If they let you make the contribution for which you are qualified, there will be some reason in your being there. I dare not hope when the headlines read "truce." That would be too reasonable. Only love and work make sense right now.

I am so tired and I miss you. I look for a letter tomorrow. I love you.
Dorothy

JULY 16, 1952, 9:45 P.M.

Dorothy my darling—

Tomorrow I leave for Korea, the name of a place that by Friday will be a reality. We shall not be flying, but taking a long train ride, a 4-day boat trip either to Pusan or Inchon, then by rail to Taegu where we get our assignments.

So my love, there it is. While I can't say we've had it too badly, we certainly haven't been getting the breaks in the past few weeks, but they will come. I suppose the lack of them compensates (in this strange rule book I'm making up) for our having each other. I keep repeating myself, as I can't seem to find words to tell you how much I love you. My handwriting is worse than ever.

We leave at 3 A.M., an ungodly hour. I'm all packed, taking a minimum of stuff. I don't know when I'll get to mail my next letter, so there may be a lapse of time before you hear from me. Don't worry. How long has it been taking to get the letters? Ernie is sitting opposite me writing to Jan. We dress in fatigues. If you thought we looked sorry before, you should see us now.

Goodnight my darling. I shall be careful and try to get back to Japan or the States as soon as I can. While I'm here I hope to work hard, think, and read. I love you.   Mel

THURSDAY, JULY 17, 1952

Darling—

Up on deck of a small troop transport. The sun is setting, the ship is rolling slightly, and a cool wind is blowing the paper. The water is deep blue, the sky hazy with clouds, and the spray of the ship as she plows forwards is beautiful to see. The air smells good and the roar of the waves is soothing. I can see why you enjoyed your ocean trip [to Europe on a student ship in 1948]. Were it not for the circumstances, I would be enjoying this one. I feel more aware of what is going on now.

Yesterday morning we got written orders to leave—about 2 hours after I spoke to you. At 1 A.M. we were issued duffle bag, blankets, mosquito netting, and mess gear. After returning to the barracks to wash and dress, we went to the officers' club for dinner where for the third night in a row, I had a good steak. Then back to the barracks to pack. You know how I love to do that! The duffle bag weighed a ton and we also carried a small canvas handbag. Since I shall be wearing fatigues from now on, I packed all my khakis and wool pants away in the Val pack to be stored in the warehouse.

At 2 A.M. we boarded a bus with other officers—regular army, reserves, medical men—reacting to similar feelings in different ways.

Some drunk, some jovial, some quiet—all frightened. At the RR station we loaded on a little Japanese train to Yokohama. It took us 3½ hours to go 40 miles. The train let us out right at the boat where I witnessed a marked difference between enlisted men and officers, the former carrying their own heavy duffle bags and rifles while for the price of a few cigarettes we had Japanese dock hands carry ours aboard. I felt guilty and gave the hand an extra 100 yen (35 cents).

We are eight men to a cabin, three layers of bunks, with a toilet and shower between each two rooms. The enlisted men sleep in the hold, four-layered bunks in rooms of 20 or 30 or more. I really feel sorry having it a little easier.

Three hours after boarding, with a band playing, we got underway. While waiting I took pictures and sometimes slept.

We've had several good meals and an abandon-ship drill. So far I'm hungry and seem to be a fairly good sailor. It is not too rough.

Standing at the rail as I write, I look at my clothes. They are those of a soldier. I am happy that I am not going with the mission of having to fight and kill. Even if I felt strongly about this war, I can't see why we have to cause suffering. When will people learn? Life can be good and productive. But I wonder how.

FRIDAY, 8:40 A.M.

Good morning my love—

On the top deck of the ship, my shirt off, about 20 other people doing the same thing. The sun is bright and the sky cloudless.

Had a pleasant dinner last night (kept it down), and stood on deck as the sun set. They had some lousy movie that was too hot and dull to sit through so I went up to the lounge and played the piano for about an hour. I don't remember many pieces, but it was fun. Not too many people got up and left.

The way things stand, I shall be in Korea until I collect 20 points. Then I can apply for a transfer to Japan. If I wish, I can stay in Korea long enough to accumulate enough points to come home (36). [Front line units accumulated three or four points per month, units immediately behind, two, and rear line units, one. Mel served in a two-point zone.] I want to get out of there as fast as I can so I can go to Japan and have you come over either via the army or commercially. I have already requested government housing and transfer of dependents. We are on an 8 to 10 month waiting list. I can't imagine what it will be like to be away from you that long.

7:00 P.M.

Another day has almost passed. You are about to have dinner—on the other side of the earth. The sun has set and darkness is coming quickly. I can barely make out the paper as I write. It's too hot downstairs. The sea is grey and dark, no longer blue and friendly. It is forbidding and dangerously beautiful. Like you! I've fallen in love with it. We shall some day sail the Pacific together.

I sometimes forget the where and what of the moment as we plow through the waves, no land in sight. Then suddenly we come upon a crowded Japanese fishing boat. And I remember.

Today is the 18th and the 21st is your birthday. Happy Birthday! I shall give you twenty-four kisses when I see you next. Imagine me close to you with my face and body tight against you, my lips against your cheek. Know that I am with you always, my darling.

JULY 19, 8:00 A.M.

Good morning my love—

It is hot and humid. The sea is much rougher today and we are swaying back and forth as I write. They are running short of dramamine. Lucky that the trip will be over tomorrow. Lucky for those who feel sick.

Last night one of the Jewish fellows organized and ran a service. Generally, the one chaplain on board, a Protestant, officiates at all services.

We shall be landing at Inchon at 4 P.M. tomorrow. Never before has my life depended so much on world events. I doubt if they will get far with the peace treaty. From what we hear from troops coming back, our lines are very well set. It is unlikely that the enemy could get through—and vice versa. The action going on is relatively minor, mainly patrols.

There are 250 officers on board and 2,500 enlisted men, a heterogeneous group—all branches of service, all ages, all dispositions. The class differentiation is worse than any I've ever seen. One of the movies I'm sending you will show the officers' sun deck and then the enlisted men below. Granted, most of the officers are older and can take less (myself and others excepted). It seems the higher ups just do not care. Oh well, as long as I keep my own sense of values.

4:00 P.M.

On the loudspeaker they are playing "Younger Than Springtime" from "South Pacific." I see other people writing and stopping and thinking.

Almost no breeze today, but the ocean is kicking up. Rumor has it that we may run into a typhoon. I spent most of the day sitting around talking, reading a mystery, washing clothes. When the ship rolls, showering is really a job. I am now waiting for dinner. There are 3 sittings. I am on the second. The loud speaker blares forth at irregular intervals: Now hear this. . . . Suppertime.

SATURDAY, JULY 19, 1952, 11:00 P.M.

My darling—

All the women think I'm pregnant, because of my stomach trouble last week and the weight I have gained. You should see my belly! Right after Aug. 2 I'm going to start dancing—or you'll come home to a fat momma.

Something about Mom: She told me that if you and I had been together sooner and she could have observed our relationship, she would have "learned" from me. She said that when you disagree with me on something, I accept the disagreement and go right on. She said that she always had to argue things out. In other words, she was always on the defensive. This conversation gave me some insight into her relationship with Dad and made me uncomfortable.

Can't wait till this Aug. 2 exam is over and we can get out more. I'm very restless even though I try to break up the studying. My darling, I even resorted to my pre-marital sex life the other day. It's so soon—but you seem to take that kind of thing so casually. However, I think it will be easier when I start dancing.

Your letter explained the time difference and now I know. Here I thought that you were a half-day behind us. Well, thank goodness you're not. Just think, you'll get home 12 hours sooner!

Last night I dreamed that you came home on leave for a short time.

You said you had something good to tell me. "I have been transferred from the Far East to the Near East." I was delighted.

Goodnight my love. Sleep well. Dream well.   Dorothy

My Darling—

The sea has changed to dull green and is quiet. There is no land in sight, but to the east of us is Korea. It is cooler today. We can breathe. Our cabin is hot. No window or porthole, just a ventilating shaft and fan, which is a life-saver and goes 24 hours a day. I haven't slept underneath the covers. But the ocean voyage agrees with me. No hayfever, no itchy b—— except when it gets very hot. Appetite good, though I've been curbing myself. We have been getting milk every day at breakfast, recombined powdered, but it's not bad.

Inchon is good as a port only 8 out of 24 hours. It has a 30-foot tide and if you don't get in at high tide, there is a 3-mile beach.

We've been apart only a little more than a week and the ache in my heart is already too great. Whatever the future brings, I don't ever want to be away from you again. I will have used up my "nights off once a week" for a hundred years to come. I shall be very happy to sit next to you night after night, then to crawl into bed beside you.

Tomorrow is your birthday. Blow out the candles and wish hard darling.   Mel

SUNDAY, JULY 20, 1952, 11:30 P.M.

My love—

All days have the same color and end the same way. At night when I lie down on my bed to write, I stare into space and think empty thoughts of how long nine months will be. Everybody has extended all kinds of invitations and I am so happy to have a good excuse. I really prefer staying home and studying. I would like to transport the apartment out into the country where I wouldn't hear the buses, smell the gas, and get my bare feet covered with soot. OUR home will be away from all this.

Mom and I took a stroll in Central Park while it was still cool. We walked down to 86th St. and on the way back stopped in a shady spot to read the Sunday *Times*. It's when doing something routine, like reading the Sunday papers, that I miss you most. Spent the rest of the day studying. After dinner I took Gerry or I should say Gerry took me out in the car and drove around the park. He's quite good. All he needs is practice. He has the same trouble I had at first in parking, using the clutch, and going slowly.

After spending half the evening studying, watched television—"What's My Line?" then "Information Please." Sir Gladwyn Jebb [Permanent Representative of the United Kingdom to the United Nations, 1950–54] was on and certainly is a pleasure to listen to. Also watched a good variety show emceed by Conrad Nagel [stage and screen star].

Time to close. I love you my darling. I miss you and wait for the time when we shall be holding each other close again. Goodnight. Sleep well.   Dorothy

JULY 21, 1952

Happy Birthday My Love—

Sitting on a stone in the courtyard of the camp here at Inchon, I shall write of what happens only to you, because you said you wanted to know. It won't be nice.

Disembarking was unreal. Landing barges alongside the ship, troops going down the gangplank struggling under heavy loads. The faces of the young kids revealed their bewilderment and fear. I was afraid too, as I went down, the ship looming behind me in the darkness, a hospital ship floating in the harbor.

It was 9 P.M. when we got on the barge. As we sailed through a maze of islands, the water smelled stale. We got off and walked up a long ramp, waited in the darkness, realizing that in the hills people were fighting and dying—only 35 miles from us. We got on a truck and drove through the streets of Inchon. The filth and odor were something. People were sitting in front of the buildings, just staring. To think that some of the men came here looking for sex.

Suddenly we came upon the camp, surrounded by a fence and barbed wire. This is where we were to spend the night. It was so bad that it was funny. The beds were cots, luckily off the floor. I placed a blanket over the bed, a towel where there was no pillow, smeared myself with insect repellant, and climbed into bed in my underwear. The cots squeaked when you turned. The jokes about masturbating and the plaster falling were funny to hear, but, I suppose, would not be

funny to read. I slept well as I was tired. Awoke at 6:30, dressed, and
ate, feeling dirty, but there was no place to wash. The food was served
by little Korean girls who looked clean. Then we went back to the barracks where we washed from steel helmets. Couldn't shave. I think I
may get an electric razor as you can usually get current though you
may not get water.

So here I sit waiting for orders to get on a train to Taegu. We joke,
talk, write, and wait. I'm sorry to write a letter like this on your birthday. Love   Mel

P.S. No cable office.

JULY 21, 1952, 0930 HRS

My Love—

I almost feel human again. It's 2 hours later and I have washed and
shaved with warm water. Am sitting at a table in the barracks. We will
remain here most of the day. They may be able to arrange a walking
tour around the town. There is little to see but poverty and a black market, but I might as well see it since I will be living alongside it.

If anyone ever says again that we should be isolationist, I will have
to reply that it is impossible. Until the whole world attempts to equalize
the standard of living, not by breaking it down from the top but by
building it up from the bottom, we shall still have wars. Of course just
improving health and the standard of living is not the only thing. Doing that creates more problems. When we took over Japan after the war
there were approximately 45 million people. By instituting sanitary
measures, improving medical care, and increasing food output slightly,
we did help the country, but by 1951 the population was 65 million—in
this small island with not enough increase in food production—just
more food imports.

Ah, the breeze feels good. I do not profess to have an answer, but we
sure ought not to close our eyes to the problem, and also to the fact that
a socialist type state with a decent government might be the answer.
But that is treason I suppose.

It is a strange feeling to be in this camp, with guards at the gate
checking people in and out, not being able to leave the post, as though
one were in prison. The reason is two-fold: guerilla fighters and rob-
bery. The people are desperate. While we were waiting to leave the ship,

several kids came around in a small boat and the fellows tossed them cigarettes, candy bars, and pennies.

I invested in a carton of cigarettes (90 cents) because that is what most of the Japanese and Koreans want as tips, not that many of the fellows do tip. The Koreans especially are anxious to work around an army camp for the privilege of eating decent food.

The fellow sitting next to me is writing home also. It is his son's birthday. I shall stop now and let someone else sit here and write.

I love you. I think of you. I dream of you and kiss you as I sign my name   Mel

JULY 22, 1952

My love—

I'm on a train and writing is difficult. We're on our way south to Taegu, having started out at 4:30 A.M. by truck to Yong Dong Po.

The countryside is beautiful with mountains jutting up, similar to California mountains but higher and greener. The valleys are filled with terraced rice paddies. Every inch of land is cultivated. If it were not for dogfights in the sky between Russian and US jet fighters, and artillery fire in the distance as we watched a movie last night, and guerrilla fighting, I might be enjoying it. Add to it that I am unshaven and dirty even though I showered last night. Well, it could be worse. We have been passing towns whose names I recognize—Taejon, Kimchon. The same poverty exists there. There's more evidence of war—burned and bombed-out buildings, tanks, and abandoned freight cars.

Ours is the first train to get out in 24 hours as they have been having trouble with guerrillas. We have been issued ammunition and hand grenades. I doubt if we shall have trouble, but we are ready. When you get this letter you will know all is well as I shall mail it from Taegu. I'll let you know as soon as possible where I am to be.

I love you and miss you. I'll write again today if I can, but no more now as it is hard enough to read this normally.   Mel

JULY 23, 1:15 P.M.

My Darling—

I just got your letters from San Francisco (#1 & 2). You can imagine how it felt to see them, touch them, read them. They were delivered as I was washing out my fatigues, standing nude, sweating to beat the band. I hurriedly washed, dried, and read them over quickly. I've since read them five times. I shall start to number my letters from now on. It's a good idea.

We were interviewed today and as usual it didn't mean very much. Unfortunately, I am to be assigned to a Division and that means—not to a hospital—at least for 2 to 3 months. Ernie and Gene are in the same boat. All C3150's (General Surgeons) are going to the divisions first rather than to a hospital. They need doctors to replace others up front. There is no particular danger, as I am quite far behind the front and not much is doing anyhow. I griped and complained and shall continue to do so and will write a letter every week asking for a transfer, just to remind them, but I guess that's not why I'm here. Oh well, I shall do some reading and try to get to the meetings they have in various locations.

The day is sunny and hot. I've taken 2 showers already. My fatigues are drying in the sun. An armed guard is pacing along the wall in front of me. Someone is playing the piano. There are Korean people walking about outside. A jet roars overhead. An ambulance brings in some casualties. I'm in the midst of all this. This is ME.

We shall be flying north to our final post. I hear they just fly low and slow and shove us off. Oh well, I still have a big behind, though it is getting smaller. But I shall endeavor to keep it as you remember it.

Be well. I love you.   Mel

WEDNESDAY, JULY 23, 1952, 10:30 P.M.

Melvin, my love,

I wish I could be bright and cheerful when I begin my letters to you, but I'll be crocky [slang, "complaining"] old me. How I miss you and wait for the time when I can feel really alive again. I'm busy and gay but I'm just going through the motions. People say the time will pass quickly. I know it's true—especially when you look BACK on it! As I number the letters, I think that when I get to 250, I can start to plan for your homecoming, as though I'm not planning for it every minute.

The car battery went dead again, so I paid $25 for an Exide battery. It seemed like a lot. Bill, Mom's doorman, said that you can get them for $15.00. I'll profit by this experience, but at least I know that we have a good battery.

I'm in the living room, sitting in front of a fan with two yellow roses beside me. I could lean over and smell them if it weren't too hot to exert so much effort. I hope it's cooler wherever you are.

A college friend called today to give me a choice bit of gossip. An "ideal" couple from Bucknell have been divorced. They went steady fresh and soph years, pinned junior year, engaged senior year, and married after graduation—all our illusions shattered! Feeling like a gossipy old woman, I called Jean [Toddie, my college roommate]. She said it was just the lift she needed.

Tonight watched the convention over television for a while. Listened to Sam Rayburn, the permanent chairman. When they showed Sam R. marching to the platform holding a great big Texas sign, I couldn't keep from crying. Didn't know exactly why. Maybe a reaction to our country's traditions, Rayburn's warmth, Korea, Texas?

One night closer to the time when we shall hold each other close. I love you, my darling.   Dorothy

JULY 24, 1952, 8:00 A.M.

Dorothy my love—

The sun is already high and hot. I'm sitting in my shorts, packed and ready to go in 10 minutes, as we have to be, every day between 8 and 10 A.M. Then we have to remain on the post until 2 P.M. If we've heard nothing, we're free until the next morning. I am glad we shall be flying to our next post, because as nice as the countryside is, I find it difficult to enjoy riding along wondering if the next bridge will blow up.

Last night we had a Korean floor show. While it was fun, I felt sorry seeing Korean gals trying to dance in western style, putting on a western type floor show. It was best when they did Asian dancing and sang Korean songs, some of which were beautiful. When it came to the can-can, oh well.

I hope to get settled soon. Although I don't expect to be doing much, at least I'll have stopped moving. One day, honey, we too will stop moving. My love, MY WIFE, if in the next few days you do not get mail, it is because I am moving.

Had a pair of wooden slippers cut out at the utility shop. I said, "Boysan, boysan, makee with rubber," and he put a strip of rubber over each sandal. Now I have good shower sandals.

My only thoughts now are of you. As far as what the army will do with me, that is up to them. I love you, my wife.   Mel

P.S. Enclosed is a souvenir, 100 WAN, equivalent to 1.6 cents (6,000 WAN to the dollar).

8:00 P.M.

It is a hot night, like one of those scorchers in the city, which I read you are having. No fan here. So we wait for each breeze. Some of the fellows are playing quoits. There is soft dance music on the radio. Sat around all day reading, snoozing, showering. A USO camp show arrived. It wasn't very good. Even Ann Sterling in a loose knit dress didn't help. Did she pull a boner! At the end of the show, she was trying to be nice, encouraging the boys to tune her in on television when they got back to the States. However, it came out of her mouth: IF you boys get back, tune in. . . . There was a moment of silence. Then the pianist started playing.

The sun has set. I'll go to the club for a coke, then to bed to dream of you. Goodnight, my dearest.   Mel

THURSDAY, JULY 24, 1952, 8:30 P.M.

My darling—

The temperature finally dropped and tonight it's supposed to go down to the sixties. Today was delightful—bright sun and cool breeze.

Up early this morning with mosquito bites covering one hand and one eye. Phoned your Mom. They'll be coming for dinner Saturday night and to see the slides from California and Hawaii. I drove Mom and a friend up to Lewisohn Stadium [best known as site for reasonably priced summer concerts, 1918–66] for the Claudio Arrau [Chilean pianist] concert. Gerry drove back circling through Central Park, making a three-point landing backing in to park in front of the house. I think he should be able to take his test soon.

Esther called yesterday. She had arrived home from L.A. the night before. She heard from Gene that he had seen you. She was in L.A. at the time of the earthquake and says that it was a frightening experience to have the room shaking and the furniture moving around.

Tell me if there are any particular columns or periodicals that you want. What news do you get? The Democratic Convention is playing up the fact that Eisenhower is backed by all the old-guard Republicans. Public opinion seems to be swinging away from the General, especially now that it looks like Stevenson will be nominated.

Dad's unveiling will be August 24th, the same day as Uncle Bernie's. [My father's youngest brother, Bernard, died of a heart attack one week after Dad died.] Rabbi Halpern will officiate. [Halpern was the rabbi of the East Midwood Jewish Center synagogue in Brooklyn, where Mel's family and mine were members. He had performed our marriage ceremony.]

I love you and miss you, my sweetheart.   Dorothy

JULY 25, 1952, 11:00 A.M.

My darling—

It's 99 in the shade. We sit without clothes on and perspire. Last night was difficult sleeping. Everyone is bored and restless. This is the army: waiting, waiting. We did go for a walk in the evening, but that's all there is to do unless one wants to run after the Korean chickadees, and you know how I feel about that. Unfortunately, a lot of the fellows do. It gives me a funny feeling to see young kids going out with prostitutes, knowing they are almost certainly diseased. Another horrifying thing is having some married guy with a wife and kids recount his exploits.

12:30 P.M.

Had a decent lunch. Salad, hamburger, peas, cake, and lemon-flavored cold water—gallons of that.

Some of the boys asked, "What do you find to write about? I have to rack my brains for something." I don't know how to answer. I guess these last few letters don't say much, but I can't tell them it's just my way of talking to you, knowing that in the next few days you will be reading this, imagining me here next to the window, writing. I could sit and write all day.

How are you, my darling? I hope the nights are not too long. Be well and cheerful. Work hard. Get some sunshine. I can't see how I shall get through the winter without you. It will probably be next spring before I see you. Love me so hard I can feel it all the way over here.

I just learned that my using APO 613 did not entitle me to Free Postage. Some of my letters may come back. I also should have used APO 301 on the letters I had written previously. The good old army telling me this now and delaying my thoughts of love to you. All my love,

Mel

SATURDAY, JULY 26, 1952, AFTER MIDNIGHT

My love—

Three letters from you this morning! from Inchon, postmarked Army Air Force Mail, as all your letters have been since you left the States. You write freely and beautifully, even when you're writing about ugliness. I am glad to know as much as you can tell me. It enables me to live vicariously your life apart from me.

The truce talks are forever stalemated. What with the conventions, Korea has taken a back seat in the newspapers. People take for granted that it will go on and on—needlessly, cruelly. And now you're in it, and I am too, so how hopeless and needless it is comes to us in sharper focus.

I still have so many things to tell you. Mom sees me writing on and on every night and she tells your Mom. They ask what I can have to write that takes so many words. They are pleased because they know there is understanding and love between us and that our hearts must talk on paper across the miles.

Goodnight wherever you are.   Dorothy

JULY 26, 1952, 8:00 A.M.

Good Morning Mrs. Horwitz, my love—

Now, next to a window, I court any breeze that comes through. Yesterday I got another haircut. Now my hair is so short you can almost polish my pate, but it's cool and easy to take care of. Cost all of 15 cents plus 10-cent tip. My expenses consist of soap, writing paper, coca cola, and laundry. The houseboy did my laundry for 3,000 wan, about 45 cents. He probably would have been satisfied with 2,000. I read mystery stories, a medical symposium, and write to you. I haven't found anyone to whom I can talk freely. Gene is more paranoid daily. All he wants out of life is to make money. Ernie is nice but his interests are different than mine—ball scores, etc. I get the feeling that he always wants to be "one of the boys." I guess I'm just not one of the boys. Do you mind?

After the sun set, it was no cooler and the mosquitoes came out, so we went to the club and played bingo for an hour, drank two more cokes, then I was tired. Perspiring all day. The boredom of having nothing to do. I had hoped a few salt tablets would help, but they didn't. There are no specified rounds at the hospital. The operating rooms are small, and they would rather not have visitors. I showered again, sprayed my bed, tucked in the mosquito netting and crawled in. The bugs here are not as large as those in Texas, except for the mosquitoes and the crickets. Those are enormous. The netting and repellant do not prevent us from getting bitten. So we are given chloroquine once a week against malaria. These measures are quite effective.

Get Bert or Gerry to take some pictures of you every so often and send them, hundreds of them. I also wish you would send—no rush until you get my permanent address—a few copies of *Surgical Clinics of N. America,* a tube of Desitin, and some camera equipment: A Series 6 adapter ring, sunshade and yellow filter, a series 6 haze filter, especially built for the Kodak Retina IIA that screws into the lens, and a Polarizing Screen for the Retina II. Make sure it fits the adapter that Bert has. Bert and Gerry will help you if I am too confusing.

2:00 P.M.

I keep forgetting to number the letters, so you will have to get the sequence of these first letters from the date and time.

This is a unique experience for me, one who has led a relatively soft life. At times I am frightened. I think of you, remembering how we talked our problems through. I feel sorry for those who don't have wives. My heart is full, loving you, knowing you love me.   Mel

JULY 26, 1952, 7:15 P.M.

My Darling—

Tonight at 9 P.M. I get on the train, back north to Seoul toward the front. I have been assigned to the 52nd Medical Batallion. This is a special medical installation. I'm not sure what its functions are, but I'm luckier (I think) than Gene and Ernie who have been assigned to replacement companies of regiments that may end up with an outfit on the line. I hope I may get to the evacuation hospital or a MASH unit sooner. A fellow got orders recently telling him to go up front and at the same time a letter from Washington revoking the orders sending him to Korea. He went to the CO here who told him he was sorry but "once he was here, here he stayed."

Tell my folks (I'll write them later) that I've been assigned to a unit which is way behind the lines, in no danger, which is probably true. I'll let you know the details as soon as I can.

One last coke. Washed and packed. Here I go. Love,   M.

JULY 27, 1952, 11:00 A.M.

My Love—

I am now at the 121 Evac. Hosp. outside Seoul. The train ride was uneventful. The writing is worse than usual because it is so humid my hand does not slide along the paper. Out of 25 fellows, 14 got berths on sleeping cars. I was not one. Since we still had to go through guerilla territory, I was not sorry to be able to sit up and keep my boots on. I was also happy to see a General's car on the train. That meant plenty of guards. While waiting to leave, I noticed a group of North Korean prisoners squatting at the end of the platform. They were being herded along like animals, but didn't seem unhappy. About 80% of them have TB, a good percentage have typhoid, 95% have lice and are disinfected with DDT powder. They are treated in U.N. hospitals, then sent to compounds.

The train was blacked out. It's a strange feeling to be rushing through pitch-black countryside. I've never before really been in danger. We arrived in Seoul at 7 A.M. In the fog and rain it was depressing. Bombed, burned-out buildings. Broken bridges across the Han river. It was a damp and dirty crew that came off the train.

I'm sitting in the day room of the hospital. About half the people are patients and the other half hospital personnel and transient officers. That's what I am—a "transient-casual officer." The Hq of 52nd Med Bn is down the street about 2 miles. In a little while I shall call them and see what they want to do with me. I've been up and down the Korean Peninsula three times now—once by boat and twice by train. I don't know what comes next.

I still don't feel like a soldier and I hope I never will. Nor like a doctor, and I hope I can feel like that soon.

The morale of the patients is good. I was speaking to a regular army officer who had been up on the line. He says that the Communists could not break through. They might just push us back a few miles, but their losses would be and have been fantastic. In one raid they lost 5,400 men, by actual body count, not to mention how many injured. He also stated that while we could probably break through their lines, the cost would be too great. If full scale war broke out we would have to go around them by sea—maybe. The truce talks are still fruitless and there will probably be an armed truce. For how long?

Am using foot powder like mad. I shall try to keep as clean as possible since that is the secret of avoiding trouble. When you send the small package, include a box of Baby Powder, as you cannot get plain talcum here. And tell the folks not to send any food till winter.

I dream of holding you. Imagine with me darling and it won't be too long.   Mel

MONDAY, JULY 28, 1952, 11:00 P.M.

My darling—

I am tender with the sweet fresh memory of this morning's letters from you—three—one from Inchon (after shower), one en route to Taegu, and one from Taegu (after shower). Your moods seem to correlate with the number of showers available. I'm sure it's a reflection of your surroundings, but it's amazing what feeling clean will do for the spirits. Even me, secure and clean, I rarely sit down to write to you until I have taken my shower. At that point I am in a better frame of mind and can think more clearly.

It really sounds as though you're in Korea. I am thankful every moment that you do not have to kill and that you won't be directly in the front lines. I feel so helpless. Maybe there is something I could do about this "Korean situation," but I don't know what it is. I almost wish I were a nurse so that I could be working at your side. How many times during the day I look at my watch, not to see what time it is, but rather to figure out what you might be doing at that particular hour, half a day ahead of me.

Just as I look at Mom alone in her big bed and say how can it be true, so I reach for you beside me and ask myself how the next months can be real. I love you with all the passion that is in me.

Your Mom asked us for dinner Sat. nite after my exam. Told her I didn't know. Just felt like getting away from the city. I have no idea where I want to go. I just want to go. I guess I feel that I can escape from loneliness, but of course that's wrong. I shouldn't complain, but what are husbands for? I shall close my eyes and dream that we are together. The time will pass. We have so much to look forward to, being together, making the most of what we have—together. I love you.

Dorothy

My Darling—

Good news. This morning I called Col. Lindsey [senior surgical resident at New Haven Hospital when Mel was an intern]. He was delighted to hear from me. He is a big wheel in Seoul, the Operations Chief of the entire medical set-up here in Korea. Well, I got a jeep and was driven in to see him. After we had talked a while, he volunteered that maybe he could do something for me, not right away, but perhaps soon. He said to keep in touch and he'd try to get me into a MASH unit. He is regular army from the word go—a paratrooper. He also offered me several other jobs which I declined, gracefully I hope. 1. Battalion Aid Station. 2. Command of a Collecting or Clearing Company. The latter would have meant a promotion and an important job BUT I would never get to do any surgery and wouldn't get out of Korea for 12–15 months. In addition, I don't know enough about the army to take either of them. He is a good person to know. The help HE volunteered. I did not ask, except to emphasize that I wanted to get to a place where I could do surgery. Whether anything comes of it, I can't even guess, but over here, I won't hesitate to do anything to get a good job—and to get out.

I'm on my way. I love you, my wife.   Mel

8:00 P.M.

The road to the Clearing Company was the worst I have ever seen—muddy and full of holes. Sometimes I bounced a full foot off the seat of the truck. I am very glad I kept my fat behind till I got here. As we went forward there were fewer and fewer civilians. Three or four places we were stopped by MP's (Military Police) and checked. Several large trailers passed us going the other way with tanks on them, battered by enemy fire, going back for repair. The country is rugged, craggy mountains jutting up precipitously, smaller hills breaking up the valleys. It is hellish country to fight in. It was difficult enough to drive through. This is the rainy season and the rivers and streams are high. There are crews of Korean laborers struggling to keep the road from washing out. Tucked in here and there in the canyons are army units (U.S., British, Korean, Norwegian), ammunition dumps, and airstrips. Each bridge is guarded, sometimes with tanks. The paths alongside the road are heavily mined.

We kept going for 2½ hours. At about 4 P.M. the driver suddenly stopped in front of a ragged tent and said, "How about a chocolate bar?" I had visions of some Korean mess, but inside was a British PX. I bought a bar of chocolate and politely refused a beer can full of tea.

Shortly thereafter we crossed a large bridge and arrived at this unit. The MD here is a GP, disgruntled by the situation, but pleasant, and glad to see me as I am to cut his burden in half.

We are set up in a dozen tents alongside a RR track. The one I am living in has a brick floor, wooden supports, electric light, four bunks, table, wash stand with basins, and a boy to keep it clean and get warm water in the morning. We have a radio, a sort of couch, bookshelf where I stack my clothes, a mattress, 1 sheet and blankets, and a bowl of artificial flowers. There is a modified outhouse in back. In one corner is a box set in the floor filled with cold beer, ice, and cokes. It isn't bad at all, considering. Of course, 10 miles away you can see the flash of OUR artillery and hear the thud of guns. 20 miles away, there are fellows dug into the mountainsides and in places 100 yards from them is the enemy. I am quite safe here.

I had a good dinner, on a table cloth on a tray, served by a Korean waiter. After unpacking I went by truck down the road 2 miles where the 8055 MASH unit is located. I took a shower (cold tonight because the burner was broken), read a sign that said, "This shower is off limits during nurses' shower hours." No time was given. I then met the CO of this hospital. I keep meeting interesting people in the shower. I'll have to take them more often. This Major Heilman told me that Col Lindsey had said I was to be nearby, and he invited me to look at the hospital and go on rounds with them. I don't know how often I'll be able to do the latter, because there is a dispensary sick call every A.M. But I shall be getting over there.

We are a transfer point where patients are loaded onto a hospital train. This is some train! Air-conditioned, ten cars with 3-layered pullman berths, a minor surgery car, diner, and kitchen.

So here I am. An MD is playing solitaire, another writing to his wife. They were married only 90 days ago. The other two are joking saying that the houseboy brings breakfast to the tent in the morning. And they may not be joking.

By the way, you won't receive an allotment check until the middle of August.

I am at Chongong Ni (old name Chonkok), 40 miles north of Seoul and 2½ miles north of the 38th parallel.

My darling, I can't put down what is in my heart. Know I love you and kiss you goodnight.   Mel

There have been articles in the papers about flying disks—no longer rumors, but actually seen simultaneously on radar and by pilots. Yesterday, for six hours over Washington, there were 5 of them. They travel 100–300 mis. per hr. Everyone is wondering, including me. It has been proposed that they are directed by some reasoning power. D.

My Darling—

Just finished a supper of roast veal, fresh tomatoes, peaches (no potatoes or corn for me), and candy. I'm trying hard to resist.

Went to bed last night with the roar of artillery lulling me to sleep. Awakened with artillery bouncing me out of bed, and the chatter of machine guns, the fire of a reserve infantry unit having target practice about 2 miles from here. Breakfast was indeed brought to our tent by our quiet boy O-Soo-Han who looks 14 but is 17 years old. At the dispensary, I saw 15 patients on Sick Call. It was good to be working again even though most of it is trivial—V.D., fungous infections of the foot, diarrhea, etc.

The rain which had started last night continued. You have never seen such rain. Gray, low-hanging clouds made the day dreary. After 10:00 A.M. I spent the rest of this morning drawing equipment, cleaning boots, reading.

Tomorrow a hospital train will come through. My job will be to make sure the patients are comfortable and decide where they are to go. The rain has slowed everything down. There is a tank down the road guarding the bridge and it just fired a few cannon rounds. Why I don't know, but I sure felt like falling flat. So did everyone else. However, I am lucky. Inside it is dry and comfortable. Not far from here, there are people in wet muddy holes.

I wish I had a job that worked me so hard I didn't have time to think, so I could fall into bed at night exhausted. My heart beats faster and my breathing quickens as I think of you. My body longs for the closeness of you. Be well my darling.   Mel

WEDNESDAY, JULY 30, 1952, 11:45 P.M.

My darling—

I know my man. I know that you make the best of a bad situation—even being afraid. I wish I could be near you sharing the uncertainty and disgust. We have each other. That thought is with me always and will carry me through the next months. There IS a reason for wanting to grow each day, to look forward to the next and the next until once again, we are filled with one another. To know how you love me should make me vain. But my love for you takes me so completely out of myself that there is no room for vanity. I feel a completeness I have never felt before.

Another day of study and restlessness. The bright spot is 9:15 when the mail comes. I have kept your folks "well" informed. I tell them only what they want to hear—officers' club, roast beef, and showers. My tone is always cheerful and there is never fear in my voice. So my darling you may continue to bitch to me as though we were alone in bed together.

Now it's time to close my eyes. It's tomorrow afternoon for you. Have you had lunch? Are you working? Can you take a shower? Are you close to the fighting? Are the people around you people you want to be with? You have told me these things from day to day, but I wonder now, at this moment, what the answers are. I can only think about you—sweaty, tasting and smelling good. Goodnight my love,   D.

Do you want me to send you the daily news summary from the *Times*?

JULY 30, 1952, 4:30 P.M.

My Darling Dorothy—

Another rainy day. Awake at 7 A.M., shaved, washed underwear in a helmet with hot water heated by a small gasoline stove. Breakfast in the tent, then Sick Call. Some real hot Korean babe must have been loose recently, since 90% of the 50 patients were here for VD. Some just laughing it off, others scared. With the treatment I order, I try to tell those whom I think it might influence to stay away from these Korean women. The VD here is getting harder and harder to treat.

About 10 A.M. after dispensary, the casualties for the hospital train began arriving. Those poor bastards. I can, if I try hard, justify my being in Korea, but not them. We made them comfortable, giving medication if necessary, and began screening to see where they would go, to Seoul or Pusan.

Later in the morning, my friend from the MASH came over. From what he tells me, they are operating day and night. I shall go there as frequently as I can and watch. At night I might get to do a few things.

At the bridge, the water has risen about 15 feet. I took pictures of the tanks guarding it. They have been firing all morning at large pieces of drifting material to break them up so they won't damage the bridge. When that gun goes off, it rocks things for a mile around.

The pictures I have of us are now in a little folder. I have them out where I can look at them. They are over a year old, one of them taken two years ago at Cold Spring [location of the Merson family summer home in upstate New York]. Two years. I can remember no further back. We met, loved, and grew together—changed together, laughed and cried together, LIVED TOGETHER. My woman, I want to hold you in my arms.

The rain which let up for a while has started again, the sky getting darker, the artillery starting up. I really will have to brush up on my languages what with Belgian, French, Greek, Ethiopian, and Korean troops coming through (of course U.S. and British too). My French is best, but I can say, "Dolor mejor?" Till tomorrow.   Mel

Enclosed map for you to follow.

THURSDAY, JULY 31, 1952, 11:00 P.M.

Melvin, my darling—

How I love to hear you "talk." I can feel your moods. During the one year we had of living together, we learned each other's rhythms. Now when we write, without restraint, there is meaning behind each word and although we repeat ourselves, the words are always fresh. How lucky I am to be married to you, that my life is bound to yours not by a wedding band but by mutual understanding, respect, interest, fun, sorrow—just wanting to be together fulfilling each other, growing, knowing that each moment is precious. That's how I have felt since we have lived together—looking forward to the immediate future, yet wanting each moment to last forever. As I told Mom, I have so much to write because I have to make up for what I haven't said to you all day. Now, our letters have to do even more than just "talk."

Goodnight my love. I sleep another night without you. Oh how I love you.   Dorothy

My love—

Still at the 618 Clearing Stn, but I go down to the 8055 MASH and have actually been operating. They are busy as the dickens. I shall be working most of the night, as that is the only time I can get over here. I've been talking to the CO and he is willing to try to get me into the unit as soon as there is a vacancy. Well you know the army. I might end up somewhere else, but while I'm here at least I'm doing something. My training has been good, and although I am not familiar with the army way of doing things, I can handle almost anything they have at least almost as well as those I've seen working.

Oh my darling, it is so good to work, though it is so different than anything I've ever seen or done.

Still no mail, but it will come, I know. Now back to work. I'll "khop it in" [Yiddish derivation, "take advantage of the situation"] while I can. No telling how long it will last.

I love you with all my heart.   Mel

August

In Korea and New York City, our daily mail vigil began in earnest. Letter writing had become a healthy addiction—like taking vitamins, Mel's mother said. My day, more flexible than his, never ended before I had talked with him on paper. He fit in his lines to me whenever and wherever he could.

Casualties increased. I rebelled against separating their body count from ours, as one might tally a football score. The impersonal statistics were beyond comprehending. "There's nobody alive on Siberia Hill this morning," reported a First Division Officer after our marines had gained a ridge east of Panmunjom. I wondered how many of our marines' lives it took to obliterate a hillful of their soldiers.

Achieving his much-sought-after asssignment, Mel was transferred to the 8055 M.A.S.H. as a surgeon. Nothing in all his stateside training in trauma had prepared him for the shock of operating on the wounded. His descriptions to me were graphic and emotional.

I studied for my Spanish teaching exam and devised lesson plans for the fall. I also kept the car in good repair, a matter of pride for this "girl" who had never used a screwdriver. After a year's hiatus, I once again enrolled in modern dance classes. There were weekends when, for love of music and fresh air, I went to Tanglewood, Massachusetts, the summer home of the Boston Symphony. Attendance at these summer concerts had been a tradition for both our families. The summer before we were married, Mel and I spent our first weekend together there in Tanglewood at the music festival.

The election campaign was in full swing. Although we were both registered Democrats, we prided ourselves on being independent voters.

Heartened to see both candidates cautioning against an extension of the war, I began my own campaign, sending Mel materials supporting Stevenson. Eisenhower endorsed all the Republican candidates, including McCarthy. Countering McCarthy's inflammatory rhetoric, Stevenson warned against striking "freedom of the mind with the fist of patriotism." But even this early in the campaign, Stevenson's intellect was no match for Ike's smile. Although initially attracted by Eisenhower, Mel's repugnance for McCarthy soon won him over to the Democratic candidate. He spent the next few months trying to convince his colleagues to follow suit.

Until the summer of 1952, I had dealt with uncertainty by fixing on the present. My father's death and the threat of Mel's departure had confirmed the validity of a seize-each-day philosophy. When Mel left for Korea, my focus shifted. Tomorrow became more important than today. For the first time in my memory of summers I was happy to see August come to an end.

AUGUST 1, 1952, 12:30 P.M.

Dorothy my Darling—

My letter last night was of necessity a hasty one. Now I can relax and go over the last few days with you.

Wednesday evening I went to the 8055 MASH, met a friend of mine, saw a movie, then went to the surgical tent. This hospital handles those injuries that must be treated immediately and those that are serious. Last month they did 800 cases. They have an operating room with 8 tables though only 2 or 3 are used at one time. You wear boots, pants, a rubber apron, and gloves most of the time—occasionally a cap and gown. All the wounds, of course, are dirty, so there is no need for strict asepsis. They had 4 cases to do and I helped them. It was really good to get gloves on again, smell the operating room. Patients of all nationalities come through, including prisoners.

I spent the night there, sleeping a few hours, then came back here and worked all morning. The other officers had gone to Seoul, so I remained all day, then went over to the 8055 at about 6 P.M. and worked all night. The CO told me he was glad to have the help. I assisted and later did a few cases on my own. It was exciting. For a while I even forgot where I was. Although it would be nice to work in a MASH unit, keeping my hand in and getting more credit, the approach to surgery is so different and must be because of the type of injury and the necessity for speed. You also lose a lot by not being able to follow the patient. Once he is over the immediate post-operative difficulties, he is sent further back.

The hospital train has come in so I shall stop for now.

I love you, my wife,   Mel

SATURDAY, AUGUST 2, 1952, AFTER MIDNIGHT

My love—

Another day away and I can see you as vividly as though you were next to me. I can feel the soft wooliness of your chest, the roughness or the smoothness of your face, your hips pressed against me, your thighs and legs rubbing mine as I curl my toes under yours.

This morning I was in the exam room by 8:45. No matter what I had told myself and everybody else, my stomach was nervous. I worked straight through till noon. It was difficult, but no surprises. I think I passed, but with language exams you can never tell. There are so many little things that take points away. However, my studying did help and there is gratification in that.

When I came home, there was a box of slides from Japan awaiting me. Gerry had the screen all set up and ready. Darling, each one is a work of art! The best part will be listening to you describe each scene as you saw it. You look wonderful. Even your Mom had to admit it. The slide I will enjoy most is the one of the two of us that we shall send to the folks.

Goodnight my darling. I love you.   Dorothy

AUGUST 2, 1952, 2:00 P.M.

Dorothy my Darling—

The train will be here shortly to pick up a batch of patients. One of them is a French boy with a broken arm. He seems to be uncomfortable. In my poor French I tried to tell him that we would give him something to make him comfortable. I've been systematically reviewing the surgical anatomy book that I have, as Traumatic Surgery is nothing but anatomy knocked to pieces.

We hear about Russia and the US playing basketball in the Olympics. That is the way this rotten mess should be settled. Draw up the conditions first: What will happen when either side loses? Then play it out on the basketball court!

7:00 P.M.

Wheeee I finally got some mail from you, letters #11 & 12 dated July 18 and July 19. The others in between will probably come as one package.

AUGUST 3, 1952, 2:30 P.M.

The 3rd Division Band came to meet a trainload of replacements. The General was there to greet them. They all came by helicopter—very impressive. Then he spoke to them. What a meathead! Don't know his name, but here were a bunch of kids coming to Korea to fight and he addressed them as if they were boy scouts: Keep your jackets buttoned. Don't litter the ground. BS! Anyhow I got off a roll of movie film of this to be developed and sent to you.

Sometimes I think I ought to request front line duty in order to get 4 points a month and be in Japan sooner, but then I think it isn't worth the gamble.

MONDAY, AUGUST 4, 1952, 7:00 P.M.

My love, my Darling Wife—

I am as close to being happy now as I can be. The sun is setting, reflecting off the surfaces of a dozen letters. When I was in Seoul today, I got this packet of mail, #3–9 from you and some from my folks and your Mom. I've read them over three times already.

I last wrote from the hospital train as we rode through the country-side, rolling hills on either side and endless rice paddies with toiling Koreans knee-deep in water, and the many children either playing or asleep in one of the primitive thatched tents, about 4' x 4', that are set up to provide shady places to rest. They wave and smile, standing there with their dirty feet, most of them nude. Many are from orphanages. They pay for this war so much longer than their elders.

At Yong Dong Po I visited the other section of the 618 Cl. Co. at the airfield. I called them and they sent a jeep for me. It is ludicrous to call and have "James the Chauffeur" come to pick me up.

The fellows at the air strip are living quite comfortably. Quonset huts and concrete floors. I met two interesting people, one, a lieutenant from Ohio. He did have style, but he acts as though he has a bee in his rectum. Surly, rude, never smiles, unhappy, doesn't speak clearly,

mopes, bitches. He has less to do than we have. Maybe that is the reason. The other lieutenant is the exact opposite. Friendly, cheerful, but I
think dumb. He's originally from Virginia and then had one year of
general practice in a town in Maine. He loves to hunt and fish. He
bragged of the hundreds of birds he had killed, but "really disliked doing it." He only did it because he liked to see his hunting dog in action.
Maybe I'm just impatient with people, but I think I can get along with
him the best of any I've met this past week, although he talks too much.

You ask about my uniform and whether I've learned where or when.
Yes, I know now. I even know how to take apart and put together the
pistol I carry. Not that I could shoot anyone. Or could I? I don't know
how frightened I might get, but we are told that an armed soldier has
NEVER gotten into difficulty with guerrillas or political fanatics. So I
wear the pistol. I don't care if my uniform—those scrawnchy fatigues—
is pressed, just clean. I don't have a fancy cap, just clean. I don't care
about a dress uniform to put all my ribbons on when I get back. You'd
be surprised how many I've accumulated just by being here. I'd almost
look like a maypole. The above words sound a wee bit bitter, as I write
them. I'm really not. I just feel hopeless, helpless. And if I feel that way,
what about the fellows out there where it's thundering. Maybe they will
sign a truce. We bomb and bomb and bomb. The enemy is not being
supplied. We hear their morale is low, but they'll fight anyhow, because
if they don't, they have nothing better to turn to.

I'll read and re-read your letters. Pepto Bismol and no toilet paper.
Colored slides. Over-exposed movies. Spanish vocabulary. Your dancing. Bitch to me. Laugh with me. I've spoken with you, talked it out. I
feel better, as always, my dearest one. Cross this year off. No. Don't do
that. We'll continue to move through time together, because we are
apart only physically. Sleep my love and dream with me of a good life
together.

I love you.   Mel.

TUESDAY, AUGUST 5, 1952, 1:00 A.M.

My darling—

Do you snore? you want to know. My darling, your breathing is as
calm and peaceful as a child's, an angel's. Just tell those guys that! Of
course once in a while, when your allergic nose is stuffed up and you
have forgotten to sniff the inhaler and your pyribenzamine pills have

run out, you might let a few wheezes sneak through. However, if they feel that you are a menace to the sleep of hard-working army medics, it is their patriotic duty to ship you home, and if the latter is impossible, I shall be delighted to act as a snore-shielder, to sleep with you and turn you over. Okay?

Bought a Korean map at Macy's for 35 cents. It has been frustrating not being able to find on the daily *Times'* map the places you've been mentioning. But of course it is actually a good sign, because as yet you are not in locations where, according to the papers, there is extreme danger. Incidentally, this map includes Japan. I hope we shall be using it soon my darling.

10:15 P.M.

Melvin, my darling—

Nowadays, I do quite a bit around the house, because Mom is working so hard. I like to see her take it easy when she gets home. Her decorator was in tonight, and I excused myself. 15 minutes in the room with her is enough.

And the days go on in the same manner except that there are big changes. Dad is gone. I miss him. It's difficult for me to tell that to Mom, even though I know she would like to hear it. In my heart there is a big void since you left. The only meaning that the days have is their passing and making weeks into months.

I love you, my husband.   Dorothy

WEDNESDAY, AUGUST 6, 1952, 9:00 P.M.

Hi Honey—

Good news tonight. As of this weekend, I'm being assigned on temporary duty to the 8055 MASH. The move was initiated by my friend Col. Lindsey, as well as Maj. Holleman, who is CO of the unit. By next Monday I'll be moved over and working a regular schedule. Going over there in my spare time paid off, as well as my having gotten along with Lindsey when I worked with him back at New Haven Hospital. So I move again.

After sick call this morning, I came back to our tent and studied anatomy for two hours.

You can now address mail to me at the 8055 A.U. M.A.S.H., APO 301, c/o PM SF, Cal. The boys here will send down any mail that comes.

This war continues and less and less appears in the US papers. I'm sure people forget that bullets are still flying and people are getting shot and killed. But that is human nature. The MASH will continue to work as it takes care of all accidents—jeep, appendices, etc. even if and when an armistice is signed.

Before they gave the final word on the orders, they asked me if this is what I wanted, if I would mind working long hours. I just smiled and you know what I said. I hope I'll be able to get Board [American Board of Surgery] credit for this time. There should be no reason not to.

"News from the U.S." No rain in many states. Eisenhower speaks. I agree with the editorial that commented that his speeches have not matched his smile. I still haven't decided. Good night and good morning.   Mel

FRIDAY, AUGUST 8, 8:00 A.M.

Good Morning Dorothy Darling—

The sun is already high, the day clear. I've washed, shaved and now what better way to start the day than writing to my darling.

During sick call yesterday, the MASH called to ask if I could give them a hand. The pre-op ward was full—about 30 patients waiting to be operated on, and more coming in all the time. 4–5 operating tables going at once and anesthetists working two patients at once with the aid of a technician. I found the CO. He said, "Pick up a knife and get going." And that's what I did. Most of the work you do yourself. I worked from 9:30 to 4:30, stopping a half-hour for lunch. When the afternoon ended, the ward was empty, just one or two still coming in.

I suppose there had been a battle somewhere the previous night. Many of the patients were from a Greek Battallion, so you can imagine the language barrier. I'm getting the idea of army methods and have been able to cope with most of the problems. For those I'm not sure of, there's always someone around to ask. Hot, sweaty, and tired, I ate supper and took a shower. Ah yes, my mood is always better after that. When I returned to the 618th, I felt I had accomplished something and learned something.

As I sat and read all the letters (I'll be re-reading them today), a trainload of men and tanks came by. The wheel on one of the cars was on fire. I took some pictures. A truck brought in two people with heat exhaustion and a Korean houseboy brought in a bowl containing three goldfish. We bought them. One died this morning.

Four weeks ago we parted. $\frac{1}{10}$th gone. $\frac{9}{10}$ths to go. Until later, my love.

Lunchtime. The boy came with the menu. We cross out what we don't want. Since the diet is the same here as at the front, it is 4,000 calories a day. I just don't eat potatoes, bread, cake, corn, etc. They have several large ice cream making plants in Korea so the GI's (and I) can have ice cream.

I won't go to the MASH now as I'll be moving over in a day or two. The afternoon is ahead. I'll read, snooze, and play chess. I have started again after a long time. We'll play when we're together again. I love you.
Mel

FRIDAY, AUGUST 8, 1952, 10:15 P.M.

My Darling Wife—

Bed time. We dream and will be together. The words "I love you" will be written countless times and never make up for one moment apart. Now I welcome the night as it means another day gone.

Spent the afternoon playing chess and finally won a game. Read the *Stars And Stripes* [military sponsored news publication for the armed forces], catching up on the news. Ike wants to cut the budget, probably no further aid to education or flood control—just arms. We bomb North Korea and they fight on. I'm only afraid that we and they will be foolish enough not to stop. Whichever side starts an offensive, there will be disastrous results on both sides. The talks drag on. They are losing more than we are. I'm sure they are stalling, but for what? Political or military reasons. I hope our children will learn to think critically for themselves and will do something useful in this world. If we can do that my love, then we truly will have done something worthwhile.

Here in the tent the electric generator hums in the background, a radio plays softly in a corner. The three of us—Martin, Curry, and I— sit here writing, each in his own world. I feel as though I'm part of a show that will be over soon. 11 P.M. The lights are out. I am writing by candlelight. Since we have loved each other, there is a peace within me. I feel complete. No longer looking. I feel loved.   Mel

AUGUST 8, 1952, 3:00 P.M., TANGLEWOOD WEEKEND

My darling—

We have been here one whole day and if, if, if—it would have been so wonderful. At the concert, there was the usual excitement, but for me in a vacuum. I made comments on the program which I am enclosing so that you will know what I would have whispered to you had you been at my side.

I preferred the Brahms to the Schumann although I was disappointed in Rubenstein. Unless I don't understand his interpretation of the music, I found his playing sloppy. Of course I wouldn't venture to comment to anyone but you because, after all, the GREAT Rubenstein. Then, the Short Symphony of Howard Swanson, with all the power of a longer work. After the program, I read the notes and somebody else agreed with me! In 1950 it had won the prize for the best new symphony of that year. It is the kind of modern music that should be played for those to whom the moderns are new. Its length makes it easier to listen to and the jazz in the last movement gives it something familiar for novices to hang on to. After it was over, the composer came to the stage to a tremendous ovation. He is a Negro. You would have squeezed my hand until it ached.

Now I sit at the water's edge alone, my eyes tracing the dark green shore line that encircles the expanse of water. In the background are the hazy mountains. The sun is barely peeping through the clouds and the breeze has died. It is a time for being together and enjoying the poetry of life. As I write, I think of how petty all this must sound. I hope that I can send some of this peace to you. I am thankful for what we have. We shall be patient and strong. I love you. D

SATURDAY, AUGUST 9, 1952, 3:00 P.M.

Dorothy Darling—

A hot, sticky afternoon. Washed and shaved with cold water. As our little houseboy says, "Water heater—she all fuck up!" Plenty of patients at sick call today, most of them with colds, and aches and pains. Having medical care available and free, they use and abuse it as a means of getting out of work. About 60% of the patients do that, another 25% have VD and only 15% have legitimate complaints. Since I've nothing else to do, I don't kick.

Had one unpleasant task. A young kid, ready for rotation home, had been a big shot getting treated for VD 10 days ago. He came in for a pre-rotation physical. The men have to be free from lice, VD, and contagious diseases before they go home. Well, he had a recurrence of his VD. The VD bugs here are getting resistant to the drugs. So I couldn't pass him. I felt terrible watching his reaction, but I couldn't do anything except try to get him well as soon as I could. I really had a conflict, thinking he had brought it on himself, and then, well, he's just a kid. Anyhow, it will only be a few extra weeks. I now have a two-minute lecture that I give to all VD patients, changing my tone and expression to fit the patient. It doesn't do a bit of good, I believe.

Tonight we may go over to one of the other units for a "party and dirty song fest" and to meet some of the British and French officers.

Two of our goldfish have died. I guess we got took by the houseboy although the surviving one still looks peppy.

10:30 P.M.

Saturday night. I've been to a party—sort of—at "Parson Charlie," the code name of a signal company. Capt. Martin drove the jeep down. He's a short, jolly fellow, a party boy. His wife likes him in uniform. There were a Negro Signal Corps officer, about 35 years old, 2 British officers, an American officer about my age, and the two of us. They really started drinking—a case of whiskey, 12 bottles of Canadian Club—cost $17.50. Because you know how I take to whiskey and because I figured someone would have to drive back (2.2 miles) in the blackout, I stayed with two beers—3.2%. But I got as "drunk," if you know what I mean, as the rest. The British sang some dirty songs with real spirit. Example:

Mary lived in a mountain glen
She seduced herself with a fountain pen
The top came off and the ink ran wild
And she gave birth to a blue-black child
Chorus: Oh they called the bastard Steven (3 times)
Cause that was the name of the ink. (and so on)

The Negro officer was funny, drunk, picturesque as he told of his wife not writing because his kids had the measles for the second time. One of the more difficult problems discussed (and this was the tenor of the party) was how to use the word "fuck" as an adverb. The final answer was "fuckingly well done." I must admit I enjoyed myself. It was fascinating to watch the various people change under the influence of alcohol. The only effect the beer had on me was to fill my bladder. The contrast of what was going on inside that tent and what was going on 15 miles away was amazing to me as I sat there in the midst of it. This Negro officer is a lawyer, has two kids and has been married 7 years. Yet on R & R (Rest & Recreation, a vacation that is given after about 8 months, sometimes Rest & Recuperation) he went to Japan and shacked up with a Japanese girl. He loves his wife and kids. I know by the way he read parts of a letter he had gotten where he described his 3-year-old boy blowing out his birthday candles and wishing his "Daddy would soon come home." He said, "Shit man— that made the old man feel good!"

The evening went on and at 9:45 it was time to go back. Curfew is at 11. Imagine now, with me. I left the BOQ tent, buckled on my pistol, went out into the moonlight with a very drunk captain at my side, into the jeep, which I had never driven before. Got it started and then with blackout lights on, feeling my way along the road by moonlight, stopped at the gate, "Who goes there? Advance and be recognized." All just as we had rehearsed at Ft. Sam Houston, but here they were playing for keeps. Identified, we went along the road back to our tent.

I'm not a party-goer, but at least I'm not a party-pooper. I'm in a rut. An old army man like me and can't stomach good liquor. What will people think?

The night is still now. The generator has stopped. All I can hear is the faint hum of an airplane, the scratch of my pen, and the footsteps of the sentry who is about 10 yards from our tent.

Goodnight my dearest.   Mel

SATURDAY, AUGUST 9, 1952, 11:45 P.M.

My darling—

We drove to the Tanglewood grounds and walked around a bit before the concert. The music was beautiful, of course, the Bach solemn, sad, and majestic. The Copeland was powerful with interesting combinations of instruments. It always takes me a while to get used to Leonard Bernstein. At first his antics bother me and then, I can't take my eyes off him. How long can he last expending so much energy?

Mom met a number of people she knew, unfortunately some who

stirred unhappy memories, especially a woman who was supposed to have had an inoperable brain tumor. Mom is a marvel at controlling herself. Right after Dad died, I could think only of what he had suffered, what he would miss of life. Now it is Mom who is my concern.   Dorothy

MONDAY, AUGUST 11, 1952, 8:45 P.M.

My Love—

Being fatigued from work and not boredom is indeed a welcome change. The guns are booming. How can man do that to man? They come in battered, and I only stop later, as now, to reflect on the actual horror. Then it was a job to do quickly, efficiently, kindly, but not emotionally. Here am I in Korea. A soldier. But I am not a soldier. I don't feel like one and I hope I never shall. For those poor fellows who do have to feel that way, it's to save their lives.

All the others are in bed and I'm alone with you. I hear rumblings about the "light." "What are you writing about?" "Look at him smile." "What crap!" And so on. Goodnight. Be well.   Mel

WEDNESDAY, AUGUST 13, 1952, 2:20 P.M.

My Wife—My Love—

Do you feel, as I do sometimes as I read your letters, that you are leading a double or triple life, one, as you go about every day, writing the letter at the end of the day about what you did—stopping and dreaming every so often—another, as you read six or seven days later about what I am doing—living with me through my thoughts of the previous week, at the same time knowing that at that very moment I'm dreaming of you and missing you.

Awakened after a restless night. It's hot and humid. My air mattress had a flat, so that every time I turned over, a blast of air would shoot from one side to the other and slap me.

About noon the X-Ray machine broke and we started sending all the patients to the Norwegian MASH down the road. This was very welcome as it is 106 in the shade, 120 in the sun and about 180 in the tents today. Right now I'm in a pair of shorts with 2 fans going. In a few hours it will begin to cool off and perhaps we'll get some rain.

My dearest, your letters are so full of you—the Lighthouse [reading to the blind], dancing. Take it easy and work into it. Eat plenty of salt.

Each day is clear and the sun burning. You can imagine how hot it is if I, the sun worshipper, don't go out to bake. Uh oh, the fans stopped. Guess they're fixing the generators. The sweat pours off me. Have been taking salt tablets like peppermints. Ah, the fans are on again. Have one of them trained right on my you-know-what and am cooling them off. If only you were here now. Do you think anyone else is as happy with their love as we are with ours?

Am now living with three other fellows. A fourth just moved in, Dick Kamil who was at Ft. Sam with me. We get along particularly well. His wife is about to give birth, so we ordered a case of sparkling burgundy from the British PX and sent down one of our British anesthetists to pick it up. My wife, I get so excited when I think of US making babies. I sometimes can't believe that I can feel the way I do, loving you. When I get down in the dumps about Korea and being away from you, then I think, Why, she loves me—snoring, sniffling, sneezing, no hair, itchy balls, and all. She loves me. And I love her with all my being, with all the feeling, power, and passion within me. Dorothy Horwitz. Mrs. Melvin Horwitz, my wife. Can I tell you what a thrill it is and how much I love to address an envelope to you?

Kellum is mixing a martini. Not for me. I feel less like drinking now than ever—only cold coke and beer, because they're cold. But the reason I mention this martini is because of the black olive he is putting in it. I can see you popping them into your mouth one after the other, and I think, the only time I like olives is when I kiss you after you've eaten them.

Now will wander over and see how things are going at the OR. Almost one more day closer to you.

6:30 P.M.

Now, in front of the tent. The day has cooled down and there's a nice breeze. Have been watching a baseball game between the 8055 and an ordnance group. Since I would rather be with my love, I shall write letter #23a.

I remembered that you tried to find ChonGongNi on the map and found it below the 38th parallel. I can assure you, it is north. Its other name is Chonkok. You should have gotten the map I sent, so you'll know where I am. The 8055 MASH is right on the 38th, directly south of Chonkok.

Wrote to Bert wishing him Happy Birthday and had supper. No appetite. Too hot. Just had fruit juice and stewed peaches. The movie tonight is "Pat and Mike," the one we saw together in San Antone, a world and ages ago. It was good, but not quite good enough to see again, so I'll go to sleep early.

There's a little Korean orphan here that the boys clothe and feed. He's cute and bright, but a problem. About five years old, he speaks better English than he does Korean. He's beginning to think of himself as better than the other Korean kids. We're trying to find a school to send him to, but of course he doesn't want to go. No one yet is strong enough just to send him. He became fascinated with someone's partial dentures, so he showed up in the dental clinic and told the dentist his teeth were too small, that they were wearing out, and wouldn't the dentist make him a set of teeth he could take in and out.

The ballgame is going hot and heavy. We're winning.

Love you.   M

WEDNESDAY, AUGUST 13, 1952, 10:30 P.M.

My darling—

Received another reel of movie film from Korea. Interesting, but I didn't like seeing you wearing arms any more than you like wearing them. I am so thankful for the pictures. The letters tell the story and the pictures confirm it. Keep taking them. If you need any film or equipment, let me know. What you have requested was sent out and will catch up with you eventually.

After a morning of letter-writing and phone calls, I went down for some drug items, had lunch, finished reading the morning paper, and left the apartment about 1:30. My first stop was Bloomingdale's where I was to look at their modern furniture department for Mom. What a hold modern has taken. The grocery man's wife didn't want to buy Mom's old furniture because "it isn't modern enough."

I bought some black pages to add to the photo album, then to the Lighthouse where I met Pedro for a reading session. We spent an hour at the 58th St. Library looking up books for him to use for a term paper on deficiencies in the present society, especially in democracy in education. Then back to the Lighthouse where I read to him for another half-hour.

I'm going to buy a new slide box because the first one is filled. I am numbering the slide rolls so that they will be easier for you to identify and arrange later on. Gerry is splicing together the movies as they come so at least they'll be in sequence. You'll be able to title them.

Soon . . . I love you.   Dorothy

THURSDAY, AUGUST 14, 1952, 9:30 P.M.

Dorothy Darling—

I am exhausted, as I haven't been for years, like back in my intern days. Last night the guns were booming and this morning the casualties kept coming in. We worked steadily from 9 A.M. to 9:30 P.M., three tables at once, sometimes four. There were a lot of serious injuries. That slows things up. I'm gradually doing the more serious cases on my own. At first, one of the surgeons who's been here a while scrubbed with me. If only you were here to give me a back rub, I'd be in heaven.

Since some of the boys want to learn Elementary French and it will be a good way for me to brush up, we'll start using the Army correspondence course books, available free in Seoul.

My darling, can't hold my head up any longer. All pooped out. Will drag myself to the john and if I make it back, well, tune in tomorrow. I love you Dorothy, my wife.   M

THURSDAY, AUGUST 14, 1952, 11:00 P.M.

My love—

People tell me I look well. How can I tell them that it is because we have had a year of loving and that the sparkle will never leave my eyes, no matter how deep my grief, as long as you are loving me. This morning I read your letters (18,19) and I cried. Not because I was sad, but because they were so beautiful. As you say, we shall repeat ourselves, for we are not poets, but, for us, our love's spontaneity and warmth lend beauty to our words. I could fill a whole page with "I love you" and you would respond differently to each one.

It is a noisy night on 96th Street as it always is even at this hour. But why should there be peace and quiet in this city? These noises on 96th St. would be sweet to my ears if you were beside me. We would alternately curse them and bless them.

I shall write to you in the morning, while I am waiting for the mailman. Mr. Waite, the doorman, rings the bell, if I don't get there first—

just to let me know when there is mail from you. I think he enjoys seeing my expression of gratitude when I open the door.

Goodnight my love. You are right. I am beside you.   Dorothy

My love—

Had lunch with a P-51 fighter pilot who was dive-bombing some
supply dumps in North Korea when he was shot down. Luckily, he was
able to get his plane back the ten miles to our lines and belly-land on an
abandoned air strip. The plane was wrecked. He only got a scratched
forehead and lost his Zippo lighter. There was no mistaking the tone in
his voice as he said, "I sure was lucky to get back to OUR lines." A helicopter pilot picked him up and brought him here.

I look at the volume of work we do—350 cases already this
month—and think back to the New Haven Hospital where we were so
anxious for cases. Here there are too many.

The other night, six of the Jewish fellows met with the young Reform rabbi and sat around discussing kosher laws, biblical origins, how
the Bible jibes with archaeological facts, the liberal vs. the fanatic (I
hope the Inspector General didn't hear me). Rabbi Brechetow travels to
the front in a jeep. On the hood it says "Chaplain" and on the back
"Rough Riding Rabbi."

The "boysan" (houseboy) just came in, closed the door, and put up
the blackout curtain. I am more aware of the blackout here than at the
618 since I am out walking back and forth more. I'll go to bed soon and
try to get rid of this "bug." Don't worry, I'm not sick. Just feel a bit
crocky.

As I read your letters, I get all choked up, big tough guy me, a soldier. The rain patters on the tent top. A helicopter passes overhead. I
hear faint laughter from the movie. Another day. It seems ages since
we spoke or touched hands or tongues. Dream of me, as I do of you.

Mel

Melvin, my darling—

Alone in Mom's bedroom, I can hear only the whir of the air-condi-
tioning. It's finally in working order. The mosquitoes are biting again.

You should see me driving and scratching at the same time. Your suggestions about warding them off with an Aerosol bomb and Skat are good but I had the same reaction as Mom—I'd rather fight the mosquitoes! The only one I'll ever oil my body for is you.

The article by Michener that you sent is very moving. I am enclosing an item from the *Post,* just to show you that there are SOME of them printed here, but this one was on the NEXT TO THE LAST PAGE. If more like it were on the FRONT page, there might be more protests. But then the papers that printed them would be accused of being "anti-war" and there would be cries of "Communist!" People seem resigned. I wish everybody in this country could see what you are seeing now—the waste, the unreasonableness, the horror of war. What can we do to stop it! I am so glad that you are putting together rather than rending asunder. Oh, my love, my heart cries for those boys in the hell of it. Is pacifism the answer?

Visited the Spanish Museum on Broadway and 155th. During the teaching year, I urged my pupils to go and I thought that it was about time I did. The neighborhood is lovely, much grass and right near the river. Nearby are the American Indian Museum and the Geographical Society. I saw paintings, silverwork, embroidery, books, documents, and arms. I certainly would like to take the kids there sometime. They go for that three-dimensional stuff.

Yesterday I started Isadora Duncan's *My Life.* She is a most amazing character and writes with such frankness about her eccentric life that you feel that it wasn't really eccentric at all. Her freshness is energizing. I will finish it by tomorrow and send it to you.

I'm receiving your mail regularly now. I'm so happy that you got more of my letters so that you can follow my days as closely as I follow yours. Can you imagine what it was like during the last war when you sometimes didn't hear for months at a time. Goodnight, my darling.

Dorothy

SATURDAY, AUGUST 16, 1952, 9:00 P.M.

My Love—

Although I don't want you to worry, I'm a "crock with the crud." All tests at the 8055 were negative, but since they are primarily a surgical hospital, I asked to be sent to the 121 Evac Hosp in Seoul. I don't want to neglect anything. Please don't worry, though I know you will. I really only have a bad cold or the grippe, or as some of my friends from Ft. Sam who are here say—the Korean Crud. Joe Berman, the anesthetist from Wash DC is here. (We met at Fort Sam.) I've spent the afternoon playing chess with him and looking over the hospital, having had a chest film and another blood count. I'm not feeling too bad, but am not raring to go. Naturally, don't tell the folks. I'll drop them a line to say I'm real busy. Sat. night and I'm a patient. What a bother. When I'm away from you my resistance is lowered. Continue to write to the 8055, as I'll be back there in a few days, or if one of the boys comes down sooner, he'll bring the letters.

I would not have written all this if I thought you wouldn't have wanted me to. I could not bring myself to write a "make believe" letter, because I love you too much.   Mel

AUGUST 16, 11:30 A.M.

Mom hasn't decided what to do with her government bonds yet, although she will probably invest them in stocks which pay 5% rather than 3%. Even though ⅓ are in my name, I told her to do what she wants with them. She would like us to have the dividends. Actually, all this seems so unimportant, I really don't give a damn one way or the other. Some day I'm sure it will come in handy, but I don't feel like worrying about that "some day" right now. We're better off financially than most young couples and, even if we weren't, whatever you will earn I'm sure will be adequate.   D.

SUNDAY, AUGUST 17, 1952, 10:30 A.M.

Dearest—

Feel a little better but still not as though I want to do very much. I am getting a new drug: ASPIRIN. So far all tests are negative. Guess I'm lazy and don't want to work. The worst thing is knowing there is mail from you and not being able to get it. I snooze most of the day—a thrilling existence.

8:00 P.M.

Don't feel bad enough to just lie in bed, or well enough to run around Seoul. Another ? days. You know the army. I'll probably be here until Xmas. Am restless. I lie back on the bed, start back two years ago, and dream about days here and days there—Tanglewood, Cold Spring, New Haven, talcum powder, skiing, walking, the peace of the golf course. I can do this for hours.

At 6 A.M., I was presented with a urine specimen bottle and a thermometer. Still 100. After 7 A.M. breakfast got my finger stuck again. Blood count still normal. Talk with the other officers, naturally, a lot about sex. Shacking up in Japan. One young single officer really opened my eyes. Claimed he shacked up 48 times in 12 days. Wonder if he stopped to eat. I played a little chess and was beaten. Players here really know chess well. Got stationery from the Red Cross worker. She comes around twice a day with toothbrushes, soap, shaving cream, candy, and cigarettes.

We were supposed to get the tail of a small hurricane, but it failed to materialize. Spoke with a Greek officer and learned that in the Greek army regular army officers cannot get married until they are 28 years old. When I asked why he said, "General signed paper," and he shrugged.

I don't look ahead anymore. It seems as though I've been in Korea for years. Guess I'm feeling sorry for myself. But soon I'll be back at work. I'll take it easy at first and then get lost in it until the months pass.

Goodnight, my love. I love you.   Mel

SUNDAY, AUGUST 17, 1952, 11:15 P.M.

My darling—

Showed the folks your new movies and slides today. Of course everyone enjoyed every minute. I didn't bring the slide of you on the tank with a gun. Later I took Pop aside and told him. He said that it was perfectly all right to show it. I guess Bert over-dramatized what I should and should not show or tell Mom. Pop knows best. I can't wait to see the one of you B.A. swimming!

On the way out this morning, I turned off at the Holland Tunnel instead of Brooklyn Battery, so we almost drove to Brooklyn via New Jersey. The policemen were charming as they removed the iron post barriers for us to get back to where we were supposed to be.

Another week is gone. Next Sunday is the unveiling and I am not looking forward to it. I don't like cemeteries. Dad is not there. And he never liked cemeteries. It would be easier if you were here.   Dorothy

MONDAY, AUGUST 18, 1952, 11:00 P.M.

Melvin, my husband, my darling—

The room is a mess and that is a good sign. I am busy. Yesterday's *Times* is unread; this week's *New Yorker* half-read (and later to be sent to my love); shoes to be heeled; shirts to be pressed; leotard to be washed; pocketbook to be emptied; and books books books. Still haven't finished Isadora, but continue to enjoy it. Tomorrow morning I am going to put myself in order. But I shall soon be out of it which will mean that my mind is occupied. Do I make sense?

Gerry passed the road test in Stamford with flying colors. By the time we got back to N.Y. it was 2:00, barely time to get to the Lighthouse where I worked with Guion Rogers. He is almost totally blind, attends Juilliard, has sung with the Robert Shaw chorale and now is interested in conducting his own group. I played choral numbers for him and we marked them off in sections for rehearsal. This is the closest I've been to a piano in a long time, I'm ashamed to say.

I got home to find three letters from you and the famous swimming reel which perhaps should be entitled "Ecstasy" [film notorious for its scene of Hedi Lamarr running nude through distant woods]. Seeing you splashing yourself all over, scrubbing your body with soap, swimming in luxurious nudity. With the exception of one or two quick shots, the film could pass the Hays Office [motion-picture moral code established by movie moguls in 1934]. But your glorious backside shines forth in all its splendor. My Mom was in the room when we started to show the film and refused to budge. She said, "I've seen your husband au naturel before." I didn't like it, but what could I do? I really wanted your nudity all to myself.

Took a 7:00 P.M. dance class. Of course it was wonderful, but I was not. Mary Anthony now knows my name and she took quite a few opportunities to correct me, which is good. The class goes at a terrific pace and I am exhausted. Actually I stayed out of a few jumping exercises because I was short of breath. But the hips are better. They just ache, not like they're out of joint.

I'm getting woozy now and want you near me. I love you.

Dorothy

TUESDAY, AUGUST 19, 1952, 8:00 P.M.

Darling—

An interesting day. The aureomycin I'm taking knocks out the appetite, but sure has made me feel good. As I settled down comfortably to listen to Toscanini conduct Beethoven's Ninth, someone tapped me on the shoulder. A whiskey tenor female voice said, "I'm Audrey Totter. Who're you?" I looked around and there stood an over-stuffed blond slouching and attempting to smile pleasantly. Not knowing who she was, but being a gentleman, I introduced myself, told her where I was from, what outfit, then I asked her a few questions. She lives in Hollywood, is in Korea with a USO show, so I presume she is a TV or screen starlet. She's engaged to a Hollywood doctor. She said, "The fellows like to see an American girl in a stateside dress," and then she continued to make her rounds to the other patients. Before long, a Catholic Chaplain came by to say hello. More pleasantries. I thanked him. With the words, "May the Lord Bless You and Keep You" in my ear, I again turned over. The symphony was excellent. Must be a new recording. And then another Catholic Chaplain, the new hospital chaplain came by to say hello. Dinner and more sex talk.

Still get tired at the end of the day. Will decide tomorrow about going back. I kiss you goodnight.   Mel

WEDNESDAY, AUGUST 20, 1952, 8:00 P.M.

My Dearest Wife—

Strange to be sitting around in pajamas with the ambulant battle casualties, just like in the movies. Got to talking about med school. I remember those carefree days, then compare them with the years with you. The same joviality, spirit, and fun, but if you add to that love, a completeness of the 24 hours, responsibility to and for someone else, that makes a great difference. I wish we could have lived those early days together, but maybe we needed them to prepare us for each other. I remember those long rides in the car when we talked and talked and became more sure of each other. I always have to keep myself from talking too much.

The news on the radio is the same. I still haven't decided about voting. If Ike does not repudiate McCarthy, I won't vote for him.

Now goodnight. Hope to write to you from the 8055 by tomorrow. Sleep well my wife. I love you.   Mel

AUGUST 21

Talked with a new patient who has partial nerve paralysis in his foot from sitting too long on a hard stool playing poker—I mean it.

More bomb strikes. Some joker on the US Staff of Officers says we can make an amphibious landing if we want to, warning the Communists of what they know to be true. Ike says the Democrats are leading us down leftist paths. I wonder if the "middle of the road" he wants us to walk may not be too far on the other side.

Today is Bert's 19th birthday—my kid brother. I hope things happen to keep both Gerry and Bert out of the army, especially out of Korea. They say being away from home and in the army does things for "boys." Well, whatever it does, I'm sure they can do without it.

THURSDAY, AUGUST 21, 1952, 11:00 A.M.

My darling—

I shall be interested in hearing more about your Bible class when you are not too tired to write about it. It seems funny that you are exposed to Judaism so far from home. The more we know about our Jewishness, the better it is for us, for our children, and for those around us who don't know anything about being Jewish.

Time passes. The weather here is oppressive—rainy, muggy, stuffy, combined with the filthy air. I wonder how the skies are over you in Korea now. I hope clear, with the sun shining and a cool breeze to refresh you. I feel close to you as I write. Sleep well my darling.   Dorothy

FRIDAY, AUGUST 22, 1952, 8:00 P.M.
AT THE 8055 MASH

My Love—

I'm back, tired but feeling OK. I waited till noon for transportation. When none arrived, I called the 8055 and after much "Speak louder— can't hear you," I learned that they were sending a jeep down that afternoon. So I waited, read, talked to Lindsey (who is here with a foot infection). The afternoon passed. Still no transportation. With my blood pressure rising, I called again and found out that they had sent a jeep down to pick up Col. Rush, the Surgical Consultant and me—except they had forgotten me. I got on the phone again, called the Air Reserve

Team composed of about six helicopters stationed at the air strip five miles away. Told them I'd like to get to the 8055. Luckily for me they had a helicopter coming up here tonight. They were somewhat hesitant and murmured something about clearing it with the 8th Army. So I muttered that I was supposed to have gone up with Col. Rush (which was true), told them to hold the flight and I'd be right out. Quickly dressed. Called hospital headquarters and told them that a helicopter was waiting to take me to the 8055 and that I was in a hurry. Since helicopters are usually reserved only for VIP's, I was rushed out to the airport and made the flight. An exciting ride. On the way down, feeling pretty punk, I couldn't enjoy it as much. It's like riding in a soap bubble. There is a momentary pause as the motor speeds up. Then suddenly you're floating in the air above the countryside. Got a wonderful view of Seoul, a contrast between an oriental walled city and a bombed-out modern one. Flying at 70 miles an hour, we were over the 8055 soon coming in for a landing. Except for the rotor above, we hovered motionless about 5 feet above the ground and settled slowly down. The boys applauded as I arrived.

Have stopped all medication and my appetite has returned. In fact I will partake of some crabmeat and saltines soon. Then early to bed to rest up tomorrow and Sunday. Am planning to go back to work on Monday. The boys tell me it has been quiet.

And thus my dearest, what I hope will be a unique and singular episode—being ill—is over. Don't know where it came from, but I shall try to take especially good care of myself from now on.

Goodnight my wife.   Mel

FRIDAY, AUGUST 22, 1952, 11:00 P.M.

My darling—

I hope that as I am writing this you are at the 8055, back to your old self. I am happy that were a good boy and told Mama everything. Of course I worry, but I know that you will be all right and working again soon. I am anxiously awaiting the letter which tells me so. I hope that the Seoul excursion cost you another camera!

Seeing summer end means checking off another season. Yesterday was six weeks that you are gone—and we thought we couldn't last more than two days apart. Well, here we are. It does not get easier.

The Post Office would not send my package Airmail as it is over 2 lbs. The next pkg. will be wrapped smaller. The clerk said the amount of time would depend upon the Army.

The Lighthouse arranged for me to read to Robert Kupfer at his apartment. He is totally blind and working on a Ph.D. in psychology. I proofread a paper for him, gently criticizing the overabundance of "as it were's" and "be that as it may's." Then I read Spanish poetry and from Stephens' *Crock of Gold*. When school begins, I'll read only one evening a week, but the Lighthouse will decide where I am most needed.

Goodnight my love—until tomorrow. One of these tomorrows will be the day we hold each other.   Dorothy

SATURDAY, AUGUST 23, 1952, 2:00 P.M.

Dorothy, Dorothy, Dorothy, I love you,

Is that a way to start a letter? And why not. You have completely revived me. I hated to pick up the last of your letters. It was like having to say, "Good-bye for now," but there will be another one tomorrow.

The article on Korean Medicine from *Time* or *Newsweek* was fairly accurate. Still, a lot of MD's are being wasted. The figures about casualties are correct. If they can survive until they get to the 8055, they have an excellent chance of pulling through, even if they have a long hospitalization ahead.

Heard from Ernie. His unit expects to go on the line soon. He is getting 3 to 4 points a month, but is not doing any work. I hope he will be OK. By the way, he doesn't want Jan to know where he actually is, so don't let on if you should write to her.

SATURDAY, AUGUST 22, 1952, 10:30 P.M.

Melvin, my darling—

Today was beautiful, the temperature 55 degrees, and we slept under blankets last night. It would have been a shame to waste a day like this in the city, so Mom, Gerry, and I packed a picnic lunch and by 10:30 we were on our way to V. Everitt Macy Park, a lovely spot about 25 miles from the city on the Saw Mill River Parkway. I particularly wanted to get Mom away from the house as the thought of tomorrow's unveiling depresses her, as it does all of us.

We ate as soon as we got there and spent the afternoon reading, taking pictures, and just lying around. As I looked at the sky, I tried to imagine you looking up at that same sky, but it was easier for me to imagine you right there beside me on the blanket—a quick peck on the cheek, a hug, a wack on the backside, a mouthful of peach, and your lips and tongue.

Tonight I decided I would like to learn to play chess. I wonder what it would be [like] sitting across the chess board from you—one thing we have never done together.

I ache all over. I never really know how good a dance class has been until the following day. Don't ever let me give it up for this long a period of time. My weight is down a bit, so I am beginning to eat more desserts and starches. I shall probably be seesawing back and forth. It seems funny—the little cooking I do here—to be using some one else's utensils, but we are setting the table with our green and yellow plastic mats from San Antonio, since they would spoil in storage. They bring back so many memories and still make a table look cheerful!

SUNDAY, AUGUST 23, 1952, 10:00 P.M.

My darling—

Today has been a long day. I would not want to relive it. I felt numb and had to breathe deeply (as you told me to) when I saw old friends of Dad's or family I know he was close to. Otherwise, the unveiling seemed far from Dad or the feelings I have for him. It is still difficult for me to believe that he is not just away for a while. I never realized that death was so simple, yet so dramatic. It scares me, yet makes it easier to think about. If only you were here, we could discuss these things.

Who is responsible for having you at one end of the world and me at the other? and for all those poor guys whom you see—and those you never get to see. Who got us into this damn mess? Do you think it would do any good if the members of Congress were to be there at 8055 when you were getting in a group of wounded? I don't know.

Gerry is pestering me to get to bed because he wants to play golf with me at 7:00 tomorrow morning—oi!

What different lives we are living now.   Dorothy

MONDAY, AUGUST 25, 1952, 7:00 P.M.

Dorothy Darling—

It feels good to be back at work. The army will spoil me. I do the initial dressing, and aidmen finish up. They put in all the IV's. Found out the hospital gets about a dozen journals, so since we're light on patients, I spent about 3 hrs reading. I should be able to keep up with some of the literature.

This afternoon, Jim Dickson, chest surgeon [later Deputy Surgeon General and who, Mel thought, was the TV prototype for Hawkeye on *M*A*S*H*] showed us a film on cardiac surgery made in Boston while he was working there. Strange sight to be sitting on a bench in a leaking tent in Korea listening to an academic discussion.

Gave my sizes for winter clothing today. Time is passing. By the way, the GI long underwear is very itchy, so please send 3 or 4 pairs of two-piece NON-itchy warm long underwear tops and bottoms.

Just got called to see some patients. A Korean came in who had been hit by a packing case of rations dropped by plane. No broken bones, but he's got an awfully sore hip.

Now to bed. Dreams, letters, love. We have so much.   Mel

TUESDAY, AUGUST 26, 1952, 1:00 A.M.

My darling—

My whole body cries out for you and all I can do is to sit here in the living room picking my fingers.

I spoke to Jean this morning. Barbara [her daughter] has a temperature of 103 and Jean is worried about polio.

We went to see "New Faces of 1952," an excellent review—good voices, good dancing, and clever lyrics and sketches. There were take-offs on Truman Capote, Gian-Carlo Menotti's "The Medium and the Telephone" and "The Consul," and a Charles Addams cartoon. I would have enjoyed it more if you had been beside me.

What a blessing it is to write to you. How much better I feel now than when I started. I love you and give you my lips to kiss and tongue to taste.   Dorothy

TUESDAY, AUGUST 26, 1952, 9:00 P.M.

Dorothy My Love—

It is quiet at the hospital, as the rain keeps activity down. Ordered my winter clothing and picked up another pair of boots, which I waterproofed. Read medical literature and Marquand's *Bf's Daughter*—not one of his

best, but interesting. Took care of some British patients who had been hit
by mortar shell. On first glance, they looked half-dead, but they were covered with dried mud. My emergency room work has helped me.

It is getting quite cool. I sleep under two blankets and hate to get
out of bed in the morning, especially when it is such a long walk to the
john. The minor discomforts of living in this Korean Boy Scout Camp
are easily adjusted to, but missing you, not so. I love you Dorothy.

Mel

THURSDAY, AUGUST 28, 1952, 11:45 P.M.

LAKE MAHOPAC, N.Y.

My love—

After dinner, Gerry and I sat outside and talked. The weather had
cleared and the sky was tinted different shades of pink. All you could
hear was the chirping of the crickets and the steady sounds of whatever
wild life there is in the brush. I know you would have enjoyed the stillness. Gerry explained how his ideas of how he wanted to live and work
fitted so well with the profession he had chosen. He has developed so
and is a terrific person. I have really gotten to know him. I couldn't help
hoping, as I talked with him, that he gets some wonderful woman to
share his life.

As I read your eight letters, I jotted down things I wanted to comment on. You compare our feelings towards each other with other couples' feelings. Of course, you can't look inside of people or into their
homes when they are alone, but like you, when I observe other couples,
I feel as self-satisfied and content as a cow. I love you, Melvin, and am
so happy to be a part of you.

You sound as though you would prefer to come back to the States
rather than finish off the two years in Japan. Is there any particular reason? I know that you feel as I do—wherever we can be together shall be
our heaven. If it had to be the jungles of Africa or the barren soil of
wartorn Korea, I would fly, if I could, to be at your side, to see your face
daily, feel your touch nightly, breathe the air that you breathe.

You asked me what I was doing that Tuesday evening that you had
that vivid dream of our love-making. It seems so long ago that I can
barely remember—I drove Pedro to the Lighthouse, lounged on Mom's
bed and talked to her while she dressed. Sometimes, when I have a vivid
dream of you or think of something that we have shared, I have a ter-

rific desire to know exactly what you are doing or thinking at that moment. We should have studied techniques of telepathy before you left.
Speaking of study, I still haven't been able to find an evening Japanese
course that isn't exorbitantly expensive.

Stevenson for President! I guess I'll have to start campaigning since
you haven't made up your mind. I'm sure if you were here and subject
to the more liberal point of view, you would be swayed as I have. Eisenhower just doesn't seem to be doing anything much but following the
old Republican line, endorsing ALL Republican candidates including
McCarthy—even though he "might not agree with his policies." Stevenson appears to be an intelligent and independent thinker.

I'm sending you speeches that the two candidates made to the Le-
gionnaires in New York. This past week NY has been full of older men
acting like college kids at hazing time. I did see a few respectable looking gentlemen touring the city with their families. One grey-haired
man wore a necktie that said "Child Welfare." But I couldn't help thinking of all the Legion's reactionary policies. Probably liberal prejudice on
my part.

The hour is late. Right now I could write on and on. So many things
to say, all meaning I want to share as many minutes and thoughts with
you as humanly possible with pencil on paper across so many miles.
Sleep well, my darling.   Dorothy

THURSDAY AUGUST 28, 1952, 10:00 P.M.

My Love—
This morning, as I was doing a messy dressing, a crowd of people
and a photographer were walking through the ward. And so I met William Holden, here on tour to find out what kind of entertainment the
boys want. When I finished my work, I got my camera and had the professional photographer take some pictures of me with Holden. Then we
sat down and had some coffee. He's a nice fellow, speaks well, and feels
that the American people just refuse to realize that this is a war here in
Korea. We agreed. He had been a Corporal in the last war (probably in
special services division). He was in for 4 years, so he was sympathetic.
He has just come from Europe and I spoke with him about the music
festivals there. According to Holden, what the boys want in shows, in
order of preference, is: 1. more girls 2. comedians 3. popular trios, quar-
tets, etc. 4. variety shows 5. western music.

Back to work for most of the afternoon. The lull is over. Patients are coming in one after the other, many seriously injured. One group of GI's in an artillery unit had a shell blow up while they were loading the gun. It sure made a mess. One soldier was hit by a mortar shell and had the side of his head blown off and an arm missing, and is still alive. I worked on him, but I wondered if it was worth it. With 8–10 pints of blood, he looked a little better, so I sent him over to the 8063 MASH (Head Injury Unit) about 15 miles from here. It's dark and the helicopters can't go out, so he goes by ambulance, with 5 more pints of blood, an aid man, and oxygen. Why? He will probably die on the way. So I'm depressed. Another boy asked me, as I was dressing his arm, "Are you going to have to take it off?" He was lucky. It was just a minor break. So it goes.

One happier note. Dick Kamil's wife had a baby—another girl. He got the telegram today, so we had a little celebration. I love you, my wife.   Mel

FRIDAY, AUGUST 29, 1952, 3:30 P.M.
LAKE MAHOPAC

Melvin my darling,

The sun is shining. I'm sitting in the shade of a tremendous oak, about two feet in diameter. Next to me is an expanse of brush with golden rod, buttercups, and clover. The breeze rustles the leaves and there is a pleasant mixture of cool and warm. I've showered, napped, now I feel relaxed and comfortable.

It is hard to believe that next week at this time I shall be in the classroom, teaching god knows what. I think of all the things I want to introduce by means of visual aids. Yet I know that I'll be so busy with Japanese, dancing, reading to the blind, maybe piano, that I won't get around to it. Must be busy busy busy so time will fly and before I have time to teach a Spanish conjugation or learn a Japanese verb, I shall receive word from you that I'd better start packing. Oh my love, when that day comes, I shall be walking on air—I won't need a plane to fly to Japan, to go to you, to have you open your arms to me. Now, separated from you, I feel like a loose tire chain.

I met Mlle Leon in the elevator. She's an old maid, French, about 70. I used to visit with her and talk French. She is a patriotic, orthodox Jew and anti-Christian. I don't like her, but enjoy talking French with her. When I left the elevator, she said, "Mes compliments a vos parents." I said, "Merci." It was a strange feeling. She knew Dad. They had spoken occasionally. She lived in the same building, yet didn't know that he had died.

AFTER MIDNIGHT—

Feeling blue. The letdown at the end of a day. Staying in a small room with Gerry and hearing dance music blare from a large hotel across the way—playing "You Made Me Love You." It sounds so empty. I used to think it was romantic.

Today I saw leaves beginning to fall. I would tear them down myself if I thought it would hurry the seasons along. Goodnight my love.

Dorothy

FRIDAY, AUGUST 29, 2:00 P.M.

Good afternoon my love—

Am waiting for some X-rays to come through, so I decided to talk to you for a while. I miss you, my wife.

The fellow I wrote about died on the way to the other hospital last night. I was told that another fellow came in ½ hour later shot through the head and he got over to the other hospital (where there is a neurosurgical team) and is doing fairly well.

I have made an investment, and I think you will agree it is a good one. No, not a camera. Our chief houseboy is very bright and has quite a bit of schooling behind him. He wants to go to school in the US. Some of the boys helped him write to and be accepted by Brigham Young University in Utah. While I have only been at the 8055 MASH a short time, I agreed to pay $25 a year for 4–5 years to help provide financial backing for him, in addition to what he can make at a part-time job. The tuition is $150 a year. If he does well, he may get a scholarship, but with 12–15 of us pledging this small amount, it seemed like a good investment. One of the fellows lives in Provo, Utah, the location of the University, and will help him out.

In spite of the radio report that "ground action was limited to Patrol Action," I spent the morning working. If 20 or 30 men go out on patrol and 15 are injured, the action may be "slight," but not to those men.

Took care of a one-star General this afternoon. He's had a cough for about 2 weeks. Examined him, ordered a chest film, then left him to sit and wait as I treated a Puerto Rican GI private who had a bad belly wound. The Gen. was pleasant, very unmilitary. He had nothing serious, so I gave him some cough medicine—Terramycin—and told him to take a good stiff drink before bedtime. He countered, "How about before dinner too?" Who am I to argue with a General?

A respite as darkness fell and the helicopters could no longer go out. The sky was dark blue and a deep red that gradually faded. I tried a picture of it. Read some military medical journals, the *Stars And Stripes,* listened to the evening news. We now broadcast to the enemy and tell them we will bomb them. We are still having prisoner trouble. Stevenson came out in favor of Civil Rights and the FEPC [Fair Employment Practices Committee] and said indirectly that he would seek to change the filibuster. He sounds better and better. The peace talks adjourned for another week. A farce.

Then another patient, with his arm just about shot off. With one of our French nurses interpreting, I told him we had to amputate. A photographer who had been on Old Baldy had taken this fellow's picture a few minutes before he was hit and had carried him down. He took my picture: "Taking care of the wounded."

Spent the past 15 minutes talking with Dick Kamil about going home, hotels in Tokyo, and the GI bill, which will pay us money during the last 2 yrs. of residency. Dick is acting CO while Maj. Holleman is gone for a few days, since he's held his Capt.'s commission longer than the other medical officers. He just looked up from the letter he is writing and laughed, saying, "I've been in Korea a short while and I'm CO—See, give the Jews time and they run the place!"

The artillery is booming again. The longer I am here, the more I hate the sound of guns. Occasionally when a unit training nearby fires machine guns, I have to stop working and take a deep breath. I hate to see these kids brought in butchered.

I love you. I am sorry to write the way I have these past few letters, but it is only to you that I can bitch. Your love soothes me. I find happiness amidst this madness, loving you and being loved by you. Hold up your face to me and "pucker." Goodnight.   Mel

My dearest—

Saw "Robinhood," and a wonderful colored documentary, "Water Birds." In the newsreel, they barely mentioned Korea except to say that Mrs. Mark Clark was visiting hospitals in Seoul. As I looked at the pictures of patients, I had a lump in my throat, not only for you and for me, but for the fact that people know so little and care so little about what is going on there. I wondered if I would see you in the newsreel.

Do you really think that, in my Spanish class, I might slip and say Senorita Gotterer? No chance! Gotterer sounds funny to me now. Being la senora Horwitz is a part of me. Yo te amo, mi querido, mi amor.

You say there is no racial prejudice at the hospital. That reminded me of a story that Cousin Bob Weisen told about how during the last war, on the way home from the Pacific, men who had fought side by side were segregated by color on the ship. There were objections on both sides, but the army stood firm.   D.

My Love—

A brief respite. Will write this while I can. About 10 A.M. we got word that about 20 casualties were coming in. The story later was that a group of men with a reserve battalion were going on a mock problem. They started across a field, which unfortunately was mined and had not been cleared. The mines were Bouncing Betty's that partially explode, rise 3 or 4 feet in the air, then explode fully. Whereas we usually get extremity wounds from mines, these were chest and abdominal. All the helicopters went out. Back and forth. Seven men had been killed. We got another 18 men in, many seriously wounded. We worked all day and now the pre-op ward is full. The boys have been working all afternoon and will be working all night. Much of my work consisted of admitting the patients, splinting fractures, stopping bleeding, getting blood going, ordering X-rays, and then, in the pre-op ward, keeping them alive until surgery could be done, sometimes a matter of hours, then watching them as they came out of the operating room. In between, I did some of the less serious wounds to keep things moving.

Had a North Korean POW shot by his own men. He is probably an officer. Some British intelligence officers came down to question him. We have a guard on him. His wound is in his neck. We shall be keeping him here so he can be questioned. He is quite a prize. He was frightened at first, but he will get treated—after the GI's—and, I hope, give us some information. I heard that a Dutch Battalion was going to try to take a hill tonight, so we may expect to see them tomorrow if the rumor is true.

More rain. Maybe it's good for the rice.

My darling. I'm so thankful you're you and we have each other. You give me life and love in this very unreal existence. I love you.   Mel

P.S. Enclosing a letter from Aunt Ruth [Gotterer, my father's sister-in-law, who was actively involved in civil rights before it became a "movement"]. She sure is one feisty lady!

DALLAS, TEXAS

Dearest Mel,

I went to our all-Dixiecrat precinct meeting as usual last month, but I knew that this time I was going to pop off, for I had been watching them railroad in their resolutions from Gov. Shivers and his gang for four years. When I arrived, I found seven liberals whom I knew. Well Mel, the seven of us held that meeting for two hours and, on a mistake by the chairman, I got myself nominated from the floor as a delegate. Boy oh boy did we have fun. So your aunt is a politician. They give me a pain in the neck trying to tell the public a bunch of lies. If you go to the courthouse or the library of records you can read—IF YOU CAN—for yourself what is going on with the tidelands. I went to the county convention. I am vitally interested for I know that our government of these United States starts with the precinct meetings, and that is the job ahead. Getting the people out and teaching them how the electoral vote (which I would like to see abolished) works.

Our trip east was a hard one and I guess you know that Aunt Helen decided not to return with me on account of the polio epidemic.

Devotedly,   your Aunt Ruth

SUNDAY, AUGUST 31, 1952, 10:00 P.M., MAHOPAC

My darling—

No matter where I go, what I do, the ache that your absence creates is with me. I can be gay and busy, but each step I take, each page I turn, each person I talk to, there is something of you. But we must continue to write and dream knowing that the love that makes us one has enough spark in it to keep it warm across thousands of miles for many months. As I sit here on my bed in Mahopac and look at the green-flowered wallpaper, I have the desire to see you doing the ordinary everyday things. Bending over to tie your shoelace, looking into the mirror to give your tie that twist into shape, standing naked in front of the toilet shaking the last few drops of urine from your penis, blowing your nose as the handkerchiefs pile up on the dresser, putting your belt on the "right" way with strong, quick motions, spraying insecticide with a murderous gleam in your eye, swinging gracefully from side to side as you warm up before starting to hit balls at a driving range, walking towards me in your whites smiling. What I would give to be looking into the mirror with you right now as you gleefully find something on your face that will squirt. I love every physical part of you and the essence that is you, the intangible that draws you to me, that draws us together in this, our own world.

Uncle Lou [Weisen, my mother's brother] just returned from a week away with "the men." He asked me if I would "let" you go away. I said, "Of course," but I can't imagine your ever wanting to. Perhaps he has never been involuntarily separated. Perhaps it's because we're young and still newlyweds. I don't know, but it seems to me that each day of sharing brings something new and more wonderful. To waste one week of not sharing seems inconceivable.

Goodnight my love—until we meet tomorrow. We'll dream our dreams and as The Prophet in Kahlil Gibran's poem says: "give thanks for another day of loving."   Dorothy

SUNDAY, AUGUST 31, 1952, 3:00 P.M.

Dorothy, My Wife, My Love—My Woman—

The rain continued last night and the wind started to blow. The tent flaps flapped and the window flaps shook. We thought the tent would take off at any moment. The mess tent did, and I took some pictures of that.

We have five appendectomy patients. Must be an epidemic.

They questioned the POW this morning. He is a North Korean agent who crosses the lines and poses as a member of a work group. As we cannot tell one Korean from another, it was fairly easy for him. He was taking another agent to Seoul when they lost the road. They wandered around in the mountains. As their food got low, our patient suggested they try to get back. They got caught by the rain. Again our patient had the idea to surrender. That night his friend shot him through the neck and took off. The patient wandered down into the valley and was picked up by some MP's. He told them about his companion who was later caught. Fascinating to hear the interrogator at work and the patient answering. He has a tube (tracheotomy) in his windpipe. In order for him to talk, the interrogator had to put his finger on the patient's neck to block the tube. After the questioning, the POW asked the interrogator to thank us for taking care of him. We are taking care of him, but we have an armed guard at his bedside.

Some guerrillas tried to blow up the nearby bridge. Two were killed and a dozen captured. So our guards are jumpy and I identify myself quickly when challenged.

I am tired and will sleep well, dreaming of you.   Mel

September

The unfamiliar autumn of our separation arrived with its familiar medley of satisfactions and stress. For me, a new school year meant congeniality, clean blackboards, the smell of fresh paint, first-day stage fright, and tedious paperwork.

Mel was transferred from the 8055 to the 8225, an experimental M.A.S.H. with few nurses. He put on his field jacket against the cold, clearly defining the physical distance between us. I was still in cottons. With scrupulous attention to detail, he sketched for me not only his crude environment but the increasingly bloody procedures that were his routine. I described a friend's wedding. The more intense his work became, the less significant my activities appeared. Into our third month of letters, I began to apologize for the pettiness of my anecdotal accounts of life at home. Next to the life-and-death context of his routine, my idle chatter was trivial indeed. But he wanted to hear it all, he wrote. So I wrote it all, but my letters became more personal as I sought new ways to express my love and longing.

While mortar shells fell on Korean hills, peace talks continued at Panmunjom. In Vietnam, French and Vietnamese were battling Communist-led Vietminh. Even though our government was supplying the French with military equipment, not many Americans, including me, were paying attention. I was more interested in the presidential campaign than in any news outside of Korea. I expressed to Mel my confidence in Stevenson as well as my anger at McCarthy's slimy harrassment of "our" candidate.

Along with the comfort of tradition and pleasurable recollections, the Jewish holidays revive memories of tragic loss. Mel attended Rosh Hashanah services wearing a pistol around his waist. He traveled by jeep along dusty roads to a large tent. There his conviction of the irreconcilability of war and religion was sustained. Mom and I, in fashionable fall suits, walked the ten blocks along Fifth Avenue to the Park Avenue Synagogue. Preoccupied by individual and shared grief, we dreaded the intrusion upon our private sensibilities by well-meaning congregants. We went to services that September because that was our custom. The three of us, Mel in a tent, Mom and I in a sanctuary adorned with stained-glass windows, shared a ritual with our fellow Jews as we sang the songs of our fathers.

Mel and I wrote and wrote and wrote. Although friends and relatives were confounded at first by our compulsion, they came to understand how much we depended upon this not-so-mysterious rite for nourishment.

SEPTEMBER 1, 1952, 7:35 P.M.

Dorothy Darling—

Labor Day. The end of summer. Tomorrow you go to work and I haven't given you directions. I hope you didn't forget how to read a map. Please be careful of other drivers. Watch out for icy roads this winter. You may find that the chains aren't much use, or they're a bother where the streets are cleared so quickly. You probably think I'm old-maidish writing this, but start slowly. Don't race the motor. Keep your eye on the ball and bend your knees! I love you.

I have 40 patients who are very sick. In civilian life, when a patient has a major operation, part of his stomach or lung removed, he is sick. A patient here probably has dirty infected shrapnel wounds. He too may have had part of his stomach and perhaps in addition, his intestine removed, a tear of the kidney repaired, a bleeding spleen excised, and holes in his diaphragm and lung closed. Operations at the MASH are done with relatively inexperienced anesthetists. The OR is not nice clean enamel and tile, but wood, covered with dust and insects. And yet, the patients do well because most of them are young healthy males with amazing resistance and resiliance. We pour blood into them, because they lose a lot on the battlefield and while being transported. If we can get the patient to the operating table, he usually pulls through. He'll be in a hospital for a long time, but he is alive. And that is the compensation for this work. These kids are on their way back—to get well. Most of them. Maybe some of them minus an arm or leg or a piece of lung. No more guns, mud, blood, death. The look on their faces as they hear that they will be evacuated, that they are on their way home . . . there is some sense to my work.

Lunch. Worked until 3 P.M., then made rounds with the surgeon who takes over. Back to my tent. Slept for 1½ hours. Had someone take movies of me, just to finish the roll. I'm afraid I'm not much of an actor. Then dinner and back to the tent. A nice hot shower for a change. They say that there is a stove in the shower tent in winter, but I'm not sure about that walk across the field. Oh well, there's always Arid and shaving lotion.

Weird Japanese music on the radio. I'm munching sweet cookies from the PX and drinking coke. What I do miss is fresh cold milk, although our powdered milk isn't bad on cereal or in ice cream.

Think it will be quiet. Hope so. I'm a bit tired.

September begins. Soon the leaves will turn. How much fun it was to drive through the countryside with you enjoying the colors. One day. . . . No more longing. To lie down at night and know my love is next to me. I wonder if the couples who are together can imagine what it is like not being together. Goodnight my love. Reach out and feel me. I love you.   Mel

MONDAY, SEPTEMBER 1, 1952, 11:30 P.M.

My darling—

The best part of this weekend was arriving home to find a letter from you written from the 8055. I shall never tell your folks about your illness until, perhaps, you are home. They might doubt your future letters and I wouldn't want them to worry. I haven't told anybody except Mom, Gerry, and Jean, and they have been sworn to secrecy. I had to tell SOMEbody!

I've read *The Old Man and the Sea,* the new Hemingway novel which has been published in complete form in *Life* magazine. I shall send it to you as I enjoyed it very much.

Goodnight my darling. I go to sleep hoping that we shall be together in tonight's dreams.   Dorothy

TUESDAY, SEPTEMBER 2, 8:00 P.M.

My Love—

A few of us attempted to finish the officers' club this afternoon. The CO, Maj. Holleman, working on the chimney, me painting tables and chairs, hammering beat-up chairs into place, shoveling dirt away from

the front door. In my tent, I re-packed my clothes into a wooden trunk
the carpenter built for me. Gave him $5 for this and other things he has
done, though he didn't want to take it. Contributed $10 to one of the
chaplains for a fund to get artificial limbs for Korean kids. Started paying $2.25 a month for houseboy services, previously supplied by the
hospital. This includes laundry, making bed, shining shoes, mopping
out tent, getting water (hot in A.M. for shaving), cleaning up mess, generally just hanging around. I cleared out a corner of our tent where we
wash and keep glasses and covered it with old X-ray film.

Tonight I am on 4th call and will probably sleep through. We rotate
every night. #1 & 2 have to stay at the hospital. A fifth man covers pre-
op and receiving for 4 days. The schedule is not too strenuous unless we
get busy. The two men on call (1 & 2) usually work most of the night.

Goodnight. Sleep well. I shall because you, my wife, my woman,
love me.   Melvin

THURSDAY, SEPTEMBER 4, 1952, 4:00 P.M.

Dorothy My Love—

At 7 A.M. the "chopper" (helicopter) brought in 2 relatively minor
and 2 serious cases. The story they told was fantastic. They are infantry-
men on the line and had been relieved of guard duty. They went into
their bunker and (here I got conflicting info though both may be true)
and were either playing poker or lying down when in walked three Chinese soldiers who had infiltrated the lines. Our poor fellows had no
weapons. This of course was their mistake as they are not supposed to
be without them for one moment. They had left them at their guard
stations. The Chinese soldiers wanted to sit in on the game. The GI's refused and the shooting began. One of the GI's took one of the Chinese
soldiers' guns and killed him. The guards finally came and the other
two Chinese were killed. But our four fellows were sure shot up. Got
them fixed up and sent one to the 8063 neurosurgical team.

I had missed rounds so I went around myself. Coffee, sent out some
letters written yesterday, "sat" in our open air library, then slept from 10
A.M. to 3 P.M. No lunch. I eat a midnight supper which more than
makes up for it. Shaved and sat down to write to my love. I got my field
jacket out last night and wore it, except when I had to scrub. They will
be putting stoves in the tents in about a month. Good for comfort. Bad

for diet, as we plan on keeping a case of C-rations (beef stew, meat, chicken, etc.) which make pretty good snacks when heated.

Another day ending and beginning. My sense of time is really upset by working nights. If I send only two letters with the same number you're lucky.

Dorothy, I sit here, more at peace today than yesterday. The months will pass. Until the day you are with me and I hold you, we go on loving as we do, knowing we have a precious thing, this love of ours.   Mel

FRIDAY, SEPTEMBER 5, 1952, 11:00 P.M.

My Darling—

I was called to see a patient I had operated on—a thoracotomy (chest operation)—last night. He had a shrapnel wound entering the left side and crossing over onto the right. He seemed OK and I opened the left chest, repaired his lung, though I did not do any other major procedures, as it was not indicated. He was also seen by several other people who agreed. He continued to do well until early today when he had respiratory difficulty and then began to look bad. Jim Dickson and I looked him over. I had been seeing this patient hourly during the morning and then from 4 P.M. on. It was the consensus that unless we went in again, he would die. So we got him into the OR practically dead and Jim operated. He opened his chest and started to look around. The patient began to look better. But suddenly he died. We then found he had a bullet hole in his lower esophagus and any leakage from that is shocking. I know I did my best, and then we did all we could. It is depressing, since you can always say, well, maybe I could have done this— or that.

The night is cool, the moon full and bright. I am alone in the tent, happy to write freely knowing that you understand how I feel. I love you   Melvin.

FRIDAY, SEPTEMBER 5, 1952, 10:00 P.M.

My darling—

I give thanks every moment that you are not closer to the front. The farther you can be from hazardous areas, the better—the points be damned! full speed BACKWARD! I'm so glad that you're feeling well again. I hope those will be the only crocky moments you will have until I see you. Then we shall be able to cure each other of all aches and pains.

The beautiful letter you wrote to Mom about the unveiling brought tears to her eyes. Since your letter to me concerned her, I let her read it. It was the only letter of yours to me she had ever read (and probably ever will). It made her feel good, not so much what you said about her, but reading about our love.

I love you Melvin and I want to close my arms about you and feel your nearness.   Dorothy

SATURDAY, SEPTEMBER 6, 1952, 11:30 P.M.

My darling—

If Mom hadn't gotten reserved seats for "Ivanhoe" at Radio City Music Hall, I wouldn't have gone. Neither Robert Taylor nor Elizabeth Taylor can act. She is beautiful, but as soon as she opens her mouth—ugh! as though she is reading lines. The stage show was the usual—lots of glitter and spectacle. Cheap, trite, noisy—it made me dizzy. In spite of this, whenever the Rockettes start to kick in unison, I get a lump in my throat. I don't know why.

Your words make me strong, Melvin, make me proud to be your wife, to want to be a better woman so that I may come to you with more.

Darling, don't apologize about bitching. This war will go down in history as the most scandalous waste of young lives ever. If only people would realize it now and not wait for the textbooks to come out.

Now I shall rest and be up early to do lesson planning. I hope that your Sunday is a good one. Goodnight, my love. Your wife,   Dorothy.

SUNDAY, SEPTEMBER 7, 1952, 7:30 P.M.

My Darling—

Rounds this morning were a bit more extensive than usual as the chief of medicine from the Tokyo General Hospital was here. After lunch, people began arriving from a 20–30 mile radius for the meeting of the 38th Parallel Medical Society. It was truly an international meeting with practically the entire UN represented, including American MD's of my age and training from many varied units. I spent an hour reminiscing with Jim Dickson about Harvard Med School. He is gregarious, humorous, and intelligent. I've learned a lot of chest surgery from him.

At 2 P.M. went to the meeting where a Norwegian MD presided. For two hours I heard talks, some of the material not too original, but good to listen to. Paid 50 cents for my colorful membership certificate in the society. Afterwards there were cold cuts, lemonade, and cheese crackers. I was introduced to some visiting brass, one of whom is the new surgical consultant. Our officers' club held an open house for which I put on my fatigue shirt, buttoned my pants, and had a whiskey sour with the brass. I'm getting to be a real soldier, sitting with Colonels and Majors, but their brass is shined, buckles gleaming. I'm afraid honey, I wouldn't pass a Sat. morning inspection. My uniform is baggy now that I've lost some weight. I just can't get excited enough to polish buckle and bars. And I'm not sure if the buttons on my shirt and fly are in a straight line. But my underwear and socks are clean! Aren't you proud of your Lieutenant?

With people leaving, I am very envious. But my turn will come. Some of the fellows were talking about how expensive it would be to bring a wife over commercially. What good is money if you cannot really live, even if you have to do without some things in the years to come. Time together is much more precious. Money can be earned, done without. We cannot go back. Goodnight my wife, Dorothy darling.

Melvin.

SUNDAY, SEPTEMBER 7, 1952, 10:10 P.M.

My darling—

I have in front of me a picture from this Sunday's *Mirror* of a pair of eye glasses, a mask, a cap, an arm, and an ear, operating at 8055. We all think it may be you. The folks are sending you a copy for your confirmation. You can imagine the excitement it created.

We sat around and talked, mostly about you and your childhood. Oh my love, did we laugh! Mom gave me your Autograph Book from Public School. After reading about all the girls who were in love with you, I find most interesting the first page:

My Favorite
Book—*Mutiny on the Bounty*

Song—"The Star Spangled Banner"
Game—Diving
Hero— . . . .
Chum—Paul Merson
Author—Mark Twain
College—Johns Hopkins
High School—James Madison
Profession—Doctor of Surgery
Motto—Think right, live right, talk right, be prepared.

Dare we say that ⅕ of our separation is over? I look forward to the time when these letters are memories. Goodnight, my love. I'm all "puckered."   Dorothy

MONDAY, SEPTEMBER 8, 1952, 8:00 P.M.

Dorothy Darling—
    Every day I work I am happy that I've had good basic training in surgery. It supports my feeling that with this you can do most any type of surgery if you use your head. I've been doing many procedures and operations that I'd only assisted at. It may take me a little longer than someone more experienced. Although I think I do a fairly good job, I still know my limitations. Last night, I could have operated on a very sick patient who I felt would probably die (and later did), but I called someone in to do the case. Then no one could say to me, "Perhaps someone more experienced could have saved him," as well as myself saying that to me. This is a human life we are dealing with, not a lung or intestine or leg.
    Went to work at 9 P.M.—a few small cases and several others who had eaten. We had to wait for a few hrs until they had digested their meals so that they wouldn't vomit after anesthesia and get food into their lungs. In the course of the night I took care of 7 patients with wounds of the arms and legs, one with a severe face wound. I then had to open a chest on another and repair a torn lung. Finished that and ran out to post op where a patient died. Two minutes later another patient's heart stopped. I rushed him into the operating room, picked up a scalpel, and incised his chest, spread the ribs and with my hand pumped his heart for a few minutes until it started beating again. That is really an amazing sensation. To feel a dead person come back to life. He did quite well for a while, but

died several hours later. He had come in originally with shrapnel in his brain, chest, and legs. We were going to send him over to the neurosurgical unit at the other hospital, but he was bleeding so badly from his lung that we had to operate here. He was the one I called for help with. By the time we finished these cases, it was 6:30 A.M. and we had a patient with a wound of his abdomen who needed surgery. By the time we had him prepared, it was 8 A.M. In the meantime, I grabbed a cup of coffee and went to the john (hadn't had a chance all night). He had several holes in his intestine. I removed part of it and sewed it back together again. Then I found that several of the patients I had worked on during the night needed some work. It was 1 P.M. when I finished. While the post-op physician usually does those things, if I operate on a pt. I like to follow him closely, as do most of the fellows. Then for one hour, I watched a very interesting case—a chest-abdominal (lungs, heart, intestine) operation. At about 2 P.M., I was so tired, I just went to the tent and slept until 5. Still tired, but these Colonels and a General were coming from Washington to talk about "Rotation." Well, it turned out to be recruiting talk. "Join the Regular Army. While there are disadvantages, there are advantages. We think we can get Congress to pass bills dealing with the disadvantages." He asked what we had against the Regular Army. Most felt as I did. I told him that I wanted to live and practice as I pleased, that in my relatively short life I'd moved about enough, that I wanted to settle somewhere with my wife and family, be a member of a community, not pick up and move every few years. The Colonel himself said, "Now we all know that you can't quit or move if you don't like your job or where you are." Some brought up the financial angle. I didn't add that I didn't like the "army way of life"—the hierarchy. Well, no one showed any interest in the Regular Army.

I could write I love you all night, but must go. I love you.   Melvin

MONDAY, SEPTEMBER 8, 1952, 10:35 P.M.

My darling—

Mom and I talked tonight about the question of hiring Negro help at the office. Mom says she would like to but can't be a pioneer. I talked about all the ugliness in the world and what surrounds you and that skin color makes no difference there. So I took a shower and cried all through it, by that time forgetting the immediate cause and just missing you terribly. Went in and kissed Mom and told her I was sorry.

All your mention of how much blood is used makes me feel that I would like to contribute some—and get others to do it too. What do you think?

Goodnight my love. All of me reaches out to you across 9,000 miles to kiss you goodnight. Your wife,   Dorothy

WEDNESDAY, SEPTEMBER 10, 1952, 10:00 P.M.

Note of hope. The hospital CO and some others went up to Panmunjom where the peace talks are going on. They were to pick a site for the 8055 if peace does come. We would then screen and take care of our returning prisoners (taken by the Chinese) and get them in shape to be put on a train (the same trains we now use to evacuate casualties) and returned south to Pusan and the U.S. However, they had to look for this site while dodging mortar shells.   M.

WEDNESDAY, SEPTEMBER 10, 1952, 10:30 P.M.

All through the day, you are with me. Driving back and forth, during classes, while giving a test or waiting for an answer, my mind is 9,000 miles away. I wonder what the children would think if they could read my thoughts.   D.

THURSDAY, SEPTEMBER 11, 1952, 10:30 P.M.

My Darling—

I plan full periods of teaching so that they may fly by quickly. The quicker the periods go, the quicker the days, the weeks, the months—voila—Nous sommes ensemble! Ah, comme je t'aime, mon mari, mon coeur. Comme je veux que les mois passent vite. Je voudrais surtout etre pres de toi, recevant tes caresses et te donnant les miennes.

You write about liking the way "Melvin" sounds in my letters. It took me almost 15 minutes to figure out what "vin" meant. I like to write "Melvin" just as I like to call you Melvin when we are making love or talking quietly together or just when it seems to fit. And now, I feel as though every line is a night of love, each sentence a quiet conversation, and so: Melvin, I love you.

One day, we will hold each other, crying and laughing at the joy of being together, knowing that in our own small way we have done our best to make it a better world. I love you and am so happy that Midwood H.S. was built [in 1940] and that you are my husband.

FRIDAY, SEPTEMBER 12, 1952, 11:00 P.M.

My darling—

A film came. We were able to see the pictures of your routine, the set-up of the unit, the types of patients you care for. It is difficult to understand why those who pull the strings can't put an end to this horrible marionette show. I cannot believe that some must die so others shall be free—not these youngsters. I'm thinking of the difference between the surgery you are doing now and cancer surgery. In the latter, the frustration must be great because of the number of failures, as you work against an unknown trying to make it a known. In your present work although the cause is evident, you cannot eliminate it but must suffer the frustration of trying to clean up the mess.   D.

SATURDAY, SEPTEMBER 13, 1952, 4:00 P.M.

Good afternoon, my love—

Oh, the luxury of a Saturday morning, but I won't see you for lunch. I remember Saturdays in New Haven when I would have breakfast with you at home, straighten up the house, go shopping, take papers and books to the hospital, have lunch with you, sit around waiting for a call, snap pictures, sign out for a short ride or walk, then at night, squeeze onto a little cot and sleep most of the night in the warmth of our love—telephone ringing—you gone in a flash. A short while later, "What was it?" "Delivery." "Everything okay?" "Yes." "Goodnight, my love." You crawl in beside me, sometimes the smell of ether still in your nostrils.

I'm glad you received the Desitin, because now the other packages will begin to come through soon. And please darling, do think of me every time you use it. Does the baby powder cloud the other boys out of the tent?

I'll write to you tonight when I come home from Jay's [Katz, medical school roommate] wedding. It doesn't seem right going without you, but I'll enjoy myself and bring home to you all the joy and sadness of the evening.   Dorothy

SUNDAY, SEPTEMBER 14, 1952, 2:00 P.M.

The Army will not approve my request for a PCS [Permanent Change of Station] to 8055. At the 52nd Med Bn they want to keep me in their unit, on paper, so that if they get short of men here they can pull me out of the 8055, which is just what I don't want. The damn business of being neither fish nor fowl is bothersome. Oh well, down I go to Seoul tomorrow to try to get things settled.

SATURDAY-SUNDAY, SEPTEMBER 14, 1952, 1:30 A.M.

My darling—

No one can understand that I must write to you now. At the wedding a friend said, "The mail won't go out until tomorrow anyway." When I got home about 10 minutes ago, Mom said, "You can write two tomorrow." Only you know why I must write now.

It was a gala occasion and, under the circumstances, I did enjoy it. But so many waltzes wasted. My body cried out for you to be holding me moving around the floor, gliding through space as though no one else existed. Just the two of us and the rhythm and the music.

Gerry drove me down at 8:00 and I was swooshed up to the roof feeling like a Cinderella who knew that her Prince Charming would not be among the guests. When I heard the bridal march and saw Esta Mae on the arm of her father, I reached for my handkerchief. I remember so well, my darling, when you took Dad's place and he said, "She's all yours." Little did he know how true he spoke.

"No matter what happens, what sorrows befall you," the Rabbi said, "you have each other. You have your love." I must admit, my darling, that I wasn't thinking about Esta Mae and Jay at all. The ceremony was simple, flowers and candlelight, and the meal was not overdone— enough liquor and champagne, but not flowing. There was lots of hora dancing and Jay's brother, who was completely drunk, began all of them. When my attention was directed more to the candle drippings than to what was going on around me, I took a cab home.

Tomorrow there will be more words and after many tomorrows we shall put our letters away and enrich each other's lives in blessed proximity. I love you and I want you.   Dorothy

MONDAY, SEPTEMBER 15, 1952, 8:30 P.M.

My Dearest Wife—

Came back to two of your letters. My ability to keep my courage, stability, and sense of humor is because you, my Dorothy, are my wife. You are all any man could ask for in a woman—good, kind, giving, a loving heart, an intelligent, tolerant mind—in a most beautiful body. But those are words. How can I write of how I feel as I think of you.

We worked through the night last night and I got about 2 hours sleep, then drove a jeep to Seoul to see Col Lindsey. He reassured me that I didn't have to worry about the 8055. He said, "We Yale men have to stick together." He introduced me to the officer in charge of personnel, several other colonels, one, the new Medical Consultant in Korea. Talked cameras with the Dental Surgeon of 8th Army and finally met with Col. Zipperman, the Surgical Consultant of 8th Army. He was not very encouraging about my PCS coming soon, but I told him I just wanted to let him know I was enjoying the work and wanted to remain where I was. It was 4:45 when we started back through the streets of Seoul and northward into the country. People were working in the fields. The rice is ready for harvesting. It will all be done by hand. We took a few pictures. Stopped at Corps Hq for dinner. (One nice thing about the army—you can drop in anywhere for dinner, gas, or a place to sleep.)

I can sympathize with your mother and her problem of Negro help. BUT there is a N.Y. State law about it. The only question should be the competence of the worker, and that bears no relation to the amount of pigment in the skin. If your mother is worried, let her ask the girls in the office. Don't cry. Just let your Mom know how we feel. Bullets have no color line. One's dealings with others should leave no room for self-reproach or excuses. It should be honest and with the intent to do good. We have found out the value of that, but your mother's the one to decide, not us.

As for my birthday, tell people that I need nothing here in Korea. I may buy this new camera and I can send you the list of accessories, but I'm not sure. I shall ponder this weighty matter and let you know.

It is now 1:45 and I have been up and down many times in the course of writing this letter. I shall bid you goodnight and write again in the morning, after work and before going to sleep. Goodnight Dorothy. Your husband,   Melvin

My darling—

I write with the strains of "Bali hai" and "One Enchanted Evening" ringing in my ears and thoughts of you in my mind and heart. The first thought, as the show began to cast its spell upon me, was that we must see it together some day. "South Pacific." I was but a few hours away from you. We were on the island together. Each time someone fell in love it was "us." Each time they sang about a paradise, it was "us." Each time there was beauty and enchantment, it was "us." I don't have that feeling of wishing for a paradise like South Pacific. To love, to build, and to help others. I hope, my darling, as we grow through life together we can continue to feel this way. It sounds so young and idealistic. The Frenchman says, "I know what you are against, but what are you FOR?" I think we know what we are for, my love, and the most wonderful thing is that we are together in that "for-ness"—to love and live and let live.

I'm dripping away and I still don't know whether it's hayfever or cold. September is moving forward. Rush, rush, rush the time away. Work, work, work each minute through. Love, love, love as much as it is possible for two people to love one another—through every day and every minute, with every breath. I love you, my husband, my Melvin. I am in your arms and you kiss away my sniffling and we sleep and dream and love.   Dorothy

My darling—

Up at the usual time and dropped Gerry and Mom at the station plowing my way thru traffic onto the East River Drive. Out of the corner of my eye I caught a glimpse of the majestic UN building. I hope some day its actions catch up with its architecture.

The house is quiet without Gerry and it will be even quieter without me. I'm glad Mom has so many interests. There are still moments, less frequent now, when I can't believe that Dad is gone. When we show your films, I wonder what he would be saying if he were watching them.   D

Fort Sam Houston, Texas. "Doctors become soldiers?"

Fort Sam Houston, Texas. Field training.

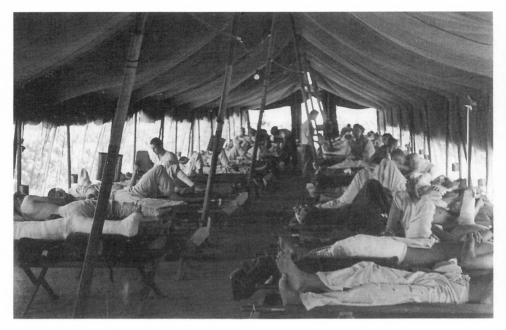

Holding Tent. 618 Clearing Company. Post-surgery. Awaiting arrival of Hospital Train to Evacuation Center for transfer to Japan.

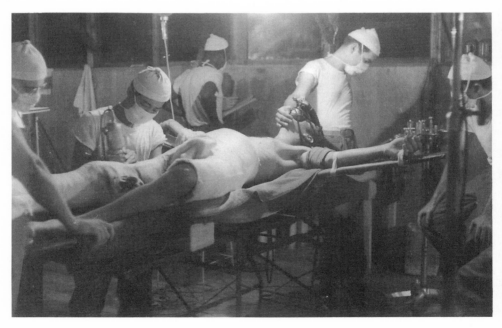

Operating Room, 8055 M.A.S.H. Surgery completed. Body cast being cut to allow for swelling.

"William Holden and yours truly." *(Photographer unknown)*

Operating Room, 8225 M.A.S.H.

First Lieutenant Melvin NMI (no middle initial) Horwitz. M.A.S.H. Korea. *(Photographer unknown)*

Mrs. Dorothy Gotterer Horwitz. Central Park. New York City. *(Photograph by Gerald Gotterer)*

"A sea of mud." 8225 M.A.S.H.

8225 M.A.S.H. at Kwandae-Ri, on the east bank of the Soyang River.
North Korea.

47th M.A.S.H.

Lee and Kim. Korean orphan houseboys. 47th M.A.S.H.

FRIDAY, SEPTEMBER 19, 1952, 4:00 P.M.

Dorothy Darling—

I have been in Korea for too many weeks now and should be used to the ways and fates of war. My heart is sick at the destruction and pain of the last 12 hours and cries out for the love and peace that is so much a part of you and me. I long for the day when I can curl up with you and not wonder if the thunder is man-made.

Last night, I had finished writing to you and went out to the john. Across the fields and over the nearby hills, flare after flare lit up the sky. I could see the flash of the artillery and tracer bullets from the anti-aircraft guns which we use as artillery. I knew then that I would not sleep the night through. However, I got into bed, one blanket under me and 3 on top, and soon was warm and comfortable. About 4 A.M. I was awakened. The story is, though unreliable, that the Chinese had taken several hills and were attacking Old Baldy again. But the facts did not count. Ambulance after ambulance came in and in 4 hours we had 50–60 casualties, 70% seriously wounded. Most could be handled by changing dressings, splinting, transfusions, and X-ray. Then oxygen, etc. But some came into the receiving room, had their clothes cut off, a transfusion started, and in 15 minutes were on the table—every conceivable type of injury, head to toe. By 9 A.M. the hospital was full, so from then on, the ones with minor injuries were dressed, splinted, sedated, and sent to the 618th to await the hospital train. We called for an extra train. They would receive their initial surgery at the 121st Hosp in Seoul, while we did those cases that had to be done immediately. That took quite a load off and cleaned out our post-op wards also. But still they came. Several extra helicopters were flown up and have been landing and taking off constantly.

When the day crew came on at 10 A.M., things were more orderly. I was able to sleep until a few minutes ago. Now I'm soaking up some sun and waiting for the mail.

This morning Chaplain Brechetow came by and was disappointed that tonight there will only be about ½ the number expected, because the people on the line will be unable to come to Rosh Hashanah services. I will try to go since we should be able to get back by 9 P.M.

I love you Dorothy.   Melvin

SEPTEMBER 19, 1:00 P.M.

My darling—

I am standing at the side of the classroom, looking out over the heads of the students. I can see the rain sweeping across the rooftops. Through the open windows I feel a cool damp breeze. It might be raining now in Korea too. I think of how we, who have never in our lives really done anything we didn't want to do, are now bowing to the will of society. No matter how individualistic we may think we are, we must compromise.

11:00 P.M.

Went to Charles Weidman's dance class tonight with Mom. I just can't get my body to do what I want it to do and thus, have to strain for it. Mom says I'm stiff. It was fun having her there. I remember the years when she used to come with me and my little suitcase and ballet costume.

Goodnight my darling. I shall be home early tomorrow morning and my only duty will be to pick out what I am going to wear to synagogue. So I shall be able to write you a "morning song." Goodnight my husband.   Dorothy

SATURDAY, SEPTEMBER 20, 1952, 9:00 A.M.

My Love—

Just a note to let you know the latest. I've been transferred to another MASH, the 8225. I report in Seoul tomorrow where my orders are.

7:00 P.M.

Since this morning I have found out a little more about the 8225 MASH, which is being reactivated as an experiment. There are no nurses, just corpsmen, some of the best taken from the other MASHes for this. I was joking with Dick as to how I would "explain my transfer to a place with no women!" This reactivation is one of Lindsey's ideas, I think, and is probably why I am going there.

Worked straight through last night, 12 hours without a let-up. Case after case. They are still fighting back and forth on Old Baldy. We were pushed off and will probably try to re-take it tonight. The guns are booming and we shall be working again. Amidst it all I keep thinking of you, of your letters, and I can tolerate this.

Last night before work, Sam Gelfan and I and 2 enlisted men (Dick Kamil was working) got into a jeep and went to services. Pistols around our waists, driving north along a dusty road, we could see the flashes of guns on Old Baldy. The tent was crowded. On wood planks set up as benches, rifles piled in corners, some men with helmets, it was a strange sight. The rabbi spoke well, and I enjoyed the melodies. There was a good Cantor who had just come in off the front line. His unit went into reserve. Somehow, I couldn't get into the spirit of it. Occasionally a particular melody would move me, but I felt no need for "religion." The artillery was distracting and in contrast to what was being read and said. Eight miles away people were dying. However, I was glad that I went. When we came out, we could see the flares over Old Baldy and the surrounding ridges lighting up the sky for miles and miles. As we drove back, several ambulances passed us on their way to the front, to return later.

I shall be sorry to leave here. I like the people and the work. Speaking of change, there is no question in my mind about Ike vs Adelaide, especially now. Ike said he would put Taft "high up in the party." I guess he is getting worried about the election and grasping at straws. Well, the Democratic machine may be corrupt, but Ike and his backers—Taft, Dewey, Nixon, McCarthy and Lodge—are not very inviting. I should get my ballot in about a week.

Now to work. The night is cold, and the day will come when we can warm each other. Goodnight my wife. I love you.   Melvin

SUNDAY, SEPTEMBER 21, 1952, 4:30 P.M.

Dearest—

A hectic night. Again we saw the flares over Old Baldy and shortly thereafter got a call from the 2nd Div. General to expect casualties. I think we had tried to recapture some lost ground, and from the way the casualties poured in, didn't do too well. I did an appendectomy about 1 A.M. and then between 1 & 5 we got in 50 cases. By 9 A.M. I could barely stay awake so I dropped into bed and slept until 2:30 P.M. when one of my friends from Ft. Sam came by. He is at a Battalion Aid Station and likes it because he is getting points. Well, after being at a MASH, the experience I've been getting is so valuable, that it makes up for the points, not to mention the proximity of flying steel at the Aid Station. Gene was transferred to a Division in Eastern Korea. I may get to see him as the MASH I am going to supports this Division. The latest MASH to be activated, it has all new equipment and is across the river from an airplane loading strip where patients are evacuated. This also means that living will be comfortable, the PX well-supplied and an officers' club available—as always with the Air Corps.

Darkness has come. I'm packed and have arranged for transportation. The helicopter can't take me and all my baggage, so I'll go down by jeep. The road isn't too bad now.

Why are we so far apart? For centuries, men and women have stood alone and far apart, under the same sky. Nothing is gained by it. The lights in the distance are fewer and the hard fighting is over. We won't be getting as many casualties tonight. I think we still have Old Baldy, but so many have died and suffered, just for a hill, a headline. Well, I am not one to judge military tactics.

Now going over to do just a few small cases, so I shall be able to rest, dream of you, think of you as a new day begins bringing us closer together.   Melvin

SUNDAY, SEPTEMBER 21, 1952, 11:15 P.M.

My love—my husband—

I'm depressed tonight. The entire holiday weekend. The idea of why Mom and I are alone on a Sunday night. And WQXR [New York's music station] was all static, so we listened to "Traviata" (on the victrola) which at times like these further depresses me.

Up at 8:00 A.M. and marked all the tests I had given on Friday while writing to you in the classroom. We had decided that yesterday's ordeal at Synagogue had been sufficient, so we didn't go again today.

At the Trans-Lux, we saw "Carrie," an adaptation of the Dreiser book, with Laurence Olivier and Jennifer Jones. He is an amazing actor, so convincing in any role he plays. Came home and I read the *Times* while Mom wasted her time on *Two Beds for Roxanne*. I guess she feels an obligation to read it because Stephen Longstreet is a relative. I haven't read anything but a newspaper since I've begun teaching.

Rather than becoming accustomed to our separation, I find it more difficult. I get more impatient. I feel less and less like adjusting to this unnatural state. I want to live with you and share each moment that is ours on this earth. I love you and could tear down the walls tonight. Goodnight my love.   Dorothy

Dorothy Darling—

From the 52nd Md Bn, a driver took me into Seoul to see Lindsey. It was the first time I had been there at night. Two miles from the city, we drove in blackout, just pinpoints of light from candles and lanterns in the native huts along the way. People sit in groups in front of small shops, an entirely different feeling than during the day, more oriental if possible. In the city, the streets are less crowded. Few people frequent the small cafes and shops. Kids and prostitutes roam the streets as MP's patrol the city. Occasionally the hoot of a train whistle blasts through the night. One can see planes coming and going from the airport across the river.

I got to see Lindsey and heard about my new job. The new MASH has its first surgeon—ME. Others are coming in the next few days. I think the entire unit will move shortly after I get there. I am looking forward to it, since I think I shall have a position of responsibility. I met Col Guinn, the Eighth Army Surgeon, who will be up on Wednesday to see how the activation of the unit is going. Also saw some of the other Cols and Majors I had met the other day when I was in Seoul (and my buckle wasn't shined). But now it is getting cold again, and I shall crawl into bed (after I shine my buckle, of course). Goodnight dearest.

Melvin

My darling—

Now, at the studio of the New Dance Group with 200 others waiting to register. Alone in a corner, seated on the floor on a piece of newspaper, apart from the chatter. Writing to you, surrounded by people, I am still alone.

Worked with Guion this morning at the Lighthouse. At a STEINWAY! I played one song for him, then spent the next hour copying music—a sloppy job. I never did learn how to write notes and could barely read them when I finished. He said it was all right, as long as someone could make them out.

At 9:40 I arrived home to find three long letters from you and two boxes of slides. Flopped into the "reading-Mel's-letters" chair. If I had had time, I would have read them over and over until the words were engraved on my heart. What a feeling—like the song from "South Pacific," "I'm in love with a wonderful guy!" She sings: "I am in a conventional dither with the conventional stars in my eyes." I can't believe that anything we feel is conventional.

When I leave my room at the end of the school day, Johnny Narciso, a cute little ninth grader, is waiting for me in the hall to walk me down the steps—just like in "New Faces of 1952" when a schoolboy sings, "I'm in love with Miss Logan," as he waits for his teacher after school. Oh well, I gotta get some lovin'!

Almost every day we receive a letter from Gerry and it makes Mom feel good. He hasn't written anything about ROTC [Reserve Officers Training Corps], but Bill Tiger [my first cousin] said that they're combining all parts of the Army—Signal Corps, Artillery, Infantry—which doesn't sound so good. Bill says they're not taking anybody out of college right now. I hope it continues that way.

Goodnight now. If it doesn't take me all night to find a parking space, I shall be in bed soon, dreaming dreams of you and the days when we shall once again be together.   D

TUESDAY, SEPTEMBER 23, 1952, 8:30 P.M.

My Love—

Am now in eastern Korea, 2 miles north of the 38th parallel, near Inge on the map, 30 miles west of Chunchon. The front line is further away than at the 8055 and it is relatively quiet. No blackout, so it's lit up all over the place. I'm happy with the switch now. Changing jobs is interesting and helps the time pass.

My tent is nestled into the side of a hill. We have clean sheets and blankets, pillow and mattress. A moderately drunken warrant officer just rolled over and went to sleep on the other side of the tent. Now that he has stopped talking, I am alone with you. Our life is made of dreams. Reality will have to wait. I stop writing and just think of you.

Awoke at 7 A.M., ate, repacked, handed in some blankets and excess stuff to lighten my load, and sent a duffle bag by jeep East. I'll have to wait a few days before I get it. Everything I need is in a wooden box. After signing 400 different papers, I was able to get over to the air strip, get a plane reservation, have a small steak for lunch, and board. They didn't weigh the box, just asked, "50 lbs?" I said, "60 or so." Probably closer to 100! This was a two-motored plane, like the ones from Boston to NY, except the seats were benches along the sides, and we sat facing the center. We put on parachutes (Air Force rule), and the ride took one hour with a ten-minute stop along the way. There are more mountains here that are higher and less eroded.

The 8225 MASH has a beautiful spot, comfortably built, but we are moving. Tomorrow at 5:30 A.M. we shall have breakfast, load, and be at our new place—27 tortuous road miles north—set up and be ready to take patients by 6 P.M. In about a week we shall be moving into pre-fabricated buildings that another unit is moving out of. It will be quite comfortable. BOQ will still be tents.

The CO here is a Medical Officer, but primarily an administrator. Two other MD's came along with me, one a general surgeon, the other an anesthetist—the crew. More doctors will be coming in the next few weeks. There are two nurses whose job it will be to train the corpsmen to be male nurses. I am the only one of the surgeons, so far, who has had training at a MASH. We shall probably not be as busy as the 8055, but they are expecting action all along the front.

We shall have the unique and dubious distinction of being the MASH furthest north in Korea, but still not in real danger, my love.

Both the fellows are from the 121 Evac in Seoul, and talking to them, I feel like a real combat veteran. What a laugh. I was up where I could HEAR the shooting! The other boys got pistols from supply. I got a sweater and 2 extra blankets. I'm sure I'll find more use for them. But I will get a pistol later, just because there's that rule about not leaving the compound without one. The equipment and supplies are new and plentiful. The CO seems pleasant, and I am hopeful of this too being a valuable experience.

I'll be up early in the morning and it will be cold. Can you remember how it felt to curl up together under warm covers, our nude bodies just fitting together. Oh love, time is passing. Soon. Soon. I love you my dearest wife and will dream of you tonight, as always.   Melvin

TUESDAY, SEPTEMBER 23, 1952, 9:30 P.M.

My darling—

Some days are worse than others. I "fell off the roof" today, but I am happy about that. This is the 3rd time I've been unwell since you're away. I wonder how many more there will be. I am planning now, unless you tell me otherwise, to tell the school at the end of December, that I may be leaving in May or June. Whatever they want to do about it, I shall leave to them. All I know is that nothing except the damn Army will keep us apart this spring.

We have so much to be thankful for, to be able to look forward to a full life, some day leaving this loneliness behind. Goodnight my darling.   Dorothy

WEDNESDAY, SEPTEMBER 24, 1952, 9:30 P.M.

My Darling—

Arrived at the 8225 and found the MASH just beginning to go up. A bulldozer was clearing the area. We unloaded and went to work getting the hospital set, the operating room in order, and by 7 P.M. we were ready for the first patient. We ate C Rations—cans of hamburger, pork and beans, hash, frankforts and beans, and cans of crackers, cookies, coffee. I don't mind them at all. By evening we had a mess tent and our personal tents, a latrine dug (four-seater with a tent over it), so now, we're ready for anything.

It has been quite an experience seeing a hospital assembled like this. In a few days, we shall move to a group of pre-fabricated buildings now used by an ROK [Republic of Korea] MASH, which they will vacate, since the ROK Division is going into reserve and one of our Divisions is going on the line. They are only about 500 yards from here.

We are right on a picturesque river. Opposite us is a Tank Battalion. The tanks come and go. We shall have showers and laundry in a day or so.

A wonderful rumor is making the rounds that we may be getting 3 points a month here, like all the units around us. We ARE quite far north.

As I meet other married fellows, and listen, again I am amazed. Most of them, including the doctors, lament the fact that there will be no nurses at this MASH. In fact, however, we shall have the two who are training the corpsmen. I need no nurses to provide female company. I do not need an officers' club or drinking companions. Just some work to do, a pen and paper, a postman to bring me words from my wife, and I shall be as happy as I can be until we are together.   Melvin

THURSDAY, SEPTEMBER 25, 1952, 4:30 P.M.

My darling—

It rained last night. Your husband is rapidly becoming an expert in keeping his bed and clothes dry. I had put my foot locker and duffle bag on boxes along with my boots. Awoke this morning to find our place, once a rice paddy, now a lake. Thru the center of the tent ran a swiftly flowing river. You've seen pictures of vehicles and men plodding along through a sea of mud. Well, that's it. You just forget about your feet and go ahead. Last night one of the fellows was trying to figure out a way of having running water to wash with. This morning—voila!—a stream. "C'est un miracle!" Had breakfast, such as it was. The mess tent was flooded. Slogged over to the hospital tents where luckily we had put in flooring and were able in the course of the day to get everything re-arranged. Fortunately, no patients came through and probably won't until tomorrow. The heaters and blowers are working in the hospital tents and that is where I am now as I dry out my boots, socks, and pants legs. Have been able to keep warm by changing socks and wearing my heavy wool sweater under a poncho.

I love you.   Melvin

FRIDAY, SEPTEMBER 26, 1952, 11:00 P.M.

My darling—

You write so often of the sunset and your natural surroundings, the stillness of the nights. How much more aware you are of those wonders of nature when you are close to them. In the apartment, all I can hear in the night is the roar of buses and the honking of horns. My only contacts with nature are my drives back and forth in morning and late afternoon. I have the same sensation I had the year we were to be married when I used to walk from the station at Valley Stream each day scrutinizing every branch, welcoming each bud of spring. And so now, the changes mean passage of time.

How petty are the details of our problems here where there is no bloodshed. If if if there were something we could do. I think history will recognize this war as an outrage. It is some comfort to know that you are ameliorating suffering.

Goodnight my love.   Dorothy

Dorothy my Love—

Friday was a sunny day and everyone's spirits lifted as the area began to dry out. About 3 P.M., I had all my stuff on my cot, trying to repack it in orderly fashion—the other boys had gone to a pistol range to fire the 45's—I was called over to take care of the arrival of our first patients from the front. Most of the corpsmen are new. The routine is different and things did not move as rapidly as they might have. With only 2 surgeons and 2 anesthetists, we worked all night until 5 A.M. when one anesthetist and the other surgeon went to sleep. We finished the remaining cases. At 5:00 A.M., an ammunition truck crossing the bridge caught fire and exploded. For 2 hours there were continuous explosions. Occasionally we could hear a fragment whistle by. I sure felt like falling flat on the floor a few times. The surgical consultant was here and was awakened by the noise. We got after him in the morning for 4 points now that we are "under fire." It was 2 P.M. before I went to bed, after receiving 6 of your letters forwarded from the 8055, and the Isadora Duncan book. I'm far behind in reading, so don't send any more for a while. The letters were just what I needed. I was exhausted and they pepped me up.

I really have been earning my money. I am tired and filthy. Haven't showered for 5 days, but tomorrow when the showers are set up, boy, will I scrub. Working has made the time pass. I didn't even know what day it was. I'll write a better letter tomorrow, after some sleep. I love you.   Melvin

My love—

Tomorrow is Yom Kipur, a mail day, and that is why I'm looking forward to it. During the last war, couples sometimes didn't hear from each other for months at a time. We must be thankful for something.

An extra hour—no longer Daylight Saving Time. I was up at 9:00 and listened to the news and weather report with Mom—same old thing. But in today's paper there was an article about three "new" proposals concerning repatriation made at the Peace Conference by the UN. Always proposals.

We left for Synagogue at 5:30 and came in just as the Kol Nidre was beginning. It's a beautiful service. Towards the end when the more familiar melodies were sung, the Kaddish, Mom started to cry. We left just before the end to avoid having to talk to people.

During the services I thought about the time when we would be living in a community, perhaps attending service, and bringing up our children so that they will know what being a Jew means. Although I am not a believer per se, I do enjoy the positive qualities of religion and ritual, perhaps the beauty, the pathos, the yearning for an ideal. Tonight I identified with the generations of Jews who had recited these same prayers before me. Although I didn't agree with everything the Rabbi said about the necessity for survival, I did feel that as long as we are Jews, we should be positive rather than negative Jews. I would like to light candles on Friday night and to have our children able to explain their Jewishness to their Christian friends. I wish you could have been with me, to have felt what I felt—or if not, then to have shared and helped me to clarify my thoughts. Last time in Synagogue I didn't sing one word because I was too choked up [in San Antonio, just after Dad died]. Tonight, I enjoyed repeating the customary prayers and melodies.

Called Paul about malpractice insurance. The army covers you while you are subject to army orders. Thus the government is responsible. Since you are doing emergency work under adverse conditions, nobody could have any case against you. Incidentally, he sent you a SECOND salami.

I have a dream right at this moment of a peace settlement and the Army assigning you to Japan and me joining you there. I want you terribly. Goodnight, my husband.   Dorothy

October

A lull in the fighting permitted Mel to travel by single-engine army reconnaissance plane to Seoul. Flying over the Punch Bowl and Heartbreak Ridge, he saw for the first time the barren embattled hills that abutted Korea's native lush greenery. In the city, he was struck by the dirt and the poverty.

At the recently activated 8225 M.A.S.H., Mel described in detail the habits and biases of his new medical colleagues. He noted that the lack of nurses was detrimental to the operation of the M.A.S.H. Subsequently he learned why this M.A.S.H., without a nursing staff, had been re-activated and why he couldn't count on the army for consistency.

The election campaign dominated the news. McCarthy persisted in his scare tactics, with Eisenhower supporting his anti-Communist stance, "not his methods." I bombarded Mel with campaign literature, and he continued his tent-side politicking. It was time to send in absentee ballots.

Modern dance classes became the focus of my long days, the only activity I looked forward to. Mel and I were both reading Isadora Duncan's autobiography, which acted as a springboard for our discussion about my dancing and our future careers. Skirting the specific issues of geographic location and the demands of a surgical residency, we did no more than generalize, putting off decision-making until we were together. There was never any conflict. I agreed with Mel: His career was number one. Although I perceived myself to be independent, my role had been defined by my generation. I was not a maverick. I would be, I wanted to be, wife, mother, and homemaker.

As I groaned about apathy on the home front, my students celebrated the Yankees winning the pennant. Only *The Telegram,* I wrote, dignified the torturous role of our soldiers with front-page headlines: "Blood in Korea . . . Politics in U.N."

Mel, now at home in a mobile army operating room, was grateful for the pot-bellied stove as days and nights in Korea turned frigid. In Valley Stream, my teaching had become routine. I marked papers to pass time and to make time pass. Occasionally, Mel and I wrote to each other in French, for practice and for fun. Into our fourth month of separation, we began our second one hundred letters.

———————

OCTOBER 1, 1952, 9:45 P.M.

My darling—

Tonight is one of those nights. I don't feel that I had any rapport at all with the kids today. The World Series was on, if you wanted it. And I didn't. Of course, my students didn't like that. I have such a variety of them, from bright to dull. It seems a waste to put in so much effort so that just a few can learn. I had such a feeling of futility. Do I really enjoy teaching? Maybe it would be different if I were teaching French or Modern Dance. I know that I'm happier doing this than I would be selling hosiery or working in an office, but I guess I am still looking. Perhaps older students would be more appealing. I guess deep down I still want to be a ballerina.

How I would like to curl up to you now and forget everything but our love. As I write and think of where you are and how many lives there hang by a thread, I feel selfish writing about my own puny broodings.

When I think of the future, I look forward to just being at your side, living and loving with you, raising healthy children, making a warm and comfortable home. That sounds like a full-time and wonderful job. Yet, I wonder how I will react to being "at home," not so much when the family is young, but later. This probably sounds incoherent, but I'm just putting it down as it pops into my head and it feels better getting it off my chest onto yours, my love. I'm sure that these things will work themselves out and won't even be problems at all, once we are together. How wonderful it is that you love your work, since you are the one who will not be having the babies. I used to tell Mom: My husband will EN-JOY his work. I would rather have less materially and have him happy in what he is doing every day. She would smile wisely. I still feel that way.

I dreamed of you last night. All I can remember is a room crowded with people and you beside me. We kept slithering all over each other, every once in a while conscious of remarks and glances. When I woke up, I was glad I had been with you. And later, for the first time in a long time I "made myself comfortable."

The three-point rumor sounds good, but doesn't make sense. If 8055 is closer to the front, why is that a two-point area? The sooner we are together the better, but it isn't worth taking unnecessary risks for the difference of a few months. I write as though you actually had a choice.

Now our letters are our reality. I love you my sweet. Work hard. Sleep and dream well. I taste you and feel you. I kiss you full on the mouth and say good-night, my beloved, my husband.   Dorothy

WEDNESDAY, OCTOBER 1, 1952, 9:00 A.M.

Good Morning My Love—
A note to say I love you.
A few cases to do last night, but by 11 P.M. it was quiet. While we do not have as many men as at the 8055 at the hospital at night (2 surgeons, 1 medical man, the latter when the surgeons are tied up), one of the surgeons can sleep in his tent if it stays quiet. This is possible since we do not do minor cases that come in after 2 A.M. but send them by ambulance or helicopter south 22 miles to the air strip and then by plane 50 miles to Wonju to an Evacuation Hospital. We evacuate patients all day since we are a relatively small hospital and have to keep bed space open.

During rounds today one of my Korean patients was trying to tell me something. He had no pain. He wasn't cold. He didn't need a urinal. So I got an interpreter. It turned out he wanted to know where his money and fountain pen were and when he could eat.

We've set up an on-call schedule now and will change shifts weekly. I'll be on days starting Saturday. Because of the small staff, we are all on 24-hour call, but will rarely if ever have to work more than 12 hours.

About 9:30 we had an air raid drill. When we first heard the siren, we didn't know if it was real or not. We turned off our lights, as we heard the vehicles being moved. They are scattered around the compound rather than being grouped in the motor pool. The generators were cut off, except those in the operating room, which at the time was empty. Some of the fellows put on their steel helmets. I had mine near-by but did not put it on as we had by then heard it was a drill. A funny sight was one of the fellows shaking cracker crumbs out of his helmet before putting it on. When the drill ended, I worked on a Korean who had shot himself in the foot.

I shall start studying and reading in earnest tomorrow, especially if it stays quiet. Haven't found anyone to play chess with, although the group on the whole is becoming more congenial. There are several new men, an orthopedist and the present acting chief of surgery. He has been at a MASH for several months and knows how things can and should run. It sure makes life here pleasant, having likable people around.

Dorothy, I love you with all my heart. Your husband (the word sounds so good),   Melvin

THURSDAY, OCTOBER 2, 1952, 8:00 P.M.

Dearest—

I am sitting at one end of the operating room, and at the other end two cases are going on. This is the warmest place available where I can write.

I got 6 letters from you today, also letters from Bert, my folks, and Barbara Kass [Mel's cousin]. I ran to my tent to read them, hungrily devouring the words of love, as I shared your week with you. I read and re-read them, laughing and crying with you. My thoughts are racing faster than my pen. I have to control myself so that you will be able to read this. But a case has come in.

5 MIN LATER

The other fellow I work with is going to do it, an accidental injury. A man was fixing his gun and shot the patient through the buttocks. Luckily, no real damage, but a sore behind. Most of the casualties today were accidental. One of our patrols returning from No Man's Land was shot up by our own troops. I am afraid many of the fellows around here get a pistol and brandish it without knowing anything about it. I have a great respect for guns. Though I know how the thing works and how to take it apart, I still never carry it around loaded, but figure if I ever need it, I'll have the few seconds it takes to load it. This way I can't hurt anyone.

Last night I had a few small cases to do and about 1 A.M. went to sleep on the operating room table in the most comfortable tent in the area. Was awakened once at 5 A.M. to treat 2 Koreans who were stealing gasoline that exploded and burned them. It takes a lot of self-control to treat them sympathetically.

Read Hemingway's *The Old Man and the Sea.* He writes so simply. You feel the vitality of his characters, and their emotions come across vividly. I enjoyed it, as I've enjoyed most of his books. Have you read *For Whom the Bell Tolls?* Don't know if it is still at 1299 [Mel's folks' apartment house on Ocean Avenue in Brooklyn] or in one of our cartons.

Warm under 5 blankets. After lunch I picked up more winter clothing—wool shirt and pants, and extra-heavy pants. The issue after this will be fur lining for our field jacket, a fur-lined hat, winter parka, and warm boots.

Back again—patient a scared kid whose story is: He was cleaning his 45 (pistol) when it went off accidentally. The bullet perforated the palm of his hand. One never knows whether it was self-inflicted or not.

My darling, I will cross a moonlit compound ringed by sentries and surrounded by war. Yet I will be able to sleep with love in my heart. Goodnight, my wife.   Melvin

My darling—

Winter is on its way. We are closer to walking arm in arm in some strange new place, going to bed at night with sighs, stretching and purring, talking over the day's events, feeling the closeness of each other's bodies until we are so tired that we fall into sleep. I still think, my darling, of how it must be for Mom to have only memories. I remember the last night we slept together, knowing that it would be the last for a long time to come and yet, not really believing it. How we clung to each other, hoping against hope that there would be just one more night and yet knowing it would be just as difficult. I remember that room at the Chancellor so clearly and the night and the days that followed. I buttoned up my suit jacket today. I can't wait to feel that March wind.

Danced tonight—first class of the fall semester. Nona Shurman (Weidman trained) teaching. At the end of class, to my surprise, Mom greeted me from the sidelines. She had come down to bring me a coat. You have never seen me dance, except when I pranced around the house. I wish I could dance every day. It makes me feel so good, a different kind of tiredness, not so tense.

Incidental intelligence: Gave the word "implied" to students as vocabulary study to be used in a sentence. Result: "The man implied for a job." Ah the joys of teaching! I have one boy in my Eng and Span classes who is really negative. Nothing interests him. No matter how funny or inspiring (hmmm) or dramatic I am, he is not impressed. Today, I finally reached him. While discussing a character in an O. Henry story, I compared him to a Charles Addams monster. The children had never heard of C.A., so I described some of his cartoons. The boy was entranced and even laughed gleefully. I think I shall submit HIM as material for C.A.

Goodnight my love.   Dorothy

SATURDAY, OCTOBER 4, 1952, 7:05 P.M.

My Love—

It is pleasurably warm in the tent now. Although I still wear my sweater or field jacket, I can sit here and be comfortable. The oil stoves are potbellied things, an oil can outside and a pipe to the stove, a carburetor to regulate the flow, and a long stove pipe. We can heat water and food on its flat top, but mainly it warms the place when we get up in the morning.

At times during the day, I lie down for a moment to dream of you, remembering things we've done together—going to theatre, dieting, feeding your Mother pills, holding your hand under the table cloth, trying new dishes. Sometimes as I walk alone outdoors at night, in boots and uniform, the moonlight playing on the hills and tents, an armed guard on the road, I can't believe I shall sleep alone on an operating room table. Now I sit in this tent, another fellow writing by the light of a gas lamp and the stove burping quietly in the corner. The one certainty is my love for you, and your letters, so filled with compassion, with life and hope, words and thoughts which bridge the gap. I love you, my wife.   Melvin

SUNDAY, OCTOBER 5, 1952, 1:00 A.M.

My darling—

You really have been working at a terrific pace and I hope that by this time, you have more surgeons, are getting more sleep AND more showers! You used to think you were busy in the ER. Your first few letters sounded as though you weren't sure of getting much work to do—quite a contrast. With all this experience you'll be ready for a Professorship when we get back to New Haven. Does your technique suffer any by the fact of having to work more quickly? Will it be necessary to re-adapt yourself to civilian surgery?

10:30 P.M.

We left the house at about noon and after a good brunch at Monte's, dashed into a cab and sped over to the Met. We had excellent seats, dead center of Grand Tier. "Peter and the Wolf" which I find a bit dull in spots was enjoyable mainly because of the reactions of the children in the audience. "Swan Lake" was beautifully danced by Alicia Markova. She is so ethereal that you don't believe she is really flesh and blood. During her performance I began to feel my neck getting stiff from concentrating so hard. "Bluebeard" was a new one for me and a lot of fun—especially John Kriza's antics. I wonder when we shall be going to the ballet together. Perhaps in Japan.

After supper, I marked papers for about an hour, then began Santayana's novel, *The Last Puritan.* Incidentally, he died recently in a monastery in Italy.

As I rode the bus back from the Met to where the car was parked, I looked out at the gaudy crowds and I disliked New York. When you are here with me, we have so many things to share even though we know how much better we feel away from the city. I would go mad if I didn't keep busy at every moment. Remember when we were trying to talk your Mom into taking a course or a job to fill up her time. I know she'd be happier.

Goodnight my sweet,   Dorothy

SUNDAY, OCTOBER 5, 1952, 8:15 A.M.

Good Morning Mrs. Horwitz—

Sitting on a box close to the stove, my backside is warm, almost as red as the stove. Since I overslept, I ran over to rounds without breakfast. Unconsciously, I guess, last night I had midnight chow of fried eggs and coffee, so missing breakfast was easy. I had the most wonderful dream, that we were back at Stowe [Vermont], at the Green Mountain Inn with the red wall paper. I chased you in your red flannel nightgown from bed to bed. The air was cold and the blankets sparked.

I felt well-rested this A.M. This husband of yours, a paragon of virtue, was the only one without a hangover. In the evening the fellows sit around talking and drinking. Liquor is so cheap. It is getting too cold to drink beer, and no one likes to get out of his sleeping bag in the WEE hours of the morning. So most of them had quite a load on by the end of the evening. I have a drink here and there, but only to reinforce my dislike of it. This drunken Warrant Officer showed up at the hospital yesterday, hardly able to walk. It was with great difficulty that I didn't just kick him out. If it should happen again, I shall drag him over to the CO. I don't care if he drinks himself to death in his tent, but showing up where casualties are coming in, I wonder what they think and how much confidence they can have in us. Anyhow. I don't smoke, don't drink, and the only woman I want to mess with is 9,000 miles away. Too bad officers can't get the good conduct medal. Then I would have one more to wear on my long underwear when I get home.

Have a good day.   Melvin

8:30 P.M.

One of the fellows did decide to have a beer, which must have gotten warm, because as he punctured the can it shot up to the roof, spraying the tent. He figured it was a defective can and opened another. Now the place smells like a brewery. If this letter reeks of Schlitz, you will know why.

You write of how you felt in Synagogue and I understand. I think, my darling, that I have less feeling for religion than ever before. But I also feel more strongly about being Jewish and part of a community. I think I would like us to be members of a Synagogue and especially for our children to have a good Jewish education so they know and understand their culture and religion and, as you say, can explain it to their non-Jewish friends and be comfortable as Jews. I will want to go to Synagogue on some of the holidays and take our children, not for the religion as much as for the culture and ritual. Although you have more of a feel for it than I do, I know that we both want the same things out of life as Jews.

This has been a mixed-up letter, but I can't concentrate—too much talk and noise. Goodnight my love. I am with you always.   Melvin

OCTOBER 6, 1952, 11:00 P.M.

Tomorrow I shall open a checking account with your army check. So far, we have put only $350 in the savings account. The rest of our millions has gone for car expenses and insurance. I can't think of any other big things stateside for which we are handing out dollars—but the money sure seems to go.   D

TUESDAY, OCTOBER 7, 1952, 11:30 P.M.

My darling—

I love you. I want to be with you. It always comes back to the same motifs, like musical compositions. I think we are Beethoven—not Bach, not Prokofieff, certainly not Shostakovitch, aspects of Brahms. I am talking about the "we" which is beyond the "I" and the "you." Anyone else reading this might think I'm nuts, but you understand. And even if you do think I'm nuts, you still love me. Isn't it wonderful? We can write whatever nonsense comes pouring out.

This morning I felt so close to you. It suddenly dawned on me that the letter I held in my hands had been in your hands just 7 days ago. I smelled it and put it to my face.

Usual school day. The Yankees won the series and the kids were all excited. I let them listen to the last inning (getting soft!).

Spent an enjoyable evening with Viv and Jo Goldreich [Vivian, a college friend]. There are many things to talk about. They are warm people and think of others besides themselves. Tonight we planned (subject to your approval, of course) a weekend jaunt to Bucknell so that you and Jo would have the pleasure of seeing the beauty of the "300 acres set apart." (They have a golf course too!)

I shall sleep now. Crawl in beside me and warm yourself. We shall radiate heat until we don't need blankets. Goodnight my sweet, my love.   Dorothy

WEDNESDAY, OCTOBER 8, 1952, 9:00 A.M.

Good Morning My Love—

I have gained a minor reputation as a correspondent. I don't feel like reading. The day is gray and foggy. There is one case waiting to be done—a young fellow with one foot blown off. The other probably will

come off, and one hand is injured. He has received 12 pints of blood
and is coming around, so that we may be able to operate on him. As
you can see, the morning hasn't started happily. Except, the appendectomy I did wants to eat and that is a good sign.

7:30 P.M.

When shall this stop? When will we be together?

It's like a dream. I go to a movie and sit with 50–60 fellows as they
hoot at Marilyn Monroe. Oh that the day will come when I can put on
a suit and collar and tie. At the movie tonight, one of the men did just
that. It looked so strange.

This morning was one of the most depressing I've had. I wrote
about this boy, almost dead. We had given him 14 pints of blood and
then had to take him into the operating room—or we never could—so
three of us and 2 corpsmen worked on him. Speed was essential since
he could not take much anesthesia—or surgery. It was horrible to remove his dressings and see what we had to do. I write of this not to
sicken you, but to give you a feeling of what I felt. One of us amputated
one leg below the knee and I did the other above the knee. Fortunately
his hand was just shot up a bit and will be OK. Total operating time 1
hour 30 minutes from the time he was brought in to the time he was
taken out, including anesthesia, preparation, casts, etc. He is alive and
in fact looks surprisingly good tonight—BUT—an 18-year-old kid.
That was our morning's work. In the fog of his shock and medication,
he still doesn't realize what has happened. Tomorrow we have to tell
him. Oh hell—we sell cigarettes and soap to Koreans at our PX. They
sell it on the black market. Our soldiers buy Korean money on the
black market. And people are worried about what to buy me for my
birthday. Tell them to give a pint of blood and contribute some money
to a children's relief fund. That will make me feel the best. I buy cameras and worry about showers, but I guess I'm just bitter right now. Maybe by morning I'll feel better.

I hope there will be someone to love this boy some day, that he will
have the strength and courage to get artificial limbs and walk—or in a
wheel chair—live some sort of life—not die slowly over the next decades.

If, when we are together, you find me sometimes just staring at you,
you'll know that I am making up for all those times when I wanted to
be able to do just that. My dearest, I am so lucky to have you as my wife,

to be your husband, to make me strong, complete, with meaning and purpose to my life. It is late. I am tired. Now to bed to close my eyes and dream of snuggling next to you, feeling your warm backside fit comfortably into my abdomen and thighs as I press close to you, my arms about you feeling your smooth skin, kissing your neck and tenderly holding your breasts, feeling the cares of the day slip away, as we are alone together, warm and secure. Goodnight darling.   Melvin

THURSDAY, OCTOBER 9, 1952, 10:30 P.M.

My Darling—

Another day. I miss you my love. I try to forget the morning rounds when somehow I ended up being the one to tell the boy that we had amputated his legs. I did my best. The kid is still dazed. I wonder if he does realize what it is all about. He is out of danger—for the moment.

I finally got a shower across the river at one of the neighboring outfits, as ours is not working. The laundry is working, and I sent out a lot of dirty clothes. After dinner sat around talking to one of our new MD's, a real celebrity—Bobby Brown. He played 3rd base for the Yankees even while he was in Med School. The big wheels don't know what to do with him. As he puts it, "I seem to embarrass the generals." They would love to leave him in Japan to play baseball, but pressure from publicity and the doctor shortage made them send him to Korea. He is a 3100 (General Medical Officer) and interested in Internal Medicine. He knows about a MASH and requested it. His wife just had a baby while he was on his way over. That makes 3 of the fellows here in that position.

I labeled some slides which I shall send out tomorrow, then played bridge for a while. It was fun. I smiled as they said, "Yeah—bridge is a good game when you and your wife have nothing to do and go over to visit some friends." I didn't say that we have so much to do, that for the next ten years I'll be showing 4,000 slides of Korea, and for 10 years after 4,000 more of my wife and children (I hope and pray!!). Maybe one day we will play bridge, but not for lack of something to do. We have two pianos to master, reading, talking, listening to music, loving and and and

The light in the tent is poor and my eyes are closing. Oh how I love you, Dorothy, my wife.   Melvin

SUNDAY, OCTOBER 12, 8:30 A.M.

Good Morning My Love—

The sun is bright, the ground covered with frost. Everyone walks around huddled in his coat.

I curled up last night on an operating table in front of the heating vent and slept for a while. Then got a few patients in and worked from 2–4:30 A.M. Slept again until 7 A.M. A cup of coffee. Rounds. Now back in my tent, I shall try to get some sleep.

I enjoyed Isadora's *Life,* more so since you have stimulated my interest in Modern Dance. She was maladjusted and perhaps mentally ill at times. It reminded me how close genius and madness are. I wonder if that has to be true. Is the person who is adjusted in our society so stifled that he cannot create? Is the maladjustment a product of a society that does not support or nurture the poet, musician, artist, creator? She had an obsession to dance and what totalled up to an unhappy life. When one of the several men in her life told her he found "life itself worthwhile," she was surprised. She was always looking for something, and indeed found it only in her art. She said that loving one man was like listening to one composer. Unfortunately for her, she never had a good love—like ours, which is changing, growing, as varied as listening to many composers. Idealistic, creative, impassioned, and determined, she was fascinating to read. I wonder if she had had someone who dominated her, yet encouraged her in her work, whether she might have had a happier life.

I shall return the book Parcel Post. I'm afraid no one around here shows much interest in it.

7:10 P.M.

In your letter of ten days ago, you wrote that you were depressed, that you're not accomplishing anything. I too, in spite of my pre-occupation with my work, get that feeling, wanting to do something else. What I'm not sure. Together, our life would be settled—that would be enough at least for a while, depending on where we were living, the people around us, and most important, what YOU wanted to do. I grant you that in our society it is most important that I, the male, enjoy my work, as well as make a living, but in "our" society yours and mine, my dearest, we must both enjoy what we are doing. If you feel you want to teach or dance or teach dance or climb mountains, we shall talk it over and figure out a way so that we both will be satisfied and comfortable. I paraphrase: We shall approach each problem, mull it over and arrive at a solution that satisfies us, so that the problem doesn't hang over us. Then we'll go on to the next problem, secure in our love and in our ability to meet what life has to offer, good and bad. [When Mel was in high school, his father gave him a copy of the quotation that he restated here. He carried it in his wallet until it disintegrated.]

When I finished writing this morning, I mailed the letter and a box of slides. Then I crawled into bed. It was cold and windy. The tent seemed about to blow away at times. I slept and dreamed of you—in Willimantic in that old-fashioned bed in a cold room, our bodies warm under the covers. I awoke later, my body straining and my back arched as I pressed against the image of you. I rolled about in bed, face down, face up, the excitement overwhelming me. Here it is more difficult if not impossible to "make myself comfortable," and my body hasn't done it in a long time. I lay there, gradually calmed down and slept.

I awoke, got dressed, went over for a shower—good warm water and cold air—invigorating. Came back, read for a while, then it was dinner time. Back to the tent. Read the paper, some medical journals, and rather than go to the movie—I just don't have any patience for them now—I sat here alone, with my wife, my love, and my dreams.

Work here has been keeping us busy, but not rushed. My patients have been doing well. That boy with the double amputation is only fair, but I think he will pull through.

The other area is being built rapidly. The frames for the tents are going up one by one, and we should move over soon. They have some KSC (Korean Service Corps) laborers who look and dress like North Koreans. It's eerie to see them. Took some movies.

Things are getting hectic as the whiskey flows. I shall have a beer in the spirit of things. My heart is with you. This is my life—our letters and our love.   Melvin

SUNDAY, OCTOBER 12, 1952, 2:30 A.M.

My love—

Your wife is getting to be a dirty stay-out, as you can see by the hour. Tonight we visited the Newmans [my father's sister Helen and her husband Dave]. It is always difficult to tear ourselves away from them.

As we drove home, the moon was bright. There was a couple in the car in front of us. He was looking straight ahead, concentrating on the road. She was snuggling up to him, pecking him on the cheek, the neck, burying her head on his chest. For us, those days (nights) are far away.

Jean dropped by yesterday to pick up directions to the Met for our ballet date Friday night. She wound up leaving without them. I called to her from our 5th story window and threw the card out the window to her on the street below. We watched it travel round and round with the breeze until finally landing almost at her feet.

I spoke to your Mom and the news was "no mail."

The day at school was relaxing. I gave tests. Now I have all those papers to mark. In English, we were comparing American wages to wages in other countries. I cited the case of your Korean boy. For the first time in one of my classes I said, "My husband is in Korea." Nobody seemed concerned or surprised. I really don't believe these kids have any idea of what's going on there. Most of their fathers were in WWII and their older brothers aren't old enough to be in the army. Mary Smith [English teacher at Valley Stream] has a brother-in-law who had been in Korea. It used to annoy her that when she talked about him no one seemed interested. She said that now that he is back, she herself is not as concerned about Korean events. I'm sure her reaction is a natural one. Mine is slightly different. I really don't expect people to be genuinely concerned about Korea unless they have someone there. Although there are occasional human interest features about the fighting, memories are short.

10:30 P.M.

Pop thinks that since I put the time at the top of my letters to you, I should put the time at the bottom as well. We all had a good laugh. Maybe it's a good idea.

Jean was in her seat waiting for me at the Met. We enjoyed the performance. For me, it was the culmination of my dance lesson. I had struggled for an hour and then, I was seeing perfection on the stage.

Gerry and I went down to Barnes and Noble yesterday where I bought a book of nursery stories for Barbara (Toddie), a Japanese conversation and grammar book, *Absalom, Absalom!* by Faulkner, a book of folk dances, and a review of English Medieval History (I'll be teaching *Ivanhoe* soon). It all came to $7.00. Gerry bought a book for his comparative anatomy course which he loves.

Evening at the Newmans—Gerry spent a good part of it pouring over a human skull with Dave [an ophthalmologist] and I saw the tail end of Tallulah Bankhead's debut on television.

Today Aunt Dora [Gotterer, my father's sister], Gerry, Mom, and I walked over to City Center. "Aida"—the first time I've seen it—is a colorful opera. The voices were excellent, and there were some good dancers in it, including Glen Tetley from my Colorado College summer of '47.

Pop came over at 7:00 and we had a cold supper. Your Mom had gone to Scranton to a "Pidn ha Ben" [a celebration for the first-born male child]. We looked at slides and movies that Pop hasn't seen. Tonight I wanted you 3-dimensional. The months behind us seem long and the months ahead longer. Now I shall brush my teeth, cold cream my face, take off my hairnet and bobby pins and house dress and crawl in between clean, cool, vacant sheets.   Dorothy

TUESDAY, OCTOBER 14, 1952, 8:30 P.M.

My Love—

Letter #90. Somehow the numbers I'm writing now are ahead of those I'm receiving. I think I left out 10 somewhere. Oh well, you will love me even if I don't number properly. You can make out our income tax reports.

Yesterday, as few patients were coming into the hospital, I asked the Col. and the chief of surgery for permission to go to the 8055 to get my camera. Got a ride north about 5 miles and spoke to the Operations Officer at the small airstrip where they have Piper Cub and light plane types used for artillery spotting and as couriers. Over the mountains we flew in this small plane, over the Punch Bowl, where our artillery and units are dug in. On a high ridge is the MLR (Main Line of Resistance) with bunkers, and over and beyond that valley another ridge—on that one, the Communists. The views are magnificent, but the thought of what is going on below unbelievable. Several of the ravines are filled with smoke to obscure direct enemy observation of vehicle movement. The mountains are higher here in the east. Often we passed over a narrow river that widens. Then a valley and a plain appeared, at the head of it a small Korean village. The fields are tilled to the top of the mountains where sometimes there are village cemeteries. In each village are splotches of red, which is the pepper crop drying. The rice fields are a mosaic of harvested and unharvested fields. Interspersed with these villages are army units. On several mountain tops and ridges are empty bunkers and artillery outposts. Some of the mountains are brown, bald of trees and vegetation, and pock-marked from artillery. One can see where battles were fought. Heartbreak Ridge is a bare hill amidst beautiful greenery. Towards the west, the land flattens and the hills are eroded. The people have taken the trees and bushes for firewood. The Hwatchen Reservoir spreads out its enormous fingers among the mountains, converging to a large lake, dam, and hydroelectric plant. Quite a contrast to the primitive farms. Then Seoul. We landed on a light plane strip that was a former race track. In the center are small farms. I thanked the pilot and got a jeep ride to EUSAK Headquarters where I inquired about a helicopter to the 8055. None were available. It was 2 P.M. and I was hungry. So I went to the snack bar (an 8th Army luxury) and ordered two cheeseburgers and coffee. Had a haircut, went out to the 121 Evac to see Joe Berman and spent the night there. They have quarters for transient officers. Talked with Joe and some of the other boys, one of whom went to college with me. I had a pleasant evening throwing the bull and eating crackers and jam. They do many cases at that Evac, but most of them are minor, cleaning out superficial wounds. This is really not very helpful for learning surgery. I slept in their BOQ on clean linens. They have it soft, living in Quonset Huts, big gasoline heaters, hot and cold water in the showers. In spite of that, I would rather be where I am.

Joe and I walked around Seoul. Today was a school holiday, an athletic event for the children. All the people were flocking to the stadium. I'm sorry I didn't have time to go. Many children run after the GI's yelling "chop-chop" (chocolate). Some beg and steal.

When we got back to EUSAK, we had lunch, and I went out to the race track to get a plane back. The fellow flying got the plane up, then practically flew with no hands all the way back. I sat next to him and he gave me earphones. I expected to hear directional signals, but instead listened to Beethoven's 9th Symphony.

Now back at the 8225. Picked up your seven letters, had supper, a shower, and started this letter. Been interrupted several times by people coming into the tent to borrow books or one selling liquor, of which many of the boys made much. I've been playing with my beautiful new camera, an exact replica of a Leica. I've got some gadgets in addition. The Japanese have never signed an international copyright or patent agreement, therefore copy almost everything, at much lower cost, of course.

I love you, my woman.   Melvin

TUESDAY, OCTOBER 14, 1952, MIDNIGHT

My darling—

I was up at the usual time, worked till the usual time, left at the usual time. My day does go quickly. I dislike the paper work and the routine planning. I enjoy the actual teaching. And it's better than working at Bloomingdale's.

Mom is ordering *The Caine Mutiny* through Book of the Month Club. Since you are so enthusiastic I shall certainly read it after I finish *The Last Puritan.*

Goodnight my darling.   Dorothy

WEDNESDAY, OCTOBER 15, 1952, 5:30 P.M.

My Darling—

Today was rainy and the ground quickly turned to mud. The wind howled. We were alerted for winds of 50 m.p.h. Although they were not that strong, they whistled through the tent which flapped and fluttered, but stayed up.

My impressions of the fellows haven't changed much. I dislike Rick. He is tense, emotional, and crude. I can't relax with him. Neither his sense of values nor his morals are admirable. At the 121, his "friends" have a poor opinion of him. Harvey, the anesthetist from North Carolina, and I get along well. We argue about most everything—political and military—but in good spirits. Ken Schoenfeld, the orthopedic surgeon, in his early 30's, is pleasant, but hasn't grown up. However, he knows orthopedics and while he doesn't show as keen or quick thinking as Dick Kamil, I can learn from him. Thornton, the fellow with the guns is just plain scared. He sleeps with a loaded pistol at his bedside every night and drinks a great deal. Harvey and I unloaded his gun so he wouldn't kill anyone. Ryan, the Supply Officer, is intelligent with a wry sense of humor. He and I are the only "liberals" in the tent. Anderson, the other anesthetist, is competent. We've had a lot of long talks. I really can't say I've met anyone here I can feel close to.

The army surgical techniques are basically the same as in civilian surgery. The problems are different, the emphasis slightly different. For example, at New Haven, if I were taking out a gall bladder, I would be especially careful of sterile technique, the placement of the incision, and how I opened the abdomen. Here in Korea, we have a traumatized patient with dirty wounds in a dirty operating room. We may also have bleeding in the abdomen or openings in the bowel, so time is an important factor. Though we never sacrifice good surgery for speed, we enter the abdomen rapidly. The method of closure is different too. I will have to re-adjust, but not re-learn. In fact, many of the the tricks I'm learning, the knowledge I'm acquiring, are directly applicable to civilian surgery.

I'm cramped now from writing leaning on my knees. I love you, my Dorothy. Every fiber in my body aches for you. One day, tomorrow will be today.   Melvin

THURSDAY, OCTOBER 16, 1952, 9:30 P.M.

My darling—

The Telegram has had war articles on the front page every day. I feel that every paper should—don't know whether it would do any good. Yet, here's the rub—Top headline: "Blood in Korea. . . . Politics in U.N." Second head: "Scared Allies Veto U.S. Plan for Acheson Tough Talk." From the articles it seems that *The Telegram* is using the horror of Korea to criticize Acheson and his policies. All the allies are sitting tight until the election before taking any stand on the armistice issue. I would agree with *The Telegram*'s criticism of indecisive diplomats while boys are being killed—if I didn't think they would change their line completely if the Republicans got in.

This weekend, when I can fit it in, I shall be making up marks that are due Monday. So often, when I am trying to cram conjugations into unwilling heads, I feel that I am wasting my time. But I guess it must fit somewhere.

Goodnight my love. Sleep well. Dream well.   Dorothy

THURSDAY, OCTOBER 16, 1952, 9:00 A.M.

Good Morning My Darling—

Just a note to say I love you on this cold sunny day, so far from you. Last night the tent shook and about every hour we went out to tighten the ropes, but inside it was comfortable. Had some cheese, salmon and crackers. Discussed the Negro Question with this fellow from North Carolina. He is a fairly liberal southerner, though several strong feelings, based I'm sure on his background, still remain. He just wouldn't CHOOSE to live in a tent with a Negro officer, but would if the situation arose. He admitted he would rather do it than live in the same tent with the inebriate Warrant Officer. It was a good discussion and only fell apart when some of the other fellows became emotional: "Would you want your sister to marry a Negro?"

7:00 P.M.

Right now I'm hot on one side and cold on the other.

No mail again today except my ballot. Voted for Stevenson and Counts, and the remaining predominantly Liberal Party candidates where they were nominated by both Democratic and Liberal parties. I always get a good feeling when I vote. It's hard to explain, but I feel— shall I use a cliché—like a "free man."

In Kenneth Roberts' *Lydia Bailey,* one character, talking about travel in Haiti in the late 1700's, says, "They say any white men that travel in Haiti do so at great danger." Another answers, "That's what every stay at home thinks. You can travel in safety, anywhere on earth, if you keep a smile on your face and act like a decent human being." I think I was somewhat afraid to walk the streets of these oriental cities, but now I realize that the above statement is true. I learn more by walking the streets and seeing how people live. I am hoping to get a chance to fly to the seacoast. It is supposed to be beautiful. I shall, if I get there, shout out across the seas of my love for you.

Now time to go to the hospital. It has been quiet here lately, and I hope it stays that way. Enough accidents and appendices come in to keep our hands in. I hate to hear the artillery roar and echo over the mountains.

I love you.   Melvin

Hello my love—

Coming home I had a real scare. I started to make a turn—without looking—and a bus had to swerve to avoid me. I put on my nice tight brakes and stopped about 1 ft. from him, but you can imagine the thoughts that went through my head. You should have heard the bus driver! He got out and gave me hell. I just kept saying, "I know. I was wrong." Well, my darling, even though I felt a bit shaky afterwards, it was a worthwhile experience. I think I was getting too confident. I WILL be careful. Please don't worry. Wait until you hear my next "event of the day." One of our (my) New Haven checks BOUNCED! I had been letting the account run out and didn't realize it was so low. The check was for $6.00 to the N.Y. State Teachers Association—of all things. Perhaps they'll think I need a raise.

Your letters are so filled with your goodness and your poetry. Goodnight, my husband.   Dorothy

Ma Cherie—

Aujourd'hui j'etudie ma premiere lecon en francais. Now don't go all out and write a complete letter back in French, as I'm just getting back to it. A trailer unit came by with the Army courses—cost me $2. It is a nice opportunity for someone who wants to study and get credit for it. Many of the boys do get high school and college credit. Je t'aime ma femme.

I went to the movie tonight and was glad I did—"Lovely to Look At," an adaptation of Jerome Kern's "Roberta," with Kathryn Grayson, Howard Keel, and Red Skelton—good escapism. The song went, "They asked me how I knew—our love was true—I of course replied—Something deep inside—cannot be denied." And there followed a beautiful dance number by Marge and Gower Champion.

Goodnight my dearest.   Melvin

My beloved,

Saturday night, just like every other night, is a lonely one. How I

look forward to the nights when we shall be close and I can pinch you
when I feel like it. I can't imagine how we shall be able to sleep a whole
night through without waking every 5 minutes to look at each other,
knowing the pure joy of simply being together. I think of Mom. At
night before she goes to sleep, the past and the future must intrude
upon her, so she fills her time to shut them out. We fill our time to shut
out the present.

Time, time—we want to hang on to it, yet we push it away.
Dorothy

SATURDAY, OCTOBER 18, 1952, 9:00 P.M.

Dearest—

Time, time, time—we push at it to go quickly.

Boy was it cold this morning! So I hopped into my clothes and went
over to the hospital to warm up. Then about 10 A.M. we had a rush of
patients. As I happened to be there, I went to work. Ambulance after
ambulance, bringing them in now wrapped in warm bulky bags—like
sleeping bags. All is confusion or seemingly so (more so here where we
have no nurses to supervise the corpsmen), but after about half an hour
litters are being carried to and from X-ray and into the pre-op ward,
the shock sections, and on into the operating room. The admitting
ward is clear, cleaned up, records caught up, and the men settle back to
deal again with the walking patients who come down for medical and
surgical consultation and X-rays.

I spent the rest of the day making big wounds out of little ones to
clean out the dirt, debris, and shell fragments. In winter the wounds are
dirtier because the fragments carry in more clothing with them. Today
we had a group of men who were attacked by the Chinese—in their
own bunkers. The Chinks had somehow infiltrated and came about ¼
mile behind the lines, right into a large bunker, tossing grenades and
firing bursts from burp guns (combination machine gun, rapid-fire
rifle, and shotgun). Men in the bunker threw back some of the grenades, but two went off, killing a few of our men immediately and
wounding some others. In spite of this, one Lt decided that they'd better stop this activity. So he and others went charging out of the bunker,
carbines firing. One Chinese was just outside, dead from a bullet
through his head, but still standing. He had just pulled the pin from a
grenade and was about to throw it. It exploded before he fell to the

ground. Eventually the remaining Chinese were killed or captured. This was part of our day's work.

I'm afraid I lost my temper with some of the corpsmen tonight. They were just standing around, moving slowly, and didn't seem to give a damn. I don't care if they move that way when we have no casualties. But when we do they ought to work hard. They would want others to do the same if they were in the stretchers. I know I sure would. Oh, my love, if you were here, I could yell and rant and bitch to you and then perhaps go out and more calmly explain it to them. I wrote to Paul and Larry [Merson, Paul's brother] trying to paint a word picture for them of Korea and the MASH. Felt as though I was writing a "war story," as I do now, sitting in a tent, bare bulbs, dirt floor, fellows in fatigues and boots playing cribbage, one writing a letter. I shall go outside after I finish this and stand for a while in the dark under the millions of stars, bright and clear in the cold black sky. My thoughts will be of you. Please don't overdo, my wife, my sweet.   Melvin

SUNDAY, OCTOBER 19, 1952, 10:30 P.M.

My Love—

Am arguing politics. And I have no answers. What will solve the problems of Korea, Russia, inflation, future wars? How can you argue with people who say: Well, if you use the atom bomb, we won't sit here in Korea for 10 years. Try to tell them the horror of it. One fellow, Harvey, probably started it as an attention-getting device, but calmly states he is a fascist. "We shouldn't give the security to the bums who won't work." Well, he was probably successful (in his arguments) and he attracted enough attention till he's gotten so he believes it. I dislike him intensely for this. Arguing with him was impossible. The others are much more rational. Ed Svetke, the new surgeon, has many of the same views as we have, but he is the only one, although it is fun to talk with most of them. Rick is just plain stupid. He reads a statement and then repeats it, shouting.

I'm just pissed off tonight. Pardon the expression, but the newspapers are depressing. They want to use the A-bomb. Peace talks snafued. Iran and Britain. I'm happy to be able to write and bitch and have you listen. I feel better already, but wacked out, emotionally flat.

Mailed the letters and read Irwin Shaw's *The Troubled Air.* He writes frankly, clearly, brutally, disturbingly. Worked at cases intermittently

during the day, sat in the sun, and studied my French. Read some journals, then your letters.

I'm tired, but feel more at ease and will sleep. The handwriting in
this letter is terrible. I kiss you with all the love in me. Ma femme.
Comme je t'aime.   Melvin

OCTOBER 19, 1952, 11:00 P.M.

My love—

Tonight I begin the second 100 letters.

Tales from the home front:

In my English class—During the war there was an "evasion" of
France.

We got a $10 dividend from Barbizon!

Audrey's [college friend] comment: "The only thing that will protect me from the Red scourge is becoming pregnant."

Sally's [college friend] anecdote: She went out with one of my Bucknell beaux. When they got home, they stood at the door, Floyd gripped
Sally's shoulders and looked deep into her eyes. Sally was all set to put
up a fight when Floyd burst into strains of the Alma Mater.

Everybody asks about you. What can I say? "He is busy, working
hard, making time pass. Hopes to get transferred to Japan sometime in
the spring and I'll be able to join him." I've said it so many times. It's
only when I write them to you or think them to me that the impact
hits.

I want you.   Dorothy

MONDAY, OCTOBER 20, 1952, 10:15 P.M.

My darling—

Mom is out seeing "The Millionairess" starring Katherine Hepburn.
The house is quiet and smells of paint. Before 8:00 this morning, the
painters came and began to argue. Two coats? One coat? Red closets?
White closets? I shut myself in the bedroom and worked furiously.
Mom went for her driving lesson in a blinding snowstorm. Renee, the
decorator, was with the painters mixing paint. She stopped long enough
to bring me a cup of coffee and a toasted roll, which was really nice of
her.

I received two of your letters this morning, my darling, and tried to say them over to myself all the way to school. How I love to be caressed by you verbally. I'll hang the "Grin and Bear It" cartoon in the Teachers' Room tomorrow.

You mention remembering the bed we slept in last winter in Willimantic. Last night before I fell asleep, I was remembering ALL the beds we have slept in. [I nostalgically listed twenty-five.] Towards the end of the list, I began to forget, willingly, because I didn't want to get to the end of the list. I didn't want to remember those last few nights at the Chancellor after you left, when I could still feel the form of you beside me, but when I reached for you, I grasped air.

The leaves are falling fast and the color is almost at its peak. We can enjoy the shades of autumn with a feeling of joy as well as sadness, knowing that time never stops. Oh god, how I miss you.   Dorothy

THURSDAY, OCTOBER 23, 1952, 10:30 P.M.

My love—

I shouldn't complain, but since you love me and my bitches—I have only one: I'm tired and can't seem to catch up with myself.

Yesterday I spent an hour tutoring. I enjoy it because I can feel my student Roger respond to me. The hour goes quickly. His mother always asks me to stay for lunch, but I accept the $3 and politely refuse the meal. He is nervous, self-conscious, stutters, and has been completely indifferent. He expressed a desire to be tutored in English. So here I am!

Usual day teaching except that I was irritable. I sent some nice little boy to the office and was sorry afterwards. Saw 72 parents during two hours of meetings. Unfortunately, it's mostly the bright kids' parents who came.

There is one point in my drive to Long Island, just as I enter the Cross Island Pkwy from Grand Central that a lovely curve of foliage comes into view. I gauge the dates by this foliage.   Dorothy

FRIDAY, OCTOBER 24, 1:00 A.M.

My Darling—

Yesterday was quite a day because of what I heard, as you shall see. Spent the morning writing, read some journals (I try to read at least 2 or 3 articles a day) and did some small cases. Worked until suppertime.

At the table was Doug Lindsey, who had come to see the place. After the usual introductions and amenities, as we ate, we were talking of how little work we had had for the past few days. Lindsey said, "Would you like to know why this MASH was activated and moved up here so quickly?" We all waited. I wrote a few days ago of a feint made by an amphibious force off the east coast of Korea, as though they were going to try an invasion behind Chinese lines. Well—WE were supposed to have been part of it!!! We were astounded, as you can well imagine. This maneuver had not started as a fake. The tremendous collection of ships, men, and planes were meant for the real thing. Our MASH would have come in, of course long after a beach-head had been established and when troops had advanced. But that's it. There are two reasons for the change of plans, i.e., not making the landing. First, that the Chinese got wind of it and were ready, and second, the election and the desire on the part of the govt not to use that as a campaign issue. Lindsey guessed it was the elections. Maybe. I guess it's a break for us not to have gone, as I am not one who likes "moving." Our lives are not our own.

In the next breath, Lindsey said, "What job would you like to have if the peace is declared?" Before we could say, "Go home," he answered that there were four possibilities: taking care of prisoner exchange, taking care of civilian exchange, staying where we are supporting the divisions as they slowly withdraw, or being at a "rest camp." All this means of course is providing whatever medical service is necessary. I for one don't really care. IF peace is declared, I have one wish: to be with you. Whatever will further that end, I am in favor of.

Some boys from the tank outfit across the river dropped in. Trying to recount their stories is impossible since the stories themselves are not much without the atmosphere of the tent, such as one battalion being overrun by the Chinese and the MD in the aid station calling for help (this MD previously an obstetrician). When asked if he wanted more corpsmen or litter bearers, he replied, "Hell no. Send someone with guns. They're all around me!" Nothing happened to him, but as I read it over, it almost sounds tragic, not as funny as it did last night. Of "Silver Star Stratton," a physician who firmly believed he could not get hurt and therefore went behind enemy lines to bring out wounded. When fired upon by snipers, he took the rifle from his guard and shot it out with them. He received the medal, and at the same time, an official reprimand for "neglecting duties as a medical officer and acting as an infantry officer." Of how he would drive down a road exposed to enemy gunfire. Of how the Turks guarded Sandbag Castle, which was only 50 feet from the Chinese trenches. Of how one Medical Officer, a Major who had gone regular army and was trying to talk others into it, was touring some areas at the front. When a few mortar rounds came in, he turned to his driver and said in a frightened voice, "You bastard, get this jeep out of here!" The other medical officer with him (not R.A.) was too scared to say anything. When they were out of the area, the driver turned to the Major and said, "I just eat that shit up. Don't you, sir?" Is it funny? It was last night. However, hearing about what it is like, even in a story, I have less desire than ever to go to the division, even to visit, no matter how many points.

Some work has come in. Sleep well my dearest.   Melvin

SATURDAY, OCTOBER 25, 1952, 9:20 A.M.

Good morning my love—

It's a bright sunshiny day, the temperature in the low fifties. If we were together, we would dress in comfortable clothes, pack a lunch, take the car out to the country and tramp about in this crisp fall weather.

Mom is arranging the closets and says to tell you that she's keeping your Texas hat in good shape. In spite of all the paint and mess, it's curled up in readiness for you.

I'm happy that you enjoyed Isadora. I remember particularly feeling sorry that she had found no one love. I don't think that genius must necessarily be a product of maladjustment. I think of all those who are led into art through psychoanalysis, whose problems are helped by finding the right outlet for their talents. Did you ever read *Dance to the Piper* (Agnes de Mille)? A refreshing autobiography, as full of life and art as Isadora's, but quite a contrast.

Winter is almost here. I love you.   Dorothy

SUNDAY, OCTOBER 26, 1952, 11:30 P.M.

My Dearest—

I should be sleeping, but I couldn't without sharing my day with you. I am filled with longing. I don't look ahead. I just look to the mail at the end of the day.

Have just been interrupted by Armenti. I don't like him. He's self-centered, selfish and not too bright. He's dirty and flips cigarettes all over the floor. He is continuously trying to impress everyone, including our poor colonel, who knows no medicine anymore, of how much experience he has had.

It was white outside this morning, as though it had snowed, and we had to chip ice off the windshield of the jeep.

The FECOM [Far East Command] Surgical Consultant, Col. Salyer, lectured to us for an hour, then showed us a film on a chest surgical procedure. Very interesting. He seems pleasant, especially when he called General Shambura, the FECOM Surgeon, an administrative politician. He will be here for a day or so. Will make rounds with us in the morning. He and others, from what I gather from looking at shifting of units, expect this sector of the front to blow up in the near future, with the hopes of peace even less, I guess. If all the money now spent on arms and war were spent on constructive research on "how men can live together" maybe we would get somewhere. Oh, my love. I wonder if we shall ever see the end of war in our lifetime.

It is after midnight. All is quiet except for the hum of the generators. I love you.   Melvin

SUNDAY, OCTOBER 26, 1952, 12:30 A.M.

Hello my love—

How are you this evening (this afternoon, this morning) so far from me, so close to my heart. Saw a beautiful performance of "Cavalleria rusticana" and "Pagliacci." Patricia Neway brings such drama to her singing and recalled memories of how much we had been moved by her performance in Menotti's "The Consul." This was the first time I have seen "Pagliacci." The only one I have ever heard sing it is Caruso, on our records. Giulio Gari was Canio and Lawrence Winters, Tonio. Dad loved this opera and often hummed the arias.

I'm glad that you got your ballot in, and I do understand your feeling good when you vote. It is one of the few tangible reminders that we are living in a democracy. But, my love, I do believe that we do not have as much freedom as we had—especially when I heard (from the head of the department at V.S.) that the Board of Regents of N.Y.S. had "suggested" that Social Studies teachers de-emphasize current events and controversial issues like the Korean situation. This certainly is not good. Retired Judge Learned Hand spoke a good piece about this menace.

The picture of "Tiger Horwitz" will make our children believe in werewolves—so no more knives in teeth if you please. What will Mother say? What would Freud say?

Goodnight Melvin. I love you.

10:45 P.M.

My darling—

My ovaries ache. This is the fourth period I've had since you are away—one more way of keeping track. If only I could flow for a whole month and crowd four months into one.

Mom and I worked today putting things back on the kitchen shelves, then went to Brooklyn. Had a delicious chicken dinner, showed the latest black and whites and slides, the letter from Gus Lindskog [Mel's boss at New Haven Hospital], and read aloud the account of your trip to Seoul. What a wonderful afternoon! I know I can talk about you to my heart's content and no one will be bored.

We left about 5:30 taking Bert with us. He and I discussed his future in medicine. The only thing he said he was sure of was that wherever you practice he wants to practice. I can well understand his admiration and desire to be with you. But I asked, "How do you know what your wife will want?" I hope I didn't disturb him by my questioning. All this is so far off.

Goodnight Melvin. I love you.

WEDNESDAY, OCTOBER 29, 1952, 12:20 A.M.

My Love—

Last night, the excitement was one patient who bit off the end of a thermomether and swallowed the bulb. Didn't hurt himself, but could have. He was just coming out of anesthesia. A corpsman who didn't know any better took an oral temperature. We keep asking for more nurses. I hope it won't be necessary for someone to die because of a mistake before they send them to us. The boys just haven't had the experience with patients.

Built some shelves, a table, and chair. This took several hours but was lots of fun. How valuable tools and nails are here. We have beer by the truckload, but are short of nails. More army efficiency—

Got embroiled in a chess game that has taken up most of the evening except for about 2 hours when Bobby Brown dropped in. He told stories about teams and players, each one funnier than the last. We really got an inside view of big league baseball.

8:30 A.M.

The houseboys are going through the motions of cleaning up, but they sure don't do very much except stir the dust around.

As for the staff, we now have four surgeons, an orthopedist, two anesthesiologists, two internists, a supply officer, a motor officer, an Adjutant & Detachment CO, a Utilities Officer (Warrant Officer), and the hospital CO. A mixed group. At the moment, Bob Brown is the one most annoyed by our Fascist friend Harvey. Brown told me last night that "one day Harvey will make one of his funny but insulting statements when I'm not feeling good and I'll slam him one." Well, I am not alone, I guess, in my dislike of snobbishness.

The tent is filled with visitors. Harvey came in to borrow a plug for his electric razor and at that moment the generator stopped and the lights went off. Poor fellow. They are all reading the books and magazines you sent, so you might as well keep it up, about once a month or so. The *New Yorker* makes me homesick, especially the ads. I remember how we would leaf through them together.

Now, a meeting at which we shall re-arrange the night call and I'll get more sleep. I place my lips to yours and filled with love I start the day.   Melvin

WEDNESDAY, OCTOBER 29, 1952, 10:00 P.M.

My darling—

My love, my husband—Melvin! Don't say, ever, that you are ashamed for writing the way you do. We make love through our letters. Whatever is unsaid can be felt. My words come too slowly to tell you all my heart feels. How your words satisfy and stimulate, in turn, my longings. That day shall come when we are able to look back and forward—together. Best of all, we shall be able to live fully and completely in the present.   Dorothy

THURSDAY, OCTOBER 30, 1952, 10:00 A.M.

My Love—

If you can't read this, it's because my hand is tired and so am I. Ambulances and helicopters started pouring in about 4 P.M. yesterday. I went over at 5 P.M. and worked steadily until 6 A.M. I was on call so as the rush of pts subsided, one after another (doctors and corpsmen) left until at 4:30 some corpsmen and I were the only ones left. I was doing the cases under local. There were a terrific number of amputations. At times I felt more like a butcher than a surgeon.

Had one of those meetings trying to decide about a new schedule where everyone talked and no one said anything. I just walked out not caring.

I pray our children never have to go through this.

Tell the Moms I'll write in a day or so.

7:00 P.M.

Seated on my bed writing on my "bedside table." Reading Hardy's *Tess of the d'Urbervilles* and in spite of the cover, am enjoying it. A change from the modern novels.

Had supper, which I didn't eat—hash. I wasn't hungry anyhow. Our tent gets more comfortable daily. We are about to winterize it. Went over to the hospital to see some of my patients—doing fairly well. The two main problems I think I can send back tomorrow. One boy with abdominal injuries, a broken pelvis, and a paralyzed leg. He needs constant encouragement and faces a long tedious hospitalization. The other one, I told tonight, that I had taken his foot off. What a hell of a job. They look at me, eyes filled with tears, and I have to try to tell them that they will be able to walk with an artificial foot and be OK. But can I tell them of the months of pain and repeated operations and despondency. No, I can only hope and say that if they fight to get well or to walk, they'll do it. So tomorrow they go back. South. To Tokyo and to the U.S. I don't envy them. My heart is heavy at the thought of so many and yet I feel good when a patient of mine does well. I think perhaps I've shortened his hospital stay a while.

I left the hospital and in the dusk walked over to the new area. The moon had come up, the sun just gone behind the mountain. It was cool and misty. (Can you imagine it?) As I walked in the darkness of a Korean Valley, amidst war and armies—thousands of miles from you, I felt useful.

Our radio has been working and we've been getting some good concert music. Heard one piano concerto broadcast from Russia and I felt like playing. Thought about the day we shall play together and our wish for 2 pianos. The music is filling the tent as the current gets strong. I miss you so.

Talked about "going home" with Irv Graham, a wholesome, affable fellow. I feel "old" talking to him although he'll be 25 in Dec. He's a pharmacist and plans to go back to North Carolina to work. He was married only two months before he left for overseas. We were talking about what we would do as soon as we got back. He wants to go on the honeymoon he didn't have. (He went right to Ft. Sam.) As for us, I said it depended on what happened in the next few months and when we got back. But I thought we would like to go away and be alone for a while—where the countryside was beautiful and where we could just be together. Goodnight, my beloved.   Melvin

THURSDAY, OCTOBER 30, 1952, 10:45 P.M.

My darling—

Mom and I were out of the house at 7:15 this morning, Mom practicing for her driver's test. At the Lighthouse, I helped the music student memorize the accompaniment to Bach's "Magnificat" for his chorus. Because of his knowledge of theory and harmony, he was quick to pick it up. I do enjoy working with him.

We now have a white dining room and believe it or not it doesn't look bad.

Yesterday Gladys [Segal, whom I had described as a new young bombshell in the Spanish Department] and I were in the teachers' room when we noticed a stupid *Daily News* editorial on the mirror. We gleefully ripped it down. A few days ago I had come in alone and seen one. I knew it was wrong, but it made me angry so I tore it down surreptitiously. Gladys was the one to suggest it this time so I felt less guilty. Later today I overheard this conversation: "There must be some rabid Democrats around here. Twice I have put up articles which have been torn down." As I told Gladys later, I felt I, and today we, had been wrong. We had the immediate satisfaction, but actually, we should combat words with words. If we had put up a *Post* editorial next to it, we might have accomplished more.

My teeth hurt tonight and I have chewed off a few nails. I need you. Goodnight my darling.   Dorothy

FRIDAY, OCTOBER 31, 1952, 11:30 P.M.

My darling—

I sit here eyes half-closed, thinking of you in your crude surroundings reading my words, with your heart in this bare room with me. Oh my love, tell me the way! I shall fly to Korea, become a postwoman or an air hostess.

As I left school tonight, one of the teachers behind me said, "Perk up! It's the weekend!" I smiled feebly. Although weekends mean a break in routine for me, a weekend is just a weekend, until we can share it together.

My dance class was good, strenuous. I have fresh black and blue marks on my knees. Mom is worried. Said to ask you if I could get water on the knee or something horrible from all these bruises. Eventually, I'll learn to get down on my knees with enough control so as not to bump them.

I listened to Stevenson's speech on television. I like him. The campaign is hot and heavy with only a few days to go. Spirit is very high. The kids in school voted and, knowing the district, I'm sure it was a landslide for Eisenhower.

I love you, Melvin. I just ask to be with you. It seems so simple a request. I am only half a person without you. Having you gives me strength. Goodnight my darling.   Dorothy

November

November was for us a month of birthdays, which had always been accompanied by great fanfare. This year, Mom's fiftieth came and went with as little fuss as possible. Five days later would have been my father's fifty-fifth. At the 8225, Mel gave a tent party for his twenty-sixth and bitched to me about increasing fatigue and a drunken warrant officer.

The burden of fighting was shifting from GI's to malnourished ROK's whose estimated fatality rate among their wounded was 30 percent higher than the GI's. We watched with dismay as Russia vetoed India's peace proposal at the U.N. In an attempt to ascertain reader interest in the war, the *Vancouver Sun* had run the same Korean War dispatch on its front page three days in a row. Not one of its 500,000 readers responded to the "error." Mel and I were convinced that no one believed in this war. That didn't prevent me from attending the ballet and savoring a pas de deux by Maria Tallchief and Andre Eglevsky, two of our favorite dancers.

In response to a rising fear of subversion, our government was denying citizenship to long-time residents and clamping down on American citizens who had associated even briefly with the Communist Party. As a teacher, I was asked to sign a non-Communist affidavit. While questioning its morality, though not its legality, it never occurred to me not to sign. I complained a lot, but was too self-involved to become politically active.

One by one, I counted out the hours and days of each school week, calibrating their worth against the numbers scrawled on the backs of airmail envelopes. Often, Mel included "Official Daily Bulletins" in his letters. Reviling the pettiness of army regulations, he ranted against a typical directive: "Hair will not extend more than one (1) inch beyond scalp." Although his own bob was bristle-short, he objected to the army's boy-scout approach with men who were risking their lives. As he went on patching broken bodies, he felt himself further and further removed from civilian surgery.

———————

SUNDAY, NOVEMBER 2, 1952, 9:00 P.M.

Dorothy Darling—

Spent a few hours trying to keep my Korean patient alive. How he gets oxygen I'm not sure. I had to operate on both lungs, also wounds of the shoulder, a fractured leg and to top it off abdominal wounds such that we had to do an intra-abdominal operation. His lungs are the main problem now. If I can get him by the next few days, I think he'll live.

The day was beautiful, marred by the crash of guns at the other end of the valley where ordnance was testing tank guns. A puff of smoke would appear on one of the hilltops (markers on the hills are used as targets). When they fired in our direction, off to one side, you would hear the thump of the gun firing, the whish of the shell, the explosion, and see the smoke. The explosion would echo up and down this valley and the next. It was too easy to imagine what it would be like if we were being shelled directly.

One of our trucks was found bringing a load of GI food to Wonju, a nearby city, to be sold on the black market. Apparently, the MP's and CID (Counter Intelligence Division) have been watching this happen and they finally cracked down on some Koreans in our outfit—and un-fortunately, some GI's—trying to make some money. All the Koreans in the kitchen were fired and a new batch hired, probably just as bad as the others. As for the GI's, I have no sympathy for them—here—where supply is so great a problem.

I stop during the day and think of you. I remember one night at Cold Spring as we stood behind the house in the sweet-smelling air. People are talking about Xmas now. I love you my Dorothy.   Melvin

WEDNESDAY, NOVEMBER 5, 1952, 9:00 P.M.

My love,

The only thing that seems sensible tonight is writing to you. I dreamed about the election all night and when I awakened I knew Ike had won. Honestly, I don't think it makes a difference right now who is in the White House—as long as we don't let the McCarthys gain in strength. That we must fight. I do hope that Ike is able to take some positive step about Korea. That is what his voters hoped for and that is what we all hope for now. I'm sorry about Stevenson. I think he is high caliber material. One of the liberal girls at school proposed that every once in a while the conservatives had to be elected so that they could stabilize the reforms the liberals had instituted in order to have them accepted by the great mass of people. Then the liberals come in again and make further reforms—progress!   D.

WEDNESDAY, NOVEMBER 5, 1952, 8:45 P.M.

My Beloved—
    I sit alone in a darkened tent, one light above me. The others are at the movie. I am listening to some wonderful Japanese music. It fills my body and mind and its rhythms and tones carry me to you across the miles. I feel at peace.
    We have worked all day with the radio going, listening to the returns. We heard a democracy choose a new president. It was with tears in my eyes that I listened to the result—a vote for a man and not a party or an ideal. I hope he will prove equal to the task, will be a president first, not a general first.
    One of the boys just came in and told me that he heard via the EM [enlisted man] grapevine that the division ahead of us might become aggressive tonight. That will mean work in the morning. So I shall stop now and go to sleep. My love, so far from me, I hope you are well and that your ovaries don't ache. I wish I were there to rub your back and abdomen. My wife, my dearest.   Melvin

THURSDAY, NOVEMBER 6, 1952, 10:00 P.M.

My love—
    I am still reading *The Last Puritan.* One paragraph struck me as applicable to the present problem of McCarthyism. One of the characters says: "Being acquitted is nothing in this world. Being accused is what makes all the difference. What another man may think or even know about you does you no harm, so long as your public standing is unchallenged and you pass for an ordinary person; but your best friend will drop you if he finds you are in bad odour."

Today I looked forward to going to the Lighthouse. I met Guion at 8:40 and we worked until 10:00. I played the piano part for one of the Brandenburg Concertos and a Bach cantata. He has "traveling vision"—can see cars, the edge of the curb, doorways. He has been coming to the Lighthouse for 15 years.

I was sitting in the teachers' room staring into space when someone said, "You look as though you're a million miles away." I said, "No—only 9,000."

My love, don't worry about my overdoing it. I know how much I can take. I have reached a balance now and I do relax more frequently. But you know how much better it is to keep busy. Mom's driving practice will be over in a week and that will make it easier.

You mentioned your talk with Irv Graham about "going home." I can't think that far ahead—my dream extends to the moment I see you again. Once we are together, we can live, but never too far in the future. That has become part of my (our) basic philosophy during this past year—because of Dad and because of the temporary life we lead: to make the most of every moment and to plan only for the immediate future.

Goodnight my love, as I crawl under the covers with a damp head. If you were to stroke my hair now, you would get a handful of bobbypins.   Dorothy

FRIDAY, NOVEMBER 7, 1952, 1:00 A.M.

My Love—

Having read 2 letters from you, I lay on my cot glowing. Then the ambulances started coming in. Between 4:30 and 12:30, 5 surgeons and 2, sometimes 3, anesthetists did 22 cases, about ⅓ of them serious. One I did was a drunk who had started to shoot his rifle and was shot by some other soldiers in self-defense. He refused operation, but he needed it as he had a belly wound. So I got both Colonels' clearance before operating. I hear some more ambulances coming, but we will just have to let the minor cases wait and do only the serious ones.

That accident I told you about last night did turn out to be an air raid by the Communists on some of our trucks. While I am sure it was a freak, it was only a few miles from here. While I am sure it won't happen again, I put my steel helmet in an accessible place.

I guess Ike will be coming to Korea in a few weeks—as a professional soldier, a statesman, a morale factor?

I love you. Sleep well.   Melvin

My darling—

Our latest possessions, bought at a sale, are: a collection of Heinrich Heine, a collection of Conrad Aiken (Amer. short stories), *Spanish Dancing* (La Meri), and *Folk Dancing.*

A beautiful Fall day. After lunch I shall go for a walk around the reservoir, trying to imagine you snuggled under your covers, hiding from the white cold of night in Korea. Korea. I can't connect what I read in the newspaper with you.

Read some excellent war poems, *Counter-attack,* by Siegfried Sassoon. I thought of sending them to you, but then decided against adding to your depression. A letter from you and a box of slides. There are shots of you all sunburned and healthy-looking. The slides of the amputee I will not show to the folks.   D.

Dorothy My Love—

Je t'aime. Je pense a toi. Je t'aime tant.

Thurs in mid-afternoon, the cases started coming in, at first minor injuries, so we thought only a small group were hit. We were half-way through with them when the place filled up again. It was a matter of operating, finishing, going out to the pre-op ward, picking another case, having the litter bearers bring him in, working, one after another—one a neck injury, another a leg, another a belly. They lie there—some calling to one another when they come from the same outfits. "Did you see him?" "Did he make it?" "Yes, he's in the corner." "No, he's dead." Stories of men falling on grenades to save a platoon. I had thought they were only stories. Sometimes they live. More often they don't. Their protective jackets save lots of lives. We see them come in with wounds of the extremities and bruises of the chest, back, and abdomen, where a fragment or shell hit the jacket but did not penetrate. Kids, most of them, all reacting differently to the injury and to the pain and to the horror. The ones who make the most noise are usually the ones who have shot themselves. Most of them, having had morphine, lie quietly thinking or sleeping. So the night passed and finally the ward was empty. I went to sleep. Back again in a few short hours, the place full again. Our corpsmen are working better now, but we must keep after them. Supposedly, they have all had training at Ft. Sam or its equivalent, though some are litter bearers who double as corpsmen because we are short of help. Well, the work continued through the morning hours, breakfast, rounds, trying to decide which of the patients were able to travel. It is a pretty bumpy 20-mile ambulance ride to the airfield where they are flown out, and many of them just out of anesthesia. But morphine is a good drug, and off they go. A 15-minute talk by Col. Zipperman who was visiting and back to work. Throughout the day. Case after case. And I became more tired. Necks laid open. Chests full of blood. Broken bones. Requiring judgment and skill, of which I had less as the hours passed. Finally when 7 P.M. came around, I had had enough. I went to sleep. By that time there were only a few cases left and those who had been sleeping came on and finished them up. I slept somewhat restlessly—I guess over-tired—until 7:30 this morning when I went on rounds, then to work again until about 3 P.M.

Last night was about the hardest I've worked, in actual hours and concentrated, tense work. From Thurs afternoon to Sat afternoon I did approximately 20 cases under general anesthesia, 10 under local. 15 of the general ones were major cases, which is a lot of surgery—an awful lot. In New Haven Hospital I probably wouldn't do that much in two weeks. I wish we were back in New Haven, handing out candy on Halloween.

I have clean sheets tonight, and I remember how good it was to lie together between clean sheets. I could write for hours, but the boys want the lights out and it is getting cold in the tent. Sleep well, my wife.

Melvin

MONDAY, NOVEMBER 10, 1952, 10:00 A.M.

My Love—

We talked of everything, including cars and wives. Most of the fellows said they never bitched about anything in their letters to their wives. I know that I am easier to live with here in Korea because I can talk to you about everything.

11:15 P.M.

I am really in a foul humor tonight. More bullshit. The morale at the unit is low. I was up all night and most of the morning. It was too hot and noisy to sleep much. I napped for an hour and was relaxing reading when I was asked if I wanted "to come over and see what was there." I said no, but if I was needed I would be glad to come. Anyhow I went over to do one small case, and only because Rick and Schoenfeld are piddlers and because of that (Rick especially) I work more. I am tired. When I am tired my temper gets short. The world is out of step— all but us. The irregularity of the hours makes it difficult, never knowing when you can relax. Hearing the helicopters come in and wondering if you will be called. I guess the day will come when I'll be looking for cases to do, but now I've had enough surgery. Enough cutting out blasted bodies, torn muscles and shattered bones, arms and legs. An amputation is no longer surgery to me. I dread to see them come in (maybe it's my castration complex) but we've had almost a dozen in the past few days.

I love you. Maybe I'd better not mail this, but I do, because I know you want to share every day with me as I do with you. Goodnight my love, my wife.   Melvin

TUESDAY, NOVEMBER 11, 1952, 10:30 P.M.

My darling—

Another Armistice Day goes by without hope for peace. It seems crazy—you so far away, helping to alleviate man-made suffering. I cannot accept the fact that there will always be wars.

I went down to Librairie de France to buy you a pocket dictionary (French) which I will send off this week even though, from the papers, it doesn't look as though you'll have time for study. Also bought some French plays for Helen Dowdeswell [a French teacher at Valley Stream], air mail envelopes, a kelly green jersey hat for warmth (ME, in a hat— teacher can't wear a kerchief).

Goodnight my sweet.   Dorothy

My Love, My Love—

Today is Armistice Day. Just remembered as I wrote the date. My only thought was that I hoped you got the day off.

My heart aches for a normal life—to be opposite you at the end of the day—eating, talking—what to do this evening—what do you want to hear on the victrola—the newspapers—looking through the *New Yorker*—going downtown—New Haven—Willimantic—movies, shows, window shopping—watching the college students walking along quiet streets.

As I read the journals, I feel, at times, very far from the problems I read about—pediatric surgery, gall bladders, physiology of cardiac surgery, etc. I hope I can keep up and not get too far behind in my thinking about civilian surgical problems.

I love you Dorothy. Sleep well. Dream well   Melvin

My love—

Just marked a discouraging set of Spanish papers. Don't know whether it's because we are forced to go so fast or the kids don't put any effort in or they are stupid or I am not approaching it correctly. I can't do much harm anyway.

I hope your bowels are in order. Shall I send you some Pepto? How could you have gone off without it?

Last night they showed the results of election night. I cried when I saw Stevenson because we have lost a good man. I cried when I saw Eisenhower because of what lies ahead of him and because he cannot bring you back to me now.

I imagine your presence across the room, a serious expression of concentration on a book, or a light smile as you glance up at me, or the vigorous bite into an apple, or joining arms and dancing around the room like Nijinsky and Pavlova, collapsing on the bed with laughter. Your wife,   Dorothy.

Melvin, my love—

Happy birthday my husband. Next year we shall celebrate together and I shall have to kiss you not only 27 times but also the 26 kisses which are due you this year. Will you be able to bear all that kissing? Symbolically, your birthday is a special day, but every day is special, for it means another day of loving—and now, another day bringing us closer together. I like birthdays, yours, because it's celebrating you being you. I sound wacky, but I am just crazy in love.

I was out early this morning to the Lighthouse. We had the orchestration for a Bach cantata and Guion asked me to play all the instruments together on the piano. That's difficult enough in itself when the staves are so far apart and you have to cover about 6 at one time. But on top of this the viola I and II are in different clefs so I had to transpose those 2 staves as I went along. It took us one hour to get through 16 measures. I really sweated.

I think I mentioned that Karen Stone, English teacher, has a musician husband who travels, is now in Ohio and will be during Thanksgiving. She says she misses him (lives with her mother, no children) but it would be difficult to get there over Thanksgiving. She said she thought of me last night. She was complaining to her mother about Howard being away and her mother said, "What would you do if he were in Korea?" and she was ashamed, she said. I felt like saying, but didn't, Don't you understand that I would miss him just as much if he were in North Carolina or Brooklyn, if I weren't with him? How can she stay away? How can she teach here when she knows that his profession carries him all over the country?

The trees are bare. Only here and there can you see a shrub with some rust leaves still clinging to its branches. How happy I am to see them grow more and more desolate for when they are bare and frosted they contain the promise of spring. I have never known this deep longing. I waited for the buds in 1951, but you waited with me and we were out of each other's arms for only a few days at a time. Now we yearn, imagining that the urgency of our longing hastens the days.   Dorothy

Oops—the place is in an uproar—a tiny mouse ran across the floor and 3 fellows are chasing him with hammers, brooms, and shoes. They have just set 6 mouse traps. I hope I don't get a finger caught as I search for my shoe.   M.

FRIDAY, NOVEMBER 14, 1952, 4:30 P.M.

My Darling—

The ground is mud. The fog is obscuring the mountain tops that look sad and foreboding. I am not sorry to see the bad weather. In fact, I would like to see a good snowfall, as I am afraid if the weather improves there will be an offensive. The Chinks have been probing our lines heavily here in the east looking for a weak spot. So far they have found just soft spots, but even those are productive of many casualties.

Spent all last night working. One group of 3 patients had been out towards the Chinese lines laying and repairing barbed wire when one of them stepped on a mine. It blew his foot to pieces and the fragments wounded his other leg and the other 2 fellows. However, when we took X-rays of them, there were no metal fragments to be seen. This usually looks like snow on the film. I suppose this is one of the wooden anti-personnel mines that merely explode and do not produce shrapnel.

I go through my day now like an automaton. For the past week or so I just didn't feel sociable, didn't like people. I did my work, sat in the tent at night and talked, but my mind was 9,000 miles away.

I love you Mrs. Horwitz—Dorothy—my beloved.   Melvin

9:00 P.M.

No mail today—at all. I guess the bad weather kept the plane from coming in. We are dependent on air transport for mail and any rapid courier service, as there are no trains this far east and it takes 8–10 hours by jeep to travel the 100 miles west to Seoul. The slightest bit of cloud or fog cuts out the air travel since the fields are set in the valleys surrounded by fairly tall hills and mountains and there is just one approach to the field. There are very few accidents and that is because they fly only when it is safe. The curb on flying causes us to hold patients here longer since they are evacuated by air from Inge to Wonju (southwest 70 miles) and remain at an evac hospital there anywhere from 2–20 days, then either return to duty or go further south to other hospitals in Taegu or Pusan—or go directly to Japan. There they stay usually until their wounds are healed. If the injuries warrant, back to the U.S. or sometimes sooner if they need special surgery or treatment.

Another amputation tonight. There are 6 patients on the wards right now who are amputees. It isn't a happy place. I tried to buoy up the kid I did last night. I think he'll be OK. He'll start back to the States tomorrow. What a way to go back.

11:00 P.M.

Of all things, a Korean had a tooth pulled and the socket kept bleeding, so I played dentist, improvised dental tools, packed the socket, and shipped him out.

The news is on. Now there's a possibility of the hydrogen bomb. More destruction. Have to run to the hospital. I love you with all my being.   Melvin

SUNDAY, NOVEMBER 16, 1952, 10:00 P.M.

My darling—

I still cannot recognize the need for killing. India's delegate to the UN said that the prolongation of the fighting in Korea had nothing to do with the solving of the prisoner issue. He recommended that the fighting be stopped and we arrive at a solution of the prisoner issue while the toll of lives was not mounting. U.S. could see no point to it.

Mom, Gerry, and I went to the Gottehrer Family Circle luncheon. [An organization formed by my paternal grandfather and his eight siblings. Their first purchase was a cemetery plot.] It was good to see some of the faces, but after saying hello, I felt that I had nothing in common with them. Eventually it will disband, because there aren't many members of our generation who are interested. It has grown too large. One of the second cousins was in uniform and on his way to Korea in a few weeks—a private in the Infantry. Some of the folks joked nervously, maybe he'd run into you. He looked very grim.

Goodnight Melvin, my love.   Dorothy

SUNDAY, NOVEMBER 16, 1952, 11:00 P.M.

Dorothy Darling—

For 4 hours today I forgot about the war and took a ride. Our valley runs north and south. There is a ridge of mountains on either side. Southwest of us is another larger valley with a pass to it over the mountain. Carved out of the side of the mountain, curving backwards and forwards, up and down and around, it makes even the roads in the Canadian Rockies look like highways.

Happened to hear that there was a jeep going over this pass to Yongu and coming back that same afternoon. So I put on a sweater and coat, buckled on my pistol and camera, and was ready. The top of the jeep is on and the heater working so it was comfortable. Fortunately, in a way, the X-ray machine had blown out a transformer and we weren't getting any patients for a few hours, so I got Svetke to cover for me and off I went, 30 miles southwest of here and about 30 miles northwest of Inge. The purpose of the trip was to pick up a repair man who had to check our blood refrigerator. There was a driver from Kansas, previously a construction worker, and a man from supply (pvt) to contact the maintenance man. The latter was a dancer from New Jersey who did a routine with his sister before coming into the army. He had played small club dates in Philadelphia. His ambition: to be in musical comedy in N.Y. The third passenger, moi, whose purpose was to take a ride and snap some pictures. Bouncing down dirt roads past the MP check points, we started up the pass. We saw only a few other vehicles. There are no units camped in the mountains there. We crawled up and down narrow canyons, alongside streams and tall cliffs. The grey-blue clouds covering the sky looked stern. Up and up we went, almost stopping as another vehicle came the other way, since there was barely enough room to pass. On one side a steep cliff and on the other nothing but a thousand-foot drop. No guard rails. It was thrilling. Finally, as we stood on top and looked out, I felt good. Shivering from the cold icy wind, we clambered back into the jeep and started down the other side—90-degree and 180-degree turns on the road around corners that you could not see. Down, down, down. Then, at the bottom, we were at the head of the canyon. There was one more 180-degree turn. We were level and could look up and see the road above. Another half-hour and we passed the 8209 MASH and arrived at an airstrip. Had lunch in an officers' mess named the "Waldorf Astoria." Took some pictures of the Yongu valley, which is filled with army units, and started back. After a short while we were at the base of the pass and on our way up. Feeling like an old hand by then, I could breathe on some of the turns. Up and down, then we were back at the 8225. Mileage: 64 mi. Time: 4 hrs, with one hr for lunch. I wonder what it will feel like to drive on a smooth concrete road again. I've gotten used to the dirt roads and the latrines. I suppose I'll remember to flush the toilet. I can get used to this life in a tent in the middle of a primitive country at war, but I cannot tolerate being away from you.

My dearest, I have so much to tell you. Your letters brighten the gloom of life in the army. But for them I would feel like a prisoner. They make me feel like a man.   Melvin

MONDAY, NOVEMBER 17, 1952, 11:15 P.M.

Hello my love—

It was a misty, depressing day. At least the UN is discussing the Korean question and not abandoning hope. I shall meet you in Tokyo—what hotel did you say? It doesn't matter. My plane arrives at (?) o'clock and you'll be there to meet me. I shall be wearing red roses in my eyes and wings on my back (purely functional). Never mind darling. I'm beginning my dream before I get into bed. Any resemblance between me and a drunken one is not fictional, because I am drunk with love of you. I hope you are not sad at this moment.   Dorothy

TUESDAY, NOVEMBER 18, 1952, BEFORE MIDNIGHT

My love—

At Paul and Jane's [Merson]. When I think of them going upstairs to bed together at the end of their long day, it is not with jealousy, but rather with longing. Being with our friends, knowing their sincere feelings about you, I can talk Mel, Mel, Mel. Now I shall crawl into a comfortable cot, "big enough for two," I said, "if they fit in well together," finished Paul. So I shall fit in with you darling and dream and wait. Goodnight my sweet, mon coeur, mon amour, ma vie.   Dorothy

WEDNESDAY, NOVEMBER 19, 1952, 9:00 P.M.

My Darling—

I am somewhat rested having slept a few hours this afternoon. Shaved and bathed from a helmet today since the showers have been on the blink for the past 5 days and I haven't had time to get over to the other unit to take one. I really smelled this time so I scrubbed with washcloth and soap, used plenty of shaving lotion, deodorant, and powder, put on clean clothes and felt better. When we've been working, my clothes get all bloody and full of plaster. The houseboy keeps my boots clean, and I just have to keep changing my clothes. For that reason, and also because I don't like the wool next to my skin, I don't wear the wool shirt and pants. The fatigues are much easier to wash.

Had a small case (for a MASH). A log fell on this guy's leg and broke the bone—a major procedure in the States, but a minor one here. I cleaned his wound, set the bone, put on a cast, and made it over to the movie—all in 20 minutes. Normally, he would have had a metal screw or plate put in to hold the bone. But because of our not so aseptic conditions, we do not do that here. So he will go to Tokyo and have that procedure in about two weeks.

They showed a movie about the Un-American Activities Committee in Honolulu—pure propaganda, not very subtle. An article in the papers reported that the Soviet soldier gets eight hours of political lectures a week. The US soldier gets a few posters and movies like this. No wonder it is difficult to find reasons for this police action in Korea. Although morale here is generally good, each man feels, for the most part, that he is serving a term. Among the wounded, there is never any regret about leaving Korea or the battle—just about leaving the other men in their units. There is no desire to fight the enemy or to crush them—just to survive.

My last few patients have told me, "I hope I don't have to go back on the line!" I must explain to the boy with the bad artery that he might lose his foot, giving him hope but not letting the possibility, which may become a reality, come as a surprise. When I tell them what is wrong with them, the faces of these kids are something to see. Their smiles are wistful, but most of them do manage to smile, even the boy with a wound of the penis, when I explained that he would be O.K. and he'd be able to use it "good as new." I wonder how much their values change. They are young and impressionable. When they are on intravenous feedings and feeling better, my heart goes out to them as they accuse me of starving them to death. I see them in the morning, having worked on them all night, knowing that they have a long pull ahead, but that the major battle for life is over and won. I guess it's as close as I can get to the feeling of creating something.

Back in the tent, talking and laughing. This actually happened today on rounds. Rick passes the foulest smelling gas silently. We almost have to air out the tent. We were making rounds. As we came to one patient, there was that unmistakable odor in the air. The Colonel sniffed and asked, "What is that foul odor?" The fellow presenting the case sniffed at the dressings, peeked under them looking for infection. I knew what it was and could hardly control myself. The Colonel looked so puzzled. Finally someone volunteered that it must be one of the patients who hadn't washed or who had passed some gas. You can imagine the response when the story was retold in the tent.

Do you know what just crossed my mind? The Yiddish expression: "Sleep quickly Papa. We need the bedsheet for a table cloth." Well, it came out paraphrased: "Live quickly. I need the time!" We are wasting time. Days and nights, hours and minutes. Apart. Just waiting.

As for the drinking, there was as much at the 8055. Rick, Art, and Ned usually sit around and have a few drinks before going to sleep. Sometimes they have more than a few. They use it to relax. Rick gets expansive, Art either jovial or morose and homesick. Ned, who rarely has too much, keeps his good humor. To discuss it is touchy. I just don't. Rick and Art, like a lot of others, talk of good parties in terms of how drunk they were.

If all goes well, the morning or evening of Nov. 26 will bring a surprise for you. So try to have someone home, O.K.? Your husband,
Melvin

FRIDAY, NOVEMBER 21, 1952, 11:00 P.M.

My Wife, My Love—
I haven't felt rested for the past week. Sent out some patients and worked on this one boy still here. He will be ready to travel in a day or so. His foot is still cool and he may lose it. He has done well otherwise and seems to be recovering from his abdominal operation. It took me 2 hours to change all his dressings. Had a few hours this afternoon when I relaxed and bathed out of a helmet. A trio of musicians and several singers went about the hospital playing and singing for the patients. It almost made me cry to see the patients we had (only the sick ones—the others had been sent out), many covered in plaster casts from toe to waist, battered and aged before their time—enjoying the music. Oh my love, this experience here in Korea has been a valuable one professionally, and, I guess, emotionally and morally. I think I could be a conscientious objector in another war were I not a physician. There never can

be any justification for war. The problems are not solved, but merely pushed back.

I dreamed of you last night. It was so real that my pajamas had to go into the laundry. I can see you smile. One day we shall love and there will be no pajamas. Know of my love for you.   Melvin

Melvin, my love—

I felt like being "dang-ly" tonight so I put on a hairnet, tied it back in a bun, wore old gold earrings and a black dress embroidered with gold. I don't think you've ever seen it. I looked exotic, I think. Carol (Don Oken's girlfriend) and I saw Katina Paxinou in "Electra," in Modern Greek. The chorus had dance movements that contributed to the mood and dramatic intensity of the play. I imagined the complete choreography of "Electra." I wonder if it has been done. We really felt that we had been purged in the true Aristotelian sense. Katina Paxinou was tremendous and reminded us of Anna Magnani.

I hope that the bad weather will set in and avoid an offensive. Why do you say "chinks," my love—or is that a silly question?

I go to sleep, praying for dreams of you which will fill my night with music.   Dorothy

My love—

The phone rang about 4:30 just as I had fallen into a sound sleep. I stumbled to answer it and put my hand on the stove pipe. Muttering a loud s.o.b. I grabbed the phone and growled "yes." It was for Ryan as O.D. [on duty]. One of the guards was not at his post. So Ryan got up and I went back to sleep nursing a 1-inch burn on the side of my hand.

Incidental intelligence: The Gen. of the 45th Division has been coming through the hospital telling some of the corpsmen that they need haircuts. So even the Col. now has a crew cut and all men were directed to have short haircuts. The stupidity of some of these so-called Generals. To wit—I asked this patient of mine with a belly wound and his leg shot up whether he had seen the general. He said "Yes, he told me I needed a haircut!" I swear I won't let the Gen. on the ward. He's bad for morale.

Rumor #6,796—from up front—the Chinks have pulled back a few miles and holed up for the winter. If that is true, we will have little to do and fighting will be almost at a standstill. Either they are regrouping or want to see what we will do or are just waiting to prolong this business until next spring, getting stronger again and letting the UN battle stand for a while. I certainly hope something comes of the Indian proposal, which has some face-saving value for the Chinese.

Tell Paul and Jane that their salamis finally came. We ate one last night, cutting off the mold.   Melvin

SUNDAY, NOVEMBER 23, 1952, 11:00 P.M.

I'm really concerned about this boy over on the ward and I will probably send him out to the 11th Evac Hosp tomorrow. He will need long-term hospitalization and careful evaluation that we are not set up to do here. I hate to shove a problem like this onto other people and I also am interested in following the pt, but his interests come first, so I think I'll send him along.   M.

MONDAY, NOVEMBER 24, 1952, 9:00 P.M.

Today's experiences gave me one more reason why I would never be able to tolerate the army willingly. Enclosed is today's daily bulletin. Our Col, a physician, must waste time and effort and thought on that. Why. Not because he wants the men clean and neat—that should be understood, and 1-inch haircuts need not be part of it—but because he must live in fear of what the generals say. "The General of X Corps wants spit and polish. We shall have it, even though we are not directly under X Corps." Those are his words. He lives for the approbation of others and, in typical army fashion, we are about to be a spit-and-polish organization. Fortunately, the haircut need not bother me unless mine be too short. I do what is expected, but when during the course of the meeting I was told, "When someone asks you: Will this experimental MASH work, you WILL answer: It will work and is . . ." Now that is a bit too much. Granted the army tells you what to think and say, but there is a limit. If someone asks for information about this MASH, then I'll refer him to Headquarters. But if I'm asked for an opinion, then I'll either give none, or tell the truth—not what I WILL say. I wasn't sure whether to speak out then and there. So I didn't, but waited and got the Col aside and told him just what I've written and at least got him to retract his words of what we "will" say. He couldn't tell us what we must say but what he "wanted to say" was that he wished us to use discretion in talking to visiting honchos and newspaper men. To that I agreed. I wonder if I would have let that slide—as most of the other fellows did, commenting on it among themselves—but I knew I would be writing to you tonight, and I could not be still.   M.

TUESDAY, NOVEMBER 25, 1:00 A.M.

My beloved—

I am up unusually late. A few hours ago I got into the last lap of *The Last Puritan* and had to finish it. I feel sad yet mellow having read it. Oliver says: "I should be glad to die now, if I could find something to die for. These poor recruits are told that they will be dying for their country. That's sheer cant. Nobody knows whether he's doing his country any good by dying for it, or whether his country is better worth dying for than any other."

9:30 P.M.

We used the binoculars on the screen tonight to bring you closer. And it worked. Can't you just see us here in the bedroom, focused on you and the hills of Korea? (Punch Bowl slides) We can see in detail all the army installations throughout the hills which cannot be seen with the naked eye.   D.

TUESDAY, NOVEMBER 25, 1952, 8:00 P.M.

My Darling—

Am glad to hear Ephraim is writing. It gives him something pleasurable to do. As for kissing him, in all probability it won't do any harm, but it is such a small thing that it would probably be better not to. TB is not a disease to be taken lightly. That doesn't mean you have to don cap, gown, and mask, as he is, I am sure, free of the active disease. Well honey, I think I can make it clear by saying, express your emotion and delight in seeing him in another way. Then there will be no question in anyone's mind—his or yours.

Was vaccinated (again) against smallpox (every 6 months in the Far East).

The world is mad. Only we are sane. We know what we want. When will this nightmare be over. I know not—but again Russia has vetoed India's peace plan. She is goading us I know. I don't think she wants all-out war, but I am afraid she will push us too far, especially with a General as President.

Yesterday afternoon I read Truman Capote's *A Tree Of Night,* a collection of short stories. His characters and expressions of emotion are strange. Faulkner's characters are unreal in a geometric, hard way. Capote's are much more nebulous, flowing and hazy. Each is an expression not of a whole person, but of an inner conflict. I wonder about this relatively young man (in his mid-twenties) writing this way, just as we wondered about Carson McCullers and what sort of background she had. Try to get hold of his novel *Other Voices, Other Rooms* in the pocket Signet Books #700. I am sending this pocketbook to you. The stories are brief and make good "library" reading. Not that the stories make you feel good, but it is an interesting experience to read them.

I love you my wife.   Melvin

THURSDAY, NOVEMBER 27, 1952, 1:00 A.M.

Melvin, my darling—

Today I came home late. There on the dining room table was the most beautiful array of flowers smelling of spring—pom-poms, snap dragons, carnations, chrysanthemums in yellows, rusts, whites, pinks—a fall variety, but my mind and heart said printemps. "Je t'aime. Je pense au printemps." (They left out the "p" in printemps.) It is Thanksgiving Day—for both of us. We are richer than kings.   Dorothy

NOVEMBER 27, 1952, 9:00 P.M.

My Dearest—

Because Thanksgiving was a holiday, "only general housekeeping and care of the sick" were carried on. Rounds went quickly. Then back to the tent. Suddenly, one of the boys came charging in. "Ike is over at the tank unit—there's a band, helicopters—let's go." While it seemed far-fetched that he would be here, I wasn't willing to take a chance, so I grabbed my two cameras and went. True the band was just leaving. So

were the helicopters. But no Ike. Just a unit citation by the division general. Rumor. Back to the hospital. I took some pictures of the turkeys
cooking and the tables decorated—cloths, candy, nuts, oranges. All the
unit ate in one room (no officers' mess today) and they really piled on
the food.

A poker game started in our tent and I photographed the players'
facial expressions, then went to sleep. To my surprise I slept for 3
hours. A cocktail party was in progress over at BOQ 3, so I went over
and had 3 coca-colas. A few people got high, but no one got drunk.
The best part was sitting and listening to the Paganini Violin Concerto. Gosh, I'm hungry for music. It helps fill the emptiness. I let the
melody fill me and I feel close to you. I wonder how it actually does
affect me and people in general. Certainly melody and rhythm are
part of every culture and for me, good music unlocks the frustrations
or uncertainties of my unconscious. I always feel relaxed when I listen, even if I am sad.

I didn't feel like eating supper, so I came back to my tent, had an orange, set up a "portrait studio," and took pictures for the boys. Then
leafed through the *New Yorker*. Darling, much as I love to get the magazine, I doubt if it's worth over a dollar to send it each time. Why not
just put a few together every so often and send them 1st or 2nd class.

Did the camera arrive in good condition? I did insure it.

Close your eyes, my darling. We sleep, thankful for each other.

Melvin

FRIDAY, NOVEMBER 28, 1952, 11:20 P.M.

My darling—

An incident which I think the *New Yorker* would appreciate for
"Talk of the Town." At 31st and Fifth Ave, a civilian with a cigar in his
mouth, evidently fed up with the mess, got into the middle of the inter-
section and began directing traffic. The funniest part was that everyone
listened to him. He was very solemn and things went quite well until a
policeman came along and chased him.

I bought *Pavlova* for us and, for Barbara, *Babar* by Brunhoff, a wonderful illustrated story about very human elephants. I had seen it re-
viewed in the *Times* Children's Section.

Class was good tonight. We did some beautiful movements—and I
have marks to prove it!   D

SATURDAY, NOVEMBER 29, 1952, 9:00 A.M.

My Beloved—

It is a cold morning. Fog shrouds the mountains and the smell of snow is in the air. Up north only a few miles away, the mountain tops are white and the vehicles clank about with chains. Thanksgiving is over. Winter is here. The snow is wet, damp, and clinging, in keeping with the atmosphere of war, dirt, poverty, and disease.

I hope our children will know what love really means—tenderness and understanding, companionship and closeness. We will give them our love as freely as we give it to each other. They will enjoy the beauty of the seasons, music, color, light, rhythm, melody—that the best in life is giving of themselves and sharing what they have. If I could be convinced that this is what we were fighting for, if these are the things at stake, if the cold, tired young soldier 15 miles from me were sure that these were his reasons for being here, then he would be willing, and I would be willing, to be here. But I'm not sure, and I know he is not. The world is not ready to do with less so that others can have more. I'm skeptical of people's reasons for fighting. Secret documents, memoirs, and letters published years later never show that good had conquered evil.

So we fight a war that no one really believes in. Pain and death, for what? There is no glory here unless it be when a man dies trying to save his fellow. There must be another way of going about living together. Life is precious and while it is of no value without our being able to live as free people, we throw it away too easily. I wonder if the families of the 100,000 casualties of this Korean "police action" feel any different.

9:00 P.M.

The poker game has started. It seems as though it will be a regular affair. At first it was a game for fun. As the evenings went by and people lost and won money, voices became strained and tempers tight. Now they play for money. I'm not a gambler. Money means too much and too little to me to play that way. I'd rather spend it on film or cameras. Also the cigar smoke was too much, so I came here. 5 minutes later, Irv Graham came over. He had been trying to read and gave up. If they plan on having it again tomorrow, I think I'll suggest another tent. Don't worry, my love. I shall be tactful.

Saturday night—tomorrow we shall sleep late, have a good brunch, read the papers, and spend the day together, to love and love and love. Am slap happy.   Melvin

SUNDAY, NOVEMBER 30, 1952, 1:00 A.M.

My darling—

I read in the papers of plane crashes in Korea, in Alaska—GI's, GI wives. For a moment I am frightened, but then I think of other things.

Mom and I went driving—one more little scratch on the car. She didn't stop when I yelled "stop!" I remember you so clearly saying, "Stop! Godammit. When I say stop, STOP!" Oh my love, when we are together again, no matter how much you yell "stop" I'll just keep hugging and kissing and loving you and I'll never stop. Yes, my darling, you will have to suffer.

In your Nov. 17 letter you wrote about sending Japanese Xmas cards from us. It sounds good to me. Send me your list. I'll go through our address book and include almost everybody, except relatives. [We didn't send Christmas cards to our Jewish relatives.]

I understand your statement: "I think I could be a conscientious objector in another war." I think I am one now. Nothing could justify this misery.

It is raining and there is a cold draft coming into the room—a smell of winter. I shall crawl between cool sheets and think thoughts of you to warm me.

11:00 P.M.

Last night what I thought was rain was snow, but most of it is gone by now. Only some ice and cold left with us. I hope that you have lots and lots of snow and there is an interlude in the killing.

My fingers are in bad shape. Shall I take up smoking? It would give me something to do with my hands besides keeping them in my mouth or picking at each other.

I was wearing a new bra and my nipples itched all day. Luckily, I was home so I could ease my misery.

Goodnight my love.   Dorothy

December

The army's only constancy was its unpredictability. In battle, that might be advantageous, but for the individuals who made up the parts of the whole it was exasperating. Not knowing what date might signal the half-way mark of our separation, we began to make plans anyway about meeting in Japan. Mel rejected a longer Korean stay that might have earned him the extra points to bring him home sooner. Not only did we reject the extra-point option, but we both emphatically vetoed any strategy that would prolong our separation.

With some uneasiness about changing course, I gave notice that I would quit at the end of the semester. This scheme would permit me to leave the States as soon as Mel sent me word of his transfer out of Korea. Meanwhile, I fit in as many dance classes as possible, anticipating the time when my agenda would be ancillary to Mel's, when the demands of his career would rely on my willing cooperation.

At the U.N., voluntary repatriation of prisoners was being discussed. Our gripes to each other about the drawn-out deliberations did not hasten the peace process or stop the killing. We could only control what was controllable in our own lives. We made little decisions—to pay or not to pay the "under 25" automobile premium, to read a novel or a biography, to open a can of tuna or salmon—while the big decisions were made for us by forces beyond our control. We acted as though we had a choice about the Japanese assignment. It was but one way of evoking a certainty for the obscurity of our tomorrows.

MONDAY, DECEMBER 1, 10:00 P.M.

Dearest—

Our activity the last 36 hours was the result of a patrol out to get some prisoners. They were moving across no man's land under cover of mortar fire. When it stopped, a red flare went up to signal them to the attack. It also signalled the Chinese to start counter-mortar fire. We had 18 casualties plus 4 dead. It was eerie to see them come in, faces smeared with dirt, purposely, so they wouldn't reflect light. But the rain and fog kept up all day until shortly before dinner when it changed to snow. Now the valley is a ghostly white.   M.

TUESDAY, DECEMBER 2, 1952, 11:00 P.M.

Dear my love—

I still haven't decided about February. On the one hand I do enjoy teaching and the money comes in. It bothers me to think of it going out and none from me coming in while I have the freedom to earn it. On the other hand, there is the chance to do what I always said I wanted to do—just dance—the unknown. This reminds me of my jump from Bloomingdale's to Columbia. But at Bloomingdale's, I didn't enjoy the work because there was no intrinsic value in it. I'm afraid of leaving Valley Stream for greener grass. And yet, if I don't take the step, I'll never know. The funny thing is, since I've considered leaving in order to dance, my teaching is more appealing. Is it the security? I wish I could talk to you. When we lived together, our solutions were whatever was best for us.

Tonight we projected the last batch of slides. Through my Japanese binoculars, I looked at you squinting into the sun and felt as though my lips could feel the smoothness of yours. I loved looking at the exposed part of your neck and thinking of how soft it is to bury my face in. You don't look as though you have put on any weight—slightly older and handsomer. You are my man. I live only to be your woman. Goodnight my darling.   Dorothy

TUESDAY, DECEMBER 2, 1952, 9:00 P.M.

My Darling—

With a startling suddenness winter has come. Awoke to the blinding glare of 5 inches of snow covering the hills and paths. I must retract what I wrote last night. The snowfall is beautiful. Trees laden, drifts whirled into varied patterns by the wind. The air fresh and clear. By 10 A.M. the clouds had lifted and the sun was brilliant as it reflected from the hills around us. I wanted just to get out my skis.

½ our casualties were accidental today. One of them was supposed to rotate to the States. Was at a party, got drunk, and shot himself in the hand. Another 2 were shot by one bullet when a rifle accidentally went off. Some of the SIW's (Self-Inflicted Wounds) are accidents, others deliberate, and I believe still others, while seemingly accidents, are unconsciously deliberate.

After a late lunch, I put on my shoe pacs (rubber shoes with leather boot tops), heavy jacket, outer field jacket, cap and gloves, loaded a dispatch case I use as a camera case, and tramped off to take pictures: the unit, people working, the hills, snow, and sky. If there are too many shots, just explain to the folks that each view is different and I want you, my love, to see them with me and feel the peace and beauty that I feel.

Came back to the tent, unloaded the junk, and went down for a shower. The water is warm, but the wind whistles through the shower tent. No mail from you today, and I felt as though I had missed seeing you. A package with coffee did come from the folks. The temperature, which had been in the 20's, began to fall, so I put on a sweater, turned the stoves up, and sat down to read *Giant* by Edna Ferber, which I had borrowed. Read about 50 pages before supper and gave it back. There are too many books in this world to waste time on one I don't like.

Wish I could have been at the theatre with you ("Electra") and felt the excitement and drama of the play. Seeing the "Playbill" was one more reminder of how far I was from all that. I can get along without theatre and plumbing, but I can't get along without you. I even get to calling the enemy north of us Chinks. I am wrong. It is a lazy terminology, and I shall try not to use it. I'll have to come home. Am getting into bad habits.

Read Huxley's *After Many a Summer Dies the Swan.*

Hold me my love as I hold you to me.   Melvin

WEDNESDAY, DECEMBER 3, 1952, 11:15 P.M.

My Darling—

After one week, the flowers are still alive and beautiful. I have weeded out the faded ones and continue to water. I look for symbols of time passing in everything. In the midst of a teaching day, often, I think to myself—I am one hour closer to Melvin. This morning when I started out, the car mileage was just over 32,000. I figured, on the basis of 5 months more of my usual driving, 50 miles per day, I was about 7,500 miles from you. When the mileage approaches 40,000, we will be making definite plans. I am silly, and you love me!   Dorothy

WEDNESDAY, DECEMBER 3, 1952, 10:00 P.M.

Dorothy Darling—

It is cold here tonight. Had to make sure the patients were covered well with blankets. Fortunately the ambulances are heated, but you can imagine some of the casualties when they are first brought in. A new problem now—frostbite and trenchfoot—but nowhere nearly as much as during the first winter the UN was in Korea. Now they are not only more warmly clothed and have proper footgear, but have bunkers to keep warm in.

A fire broke out near the motor pool in one of the gasoline heaters. Since there were plenty of people trying to get it under control, I ran and got my camera. Even when sand was dumped on it and it was covered with a tarpaulin, it just burned through. Our own carbon dioxide extinguisher didn't work, so it burned until some men from the anti-aircraft unit came over with theirs to put it out. Some excitement!

No mail again today, except for the enclosed letter from Kodak. Apparently one of the pictures I took exposed some of the patient's anatomy [male genitalia] in the OR. Arne Schairer got the same letter. We cannot figure out just which pictures did it, but I shall send a note explaining that I am a physician.

Now it is late and cold. The warmest place will be in bed. I am warm with your body—and your love.   Melvin

THURSDAY, DECEMBER 4, 1952, 9:30 P.M.

My darling—

I got to the Lighthouse at 8:30 A.M. Guion is usually late so I sit in the lobby and work until he comes, looking up every few minutes to see if he is there. This morning I became so involved in my work, that I didn't look up until 9:20 and found him standing there. I felt terrible.

He wouldn't tell me how long he had been there. It really brought home to me his blindness, which I'm usually not aware of. We played some lovely old English folk songs—so beautiful in their simplicity.

Don't go putting your hand on any more S.O.B. stove pipes. Who's going to pick your blister for you?

I just started *Came a Cavalier* by Evelyn Parkinson Keyes because Helen was enthusiastic about it and plopped it in my lap. I want to read *Lydia Bailey* next so that we can compare notes. I like the idea of our reading the same books, one more thing to share across the miles.

In the article you sent—Korean-U.S. Army slang—I recognized civilian phrases such as, "We've had it," and "clobber." You were the first one I heard use the word "clobber," long before you were in fatigues.

My eyes grow heavy and I long for you. Your wife,   Dorothy

THURSDAY, DECEMBER 4, 1952, 10:00 P.M.

My Dearest—

20 degrees today, the sky cloudless and the snow bright, except alongside the roads where the dust is thrown up by vehicles with chains. Armed with my camera, I went for a walk with Sid and Gaddis to the north end of the valley, up the hill overlooking the next valley. The natural beauty of the hills blanketed with snow sparkling in the sunlight filled me with nostalgia, as if on a mountain top about to start a ski run, though the air wasn't still and quiet, but was marred by the roar of guns and trucks. Then we walked back past one of the tank units where a platoon was getting their tanks ready to move up on the line, fixing the treads and loading ammunition, methodically and meticulously. Their lives depended on the proper functioning of their machines. Old-looking young men working in the cold. The tanks are horribly fascinating—large, geometric, ominous—yet so quiet as they are lined up, not moving, giving no hint of the roar and fire and destruction they are capable of. The high explosive armor-piercing shells for the big turret guns cost $144 each. Only a few of them are given for each tank on each run on the line. The rest of the shells are normal high-explosive shells.

No mail. The excitement of the sun and snow faded. I felt blue, tired, washed out. Came back to the tent and lay on my bed, closed my eyes and pictured you. Studied for an hour, reading the medical journals intensively crowding everything from my mind. An hour was all I could take, so I ate 2 candy bars.

I got absorbed in Steinbeck's *East of Eden*. It is wordy and rambling, but readable. So I sat, my feet on the sandbox that surrounds the stove, the tent quiet except for the hissing of the water in a pail on the stove. The others are playing poker in another tent.

Then, one of the boys walked in with three letters from you. Oh how my spirits rose. I am happy that the pictures are good and I enjoyed imagining you and Mom with the binoculars. My darling, my folks get so much pleasure from your being there. Don't work too hard on your papers. I read of icy roads in N.Y. Do be careful. If a day is bad, just don't go. Please. Call up and let them get a substitute who lives in Valley Stream. The price on the tire-fixing was OK. Remember that if you ever get in trouble like that you can call AAA to tow you or change the tire and not risk damaging the tire.

The quiet in the tent has ended. The boys have returned and are bitching about points and lack of replacements. Why there is a lack of replacements I don't know. The lack of men should be in the States and not here.

Goodnight my love. Dream with me of our love and our life. I am yours.   Melvin

FRIDAY, DECEMBER 5, 1952, 4:00 P.M.

My Love—

I wondered about the fellow who stole Bobby Brown's World Series ring (a gold ring with a diamond in it and Yankees and his name all over it) and later returned it to Brown with a fishy story of "someone" who was going home selling it to him for $20. Then he noticed Bob's name engraved inside, so he was returning it. Brown, of course, took out $20 and gave it to him without a word.

The afternoon is almost over, the shadows lengthening. Soon the sun will slip behind the mountain and the moon will be up to light the valley and hills in a soft silent light. I shall go out to enjoy its beauty and solitude. In the quiet and semi-darkness I feel close to you.

Melvin

SATURDAY, DECEMBER 6, 1952, 4:30 P.M.

Hello my love—

Listened to Shostakovitch 5th on the victrola today and it's not at all hard to take. I guess my ear is becoming attuned to discordant harmonies because it sounded mild. Thought of how our victrola was almost always going when we were at home—and how we would interrupt whatever we were doing to prance around or to love—all in time to the music!

The rumor about Ike being at the tank unit was amusing. Ironically, the same morning your letter arrived telling me about it, the news broke that he had been to Korea and was on his way back. This morning's *Times* mentioned that he had visited the 8055 MASH. Oh well, you have lots of slides of visiting generals!

I shall heed your suggestion about the *New Yorker* and send a few at a time by regular mail. I tire of it occasionally, particularly because I cannot discuss what I read with you and at times the wise, brittle style becomes irritating.

Tonight is another Saturday night. Mom and I are going to the Gina Bachauer piano recital at Washington Irving High School. I hope that I will be able to communicate some of the beauty of the music to you when I write later.   Dorothy

SUNDAY, DECEMBER 7, 1952, 10:00 P.M.

Dorothy My Love—

Seven December—a date. Eleven years ago I was at a football game with my Dad when we heard the requests for Colonels, Majors, and Captains to report to the front gate. It wasn't until later that day that I knew what it really meant. What does it mean today? A reminder of the folly of man—yellow-skinned or white. What a paradox for the child studying our history. We fought the Germans and the Japanese in the 1940's and now they are our allies and we fight former allies. Who has changed? We? They? I don't know. To me at the moment, another day, a Sunday, another week gone. As I sat at the movie tonight (another anti-Communist spy thriller) I was watching a movie surrounded by soldiers in a war-torn country—me—I still don't feel like a soldier. I never did like to fight. My surroundings are primitive yet fairly comfortable. Why, they have just put foot stools in the latrine so that the short fellows can sit in comfort and not have to dangle their legs. Each day is just a day, except for these few moments when I write or read words to and from my love.

I wasn't bored last night. One man stepped on a mine and was lucky enough to only dislocate his toe. Another Korean came in with no story, but with severe head injuries—and drunk. I tried to fix him up, but he died several hours later. Spent the morning doing an autopsy and found that internal abdominal injuries had killed him. No external signs, and he never complained of any abdominal trouble. I'm afraid that even if he had, we couldn't have done much for him. Then a head case and multiple wounds that took time. We sent him out to another hospital this morning for care of his head and eye injuries, since we do that work only in an extreme emergency.

Our mail in—my letters out—were held up 4–5 days because of Ike's trip. They wanted no leak of his visit before he had left.

Goodnight my beloved woman.   Melvin

[Enclosure]:

> Yuletide greetings from Korea,
> Land of lice and diarrhea,
> From mucky shores that we've half-mastered,
> MERRY CHRISTMAS YOU LUCKY BASTARD

SUNDAY, DECEMBER 7, 1952, 1:00 A.M.

Melvin, my beloved—

I am lonely tonight. The time when we shall be together is so distant that I cannot imagine it. We must be strong. Here I am depressing you when this afternoon I said that I would be sharing the beauty of to-night's music with you.

The concert was a disappointment. Bachauer is not a clean player and her playing lacks unity. There was no magic in it. She is a heavy woman who plays with tremendous force which sounded like banging at times. Mom said, "It looks like when she can't reach the notes with her hand, she uses her bust."

After it was over, we all went to Aunt Ida's [Derow, maternal great-aunt] for coffee. I listened to Uncle Ephraim and Aunt Ida talking Yiddish. I'm really sorry that I don't know more of that colorful language.

I have made some decisions re Xmas vacation. Although I told everybody I was going skiing and our brothers have made a reservation for me, I have decided to stay home and take the Xmas course at the Martha Graham school. We shall ski when we are together again and I have you to bandage any broken bones. Of course, there is no telling what will happen at Graham's. Decision #2: I shall leave Valley Stream at the end of the semester, work at Mom's office three hours a day, and cram in as many dance courses as possible, continuing my work at the Lighthouse. I wish we could have discussed it, although you did tell me to do what I wanted to. So I shall dance.

This letter has been so much "I" in it that it makes me feel small.

11:50 P.M.

I broke the news to Mom about the vacation and she was upset. Said that she wouldn't go to Florida. We argued back and forth. Finally she agreed to go. I'm glad because I think it will do her good to get away. I think her antagonism is a hang-over from the days when Dad was so opposed to my dancing. She's probably thinking, "If Dad were here, she wouldn't be doing it." Now the crisis is past.

At about 5:30, Pop, Mom, and Bert came over. We had drinks and watched your movie of the operation. Mom had trouble looking at it. This time, I didn't look at the wounds as much, but rather, at your hands working. (I think they were yours.)

We all wound up at Juilliard for the Jose Limon concert. I met a number of people from the New Dance Group and Desh Sikh, an Indian student from Bucknell who had been up to the house once or twice, since he lives at International House (in NY). It made me sad to see him, because he had known Dad and was shocked to hear about him— I pictured his visits here with Dad vividly.

Jose was dynamic! I don't know if the folks were being kind to me or if they really enjoyed it. Anyone who thinks that male dancers are effeminate ought to see him in action—whew!

Today was December 7. How many more Dec. 7ths shall we see in our lifetime? Goodnight my darling. I love you so much.   Dorothy

DECEMBER 9, 1952, 1:00 A.M.

My love—

Your letters made a somber and dreary day bright. It is a sight to see everyone looking for mail, then taking the letters, each to his own corner, opening the envelopes and reading—smiling, frowning, expressionless—each one living his own private life in the pages and the words—each leaving the confines of the tent for a few minutes. The days without mail make us realize what it would be if the letters could not come.

9:00 A.M.

Finished the Conrad stories. Read *The African Queen* by Forster. I can see where it would make a good movie. Am happy you are enjoying *The Caine Mutiny.* Am certain my appreciation of it was enhanced by being in the army. I could let out some of my frustration against all my CO's as I raged against Queeg.

Supper, a movie, one of those psychological crime dramas—not too good, but my ability to sit through them increases the longer I am here. Had a small feed. We opened up cans and had an assortment of Italian provolone, homemade butter cookies, pepperoni, salami, sardines, olives, anchovies, sweet crackers, ham pate, potato chips, black olives, beer, whiskey, and chocolate milk—a well-balanced meal.

I have just re-read the letters I got from you last night, and I cry. Me, a grown man—not tears (because people would think I was nuts) but all of me cries, in sadness because of the time we waste apart, and in joy at the magnitude of our love.

8:00 P.M.

I am lonely and miss you. The inactivity of late, the confines of a tent, the narrowness of some of the people all combine to add to my somber state. Perhaps I am tired. Can't get too much sleep when I stay at the hospital. I have never before been confined to such a small area.

The afternoon passed slowly. I ate. Came back to the tent and lay down. My eyes were tired from all the reading I have done in the last few days. I was tense. Finally I went out to the john and made myself comfortable. Oh my love, it just takes some of the tension off but as you know, the longing and ache and void remain.

That letter you enclosed requesting my signature on a petition to raise salaries of interns and residents, I'm afraid I could not sign. In principle it is good, but the amounts are unrealistic. $200 a month at the New Haven Hospital for 70 interns would be $14,000 a year. The hospital just can't afford it. If they gave it to us, hospital costs would rise and they are too high as it is. The hospital deficit was made up from the University last year. Where will the money come from? I don't know, but I don't think I'll write to them that the govt should be helping to subsidize community hospitals instead of building expensive veterans hospitals. I shall say it to you. The letter calls the $10 or $20 a month or week we get insulting. I never felt that way. They just can't pay and that's all. Maybe there is a way, but petitioning for that money is not it. Perhaps if they asked me for money to study how a hospital, semi-privately endowed (community) could go about paying its house staff, then I would be happy to contribute. Oh well, this brings up the entire problem of the cost of medical education, its length, the shortage of doctors in some areas, and the question of socialized medicine. As usual, instead of the people in the govt and the AMA [Amerian Medical Association] looking at the entire problem, they just look at parts of it. I read that the govt spent 84 million in the physical sciences, 17 million on research in the medical and biological sciences, and 3 million on the social sciences. So we have an atom bomb, robot planes, and jets, but cannot solve the problem of Germany, Korea, POW's, Russia, Iran, Indo-China. When will we learn that sociologically we are too far behind our technology and that will perhaps be the downfall of this civilization? I just work here—

Bob Brown came in and we talked for about ½ hour. He's easy to talk to and will be missed when he leaves.

Tomorrow I think I shall be feeling better. I do now having talked to you.   Melvin

Got a letter and Xmas card from Francis Marais (medical officer at the 8055). "Dickson sustained a linear skull fracture in a touch football game last week, when he ran into Johansen, the bit boy who worked in supply. He was sent to the 8063 MASH for observation and apparently is getting along well. He may be evacuated to Japan. Isn't that something?"

THURSDAY, DECEMBER 11, 1952, 11:50 P.M.

My Darling—

One of our anesthetists is on R & R and we were short. There were enough surgeons (6) to run the OR at capacity, but by noon I had given a spinal anesthetic on my patient, then operated. It was a reflection on our Colonel that he did not call EUSAK for another anesthetist until we were piled up with work, about 4 hrs before the rush ended. I gave my own anesthesia several times that day. We had some very seriously wounded people, one freak accident where the firing pin of a grenade slipped out while it was in the patient's pocket. He heard it, couldn't get it out, started to take off his jacket, then it went off spattering him and 2 men near him. Gene who had planned on watching us, found himself working.

My eyes are burning with fatigue, but I welcome it. Oh, I hear an ambulance coming in. Perhaps only one casualty and since I'm on second call tonight I'll be able to sleep. Sleep well my love. Your husband,
Melvin

FRIDAY, DECEMBER 12, 1952, 11:00 P.M.

Dearest—

Have just gone through a strange new experience—an air raid. No bombs dropped, but planes overhead. We were sitting in the tent when the siren went off, and then the lights. By the time we had put on our helmets, the phone rang to tell us of a "red" alert. We've had plenty of these before, but we're always told: "practice alert." There are two kinds. Yellow means that unidentified aircraft are in the vicinity and to prepare for a red alert. Red means enemy attack is imminent. All the lights were off except the operating room where they were working. I could hear the roar of airplane motors. I didn't know whether they were the enemy's or ours. It was awesome to see the valley go dark, hear the planes, and realize that an attack was actually possible. We went to the hospital. The patients were being taken care of, steel helmets on all of them. The next step is to put them on the floor with mattresses under and over them. We have bunkers we can move them into if it really gets hot. Most of them are pretty sick, and we let them be, on the beds, ready to move them if necessary. There too, it was strange to sit in the dark, waiting. Finally, after about a half-hour, the all-clear came. We walked back, hung up our helmets, and sat down to canned salmon and coffee.

I slept through the night, through the (wake-up) alarm, and got up at 8:00 A.M. Came late to rounds. Our Colonel, acting like a grade school teacher, (no reflection on you my dear) remarked to Rick and me that the next time we were late we would have to "reply by endorsement" which means, write a letter to him. Well, I'll be on time, because it's easier to go around an obstacle than through it. You asked what the Colonel's reaction to my stating my feelings about "What I will say." Well, poor frightened army man, he immediately told me he wasn't trying to infringe on my civil rights. And he back-tracked all the way.

After rounds I applied some plaster casts to prevent patients from being shaken up during their journey (to the Evac Hospital). Got some typhus and cholera shots. You can imagine, with no golf or love-making to loosen up my arm, it's very stiff.

This afternoon we had a staff meeting. What a farce. A formal meeting to discuss whether we should have an officers' club chartered or not. A charter means initiation fee, books and accounts, and an initial liquor investment. I'm not much interested. We wasted almost an hour.

Mail call brought a letter from you and, immersed in your words, I forgot all my gripes. You asked about the boy's foot. Still no word. As for food, I don't need any more. Tell the folks and your Mom that I'm well-stocked, even running out of space. I love you.   Melvin

DECEMBER 13, 1952, 9:15 A.M.

My darling husband, good morning!

At 8:30 A.M. there was an air raid drill. The sirens screetched, the traffic stopped, and people went scurrying into shelters. There were even planes overhead. It was sad and frustrating, that such a thing should be necessary, that the nations cannot live together without fear.

I am curious to know what motivated that letter from Kodak. It seems silly, especially if the slides were among others of an anatomical nature with wounds exhibited.

Your schedule when you're not working sounds good, with one exception. There isn't any exercise included. You ought to start a modern dance class or something to keep you fit. I'll really have to pound out that fat and those flabby muscles when we get together again.

I think somebody is sending or has sent you *East of Eden*. Too bad we can't get together on which books you have and which you don't. Incidentally, this Steinbeck novel did get good reviews. Where did you read otherwise?

I sent Santayana's *The Last Puritan* to you Air Mail.

I'm glad there's a place for you to walk by the river where you can enjoy the quiet beauty of nature, escape from close living quarters, and breathe fresh air. Don't worry about disliking people. I remember how many people I disliked in the mirthful and frivolous atmosphere of a college dormitory. I can't see how these unstimulating, narrow individuals can affect you otherwise in your present surroundings. I know that you're making the best of a bad situation. I'm thankful that you can bitch to me.

Have to pick Mom up at the airport now. Will write again tonight. I love you, my sweet.   Dorothy

SUNDAY, DECEMBER 14, 1952, 9:00 A.M.

My Darling Wife—

Read a bit from *New World Writing.* In an article on the "Negro in American Literature" there is a quote from a passage by Langston Hughes. "We younger Negro artists who create now intend to express our individual dark-skinned selves without fear or shame. If white people are pleased, we are glad. If they are not, it doesn't matter. We know we are beautiful, and ugly too. If colored people are pleased, we are glad. If they are not, their displeasure doesn't matter either. We build our temples for tomorrow, strong as we know how, and we stand on top of the mountains, free within ourselves."

If reference to a specific group is left out, it can apply to anyone, any group, or even to nations. Would that more people could feel that freedom of the individual.

Am happy to hear the pictures of the operation were O.K. The needle in the neck was the anesthetist putting a local anesthetic into the larynx so that the pt would not cough too much later when an airway was put in.

As for a victrola, there is enough current, but don't send one. I can get a cheap one here at the PX, but haven't. I've got enough junk to lug around now, and that is one additional bulky item—should I for any reason want to or have to move.

I love you. Your husband,   Melvin

DECEMBER 15, 1952, 11:00 A.M.

Good Morning Mrs. Horwitz—

As for next semester, I look at the word "frustration" and realize it is not a good one. Because if to dance professionally were a frustration of yours, then, my love, we should never have married. But to say you

wanted to dance almost full-time and do little else for a while, to gain
the experience and to see what it would be like, that is another thing. I
think you made the decision yourself (not to dance professionally) before you met me. Am I right? I am happy, dearest, that you can now do
what you may have wanted to do and to continue until we take up our
lives again together. As for working at the office, well, if you feel better
doing it and if it helps fill up your day, O.K., but don't do it just for the
money, even though I do like to hear about our bank account. I think
of it as a cushion against days when we won't be making much and
when we start our family.

Today I'm sending out a reel of film I took of the Koreans preparing
the ground for—and then GI's putting up—a small frame canvas hut.
The Koreans in the film are the KSC's (Korean Service Corps) and all
"old" men—for them—in their 30's. They are laughingly called the Korean WPA [Work Projects Administration, established during Roosevelt's
term to combat unemployment], as they move very slowly and as soon as
the foreman's back is turned, they stop working. I hope I got some of
their faces—some clowning, some camera shy. The "Jamesway Hut" is really something. Insulated walls so it is warm, windows, screens, lighting
fixtures and wall plugs. It costs about ½ the price of an almost equivalent
sized canvas tent and can be put up more quickly. I told the Col. if he
would assign me one, you and I could be very comfortable in it. (I love
you woman.) Also squeezed in a few pictures of me eating the cookies
Mom sent. Let me know how they come out, i.e., exposure, length of
scenes, etc. Is there too much of the Koreans?

Here is my kiss goodnight, and one more, and one more. Your husband (I like to write that!)   Melvin

SUNDAY, DECEMBER 14, 1952, 10:30 P.M.

My darling—
Your Mom had brunch ready when I arrived—hot soup and cold
gefilte fish as only she can make it, noodle pudding too! She really is a
wonderful cook and I wonder why she talks herself down so much. After lunch we "ate you up" on the screen. If you could see the positive reaction, it would be worth to you every minute of effort that you put
into your "art." Mom is reassured when she sees you looking so healthy.
And your letters to her have been good. She seems more relaxed. Maybe
my chatter helps a bit too.

The folks gave me a beautiful black cashmere sweater for Hanukah. I shall take a picture in that when Gerry comes in. I'll have to do some exercises before then though—you know, "You must, you must, you must develop your bust!" I am restless. I wonder what you are doing right now.   Dorothy

My beloved—

There were FOUR airmail envelopes waiting for me when I got home. I took off my girdle, relaxed in one of our comfortable living room chairs, and lived, through your words, with you. So many ideas generated in my mind as I read—memories, plans. Oh my love, we are not apart. We shall not be strangers when we meet, for we give all to each other even now, so many miles away, and thus continue to grow into each other and outward together.

It is late and I must awake at the crack of dawn. Have a bit of work to cram in before I leave at 7:15. I have so many things to tell you, always, the desire to share with you every minute aspect of my life. Goodnight my husband.   Dorothy

My darling—

My eyes are closing and I will welcome Xmas vacation when it arrives on Saturday. The classrooms are decorated and the kids are learning Spanish Xmas carols. My 8th graders made Xmas cards and a big colorful sign, "Felices Pascuas y Feliz Ano Nuevo," to hang across the back of the room.

Mom passed her driving test and the license arrived today!

After dinner I went to Bloomingdale's to get some gifts for our friends, about $5 each—electric kitchen clock, gin and vermouth, La Ina sherry and Cuantro, a little sewing kit for Mom, and some hard candies for my 8th grade "pinata." Had a black and white soda to revive me.

Got in at 10 and finished marking the papers for tomorrow. Spoke to Pop, and Bert called—just to gab.

I'm tired now my love and will close my eyes to dream complete dreams of you. Come in beside me and take me in your arms. I can just

feel you—enfolding me completely—looking into your eyes, you smiling a protecting kind of smile and the two of us snuggling closer and
closer. Goodnight my beloved.   Dorothy

FRIDAY, DECEMBER 19, 1952, 9:00 A.M.

My love—
    I am afraid for the future. I hope the people realize that war, in ad-
dition to being a stimulant, also means killing people. Ike is in the
White House talking to MacArthur—these men have been trained to
settle the problems facing them in only one way. And MacArthur, I
think, is an egotistical maniac who would try to regain his reputation as
a great general by trying to attack and drive the Chinese out of Korea,
no matter what the cost. To top it all off, we are practicing moving the
hospital. This is purely a local idea, but stems from the same feelings I
have that something may happen. I hope I'm wrong.

10:00 P.M.

    Brahms Intermezzi on the radio and their quiet melodies are relax-
ing. Had just started writing to Jay when a Major, a replacement for
Capt. Kosl, poked his head in and asked a question. I went back to the
letter and heard a cry, "Help, help." He had tripped and broken his an-
kle. He will be evacuated in a day or so. Feel sorry for Kosl as he has
waited for this fellow for 3 weeks. When my replacement comes, I'll put
him to bed and wait on him hand and foot until I leave.
    Outside the wind is blowing hard and the thermometer is about o
degrees. I would love to snuggle up in bed with you. It is so long since I
held you in my arms. Your husband,   Melvin.

SATURDAY, DECEMBER 20, 1952, 7:00 P.M.

My Love—
    How shall I start this letter? I love you so much that those words are
all I wish to put down—I love you. My day was brightened today by
two letters: 153 and 155 (Wed & Fri). They are so much you that I am
very close to you as I sit and read them and even hold them in my
hand.
    Took an hour's walk this afternoon. The wind is bitter and the sun

glaring. It felt good to walk rapidly (if only around the compound) and feel the blood in my face trying to keep my skin warm.

Kay Phillips, one of our nurses, has a Chintu given to her by Singman Rhee. She and one of the Generals here are the only 2 Americans who have these dogs that are raised on a small island off the coast of Korea. They were formerly used to hunt tigers. Well, the General brought his dog (male) down to play with Kay's (female). However, though the female was in heat and they had wanted to breed them, a mongrel on the post had gotten to her first, so . . . .

A houseboy was fired today. He had been stealing from the tents and the PX. He had been well-treated and was well-liked by the boys, who were always giving him small presents. Yet he stole. The only thing to do is fire him, because if not, every Korean in the place would start stealing even more. I wonder what the country will be like when the U.S. and the U.N. leave. We make up excuses to give them money. Every tree that is cut down for military purposes, even for Korean purposes, is paid for by the UN—us!

The Communists have been broadcasting they will be in Seoul for Xmas. I doubt it, but everyone is expecting some action on Xmas, even if just for nuisance value.

Rick is bitching about nothing to do on Sat night. He misses playing around with the nurses and getting drunk. That, he used to be able to do at the 121 Evac. I sit here and my love for you goes into these pages.
    Melvin

SUNDAY, DECEMBER 21, 1952, 12:20 A.M.

My love,
    Gerry and I talked for a long time—about school, politics, Mom, etc. He showed me Gray's *Anatomy* which he had bought on sale for $6.00, his first medical book, and some slides of the cat taken in the lab. I couldn't help comparing them with your exhibits. He has just finished looking at the movies he hadn't seen. He watched your operation twice. Said it was easier the second time.

11:00 P.M.

I made chow mein tonight and it was a strange feeling to be cooking—not for you. Dirtied up the kitchen the way I usually do—things flying all over the place. And Gerry didn't make me feel as lonely for your comments as I might have. He kept ribbing me. He suggested that you send me a pair of oriental rubbers, the stilt type, so that I could avoid the pieces as well as the liquid. Now I look forward to that day when we shall be in our own kitchen potting around together—paprika all over everything but the chicken!

After eating we went to work on the junk room, condensing, straightening up, vacuuming. I did want to get to those stockings I had put away, for fear they might rot, but there was no label on any of the cartons. So they will have to rot! I just hope that the mice don't get into the linens. We didn't find any evidence.

And now my love I shall close my eyes and will soon be in our present world of dreams. Goodnight my husband.   D.

SUNDAY, DECEMBER 21, 1952, 11:00 P.M.

My Love—

Today was an eventful one though it started off benignly enough—cold and windy. The bright blue sky had been full of bombers high up against the sun, the roar of their motors echoing loudly, the whoosh of the jets closer to us, the thunder of big guns several valleys away. Heard on the radio that there was action on the western front, and we waited. But not for long. Again the stupidity of war was demonstrated. In a combined air-ground artillery strike, one group of planes hit our own artillery installations. We handled 17 out of 70 people hit. I don't know how many were killed. Only a few of those we got were serious. Apparently, as soon as the first bomb fell, everyone headed for the bunkers. If not too many were killed it gives some indication of the ineffectiveness of our air strikes. All of us worked most of the afternoon. After supper we had to try and tighten up the tent, using some wire, as the wind seemed about to blow it down. Finally cleaned the place out. We still are short of anesthetists, since Andy is ill with what I had. He moved over to the hospital tonight, so there would be someone to take care of him at all times, for meals, bedpan, etc.

Back and forth. Lose a hill. Win one. It doesn't solve anything. Even if we pushed them back to the Yalu, we'd still have to sit there as we do now here. Short of an all-out war against China and Russia, there seems no other way to get anywhere but at a conference table. And a war would only end up there. I wonder if we would, as a nation, be acting as we do if the majority of people had experienced war directly.

I shall go over to the hospital to check the patients once more. Walking up and down a quiet darkened ward where kids and grown men lie battered and torn, by other men. Tomorrow these people will be on their way back south. And our doors will await more. One day we shall close them and pack up to go home. One day. But that is our life now.　　Melvin

MONDAY, DECEMBER 22, 1952, 11:30 P.M.

My darling—

Throughout this long busy day, I made little notes to you in my mind.

Left the car with Gerry as he had some chores to do and went out into the rain, boots and all, to the Martha Graham studio, 316 E. 66. Compared to the physical set-up at the New Dance Group, it is luxury! a tremendous studio and light airy dressing room.

I got there just in time to get on the floor—9:30. Martha appeared soon after. What an experience! She is wonderful and quite human. With all the build-up, one expects a goddess. She is soft-spoken and even has a sense of humor. She never leaves you in doubt as to what she wants you to do. She moves with such grace and yet with strength of steel. I was so keyed up that I really "got into my muscles," as Bill Bales [member of New Dance Group] says. She is quite captivating and I enjoyed every minute of the class.

TUESDAY, DECEMBER 23, 1952, 11:00 P.M.

Martha is superb! extraordinary! As a matter of fact, I was concentrating so hard on remembering her words, that I missed a few steps. We had difficulty executing a step on our left side. "The left side is the unconscious and the right locomotion." The Latin "sinister" means "left"—our word "sinister" is used as "unknown." "Zest" means lemon peel. "I want you to get more of it into your movement." As soon as class was over I dashed up to the dressing room to write down things I remembered: "You should have little flags of celebration up and down your nerves." "Don't look like the IDEA of action, but rather as though you are ready to move." "Movement is not in the mind, but is sensual." In criticizing introspective movement she said, "It is hidden, but there is no mystery," implying that if there WERE mystery in the movement it would be interesting. She is a real challenge intellectually. Although she takes her work very seriously, she doesn't seem to take herself so seriously, as do so many of her devotees. She is likable. One more thing— in working to achieve certain movements it is a common fault to strain through the neck and chin. I do it all the time. In trying to get us to control this, Martha said that she had learned through bitter experience not to keep her chin out. Perhaps it means that you have a mind of your own, but that should come out in other ways—throughout the body, in movement. As you can see, my love, I am so happy to share my enthusiasm with you. If you were here, you could massage my aching muscles.

Went to Dunhill's to buy Pop a box of cigars and to Jensen's for a sterling silver pencil for your Mom's purse, for Hanukah, from us. I'm giving Bert *Le Petit Prince* (St. Exupery) at his request.

Another few days and we shall begin a New Year, a good one for us because once again we shall be where we belong.   D

                    TUESDAY, DECEMBER 23, 1952, 8:00 P.M.

My Love—

Just like a bunch of small boys who cannot wait, we've been open-ing packages, many marked: Do not open. A small Christmas tree sits on the radio in the center of the room. Books, food, peppermint candy. I opened two packages—one a book from Jay and Ruth [Dranitzke, cousins] and the other a salami from Uncle Abe and Aunt Frieda [God-off, Mel's mother's brother and his wife]. Contrasts: kosher salami and Christmas tree angels. Andy is back from the hospital and feeling good, walking around wearing a horrible loud civilian tie, a present from an aunt of his. He doesn't know if she was being serious or not. But there is a somber note in the levity. Irv Graham got word today that his fa-ther died Dec 18. It was quite a shock since he had no indication of his being sick. He was denied emergency leave, apparently because he has 3 brothers at home. It is a shame. He's been here 12 months. Someone suggested he have his lawyer say he's needed to settle the estate. He's been taking it pretty well.

I didn't sleep last night, even though there were no calls. It was ei-

ther too hot or too cold. Awoke, made rounds—a Korean that had almost lost 2 fingers, (I had tacked them back on the day before) needed
amputation of the fingers. We had been told that a General was coming
to inspect us and we were to wear our wool OD's. I wasn't in the mood
to change, so I scheduled the case for about the time he was to arrive. A
rush of patients came in this morning—a grenade into a bunker full of
men. So I worked, had lunch, and then the amputation of the fingers.
The general had come by while I was working!

The day was clear, but the sky was filled with planes circling overhead, roaring by, then stringing out and heading north. A few minutes
later we could hear the thump of the bombs. There were more planes
today than we've seen in a long time.

Know how I love you my wife.   Melvin

DECEMBER 24, CHRISTMAS EVE, 8:00 P.M.

My Love—

"Peace on earth," people will sing. "Good will towards men." While
they sing there will be 23 men of all races and creeds lying in the hospital. 3 of them may not live until morning. My heart is heavy. When I
stand at the foot of a bed, watching a losing fight for life, I wonder if
there will ever be peace. This boy and the one next to him will never
know the true beauty and sweetness of life. If they should live, I wonder
if they ever will forget this year's end—1952. One will never walk
again—the lower half of his body is useless, with a piece of metal in his
spinal cord and one leg gone. The other, well, details are not important,
but I wonder if we are right to work so hard and to fight so desperately
for life, when the world is so careless with it. But that is wrong I know.

I finished writing last night and heard another ambulance come in.
So I took my boots off and lay down on the bed. Shortly before midnight
I had 2 cups of coffee and went to work. On one boy we worked as rapidly as we could. Each time we started another phase of the operation, we
wondered if he would live and we only worked on those wounds necessary to save his life. Others that could wait were merely dressed. We
worked on his leg for almost 3 hours, repairing one hole in the artery and
then another. At the end, we just ran out of material (his) to work with,
and his leg was lost. As I've said, he is still alive tonight, but. . . . We
worked through the night. I would sometimes take my turn to drop out
and go outside to help draw fresh blood from donors from surrounding

outfits and from our own men for those patients who needed fresh blood. (The Red Cross blood is 10 days or so old.) There is never a lack of donors. All we have to ask is, how many. The fellows here know what blood means. They see it on me, or on one of the other fellows, soaked into our shoes and pants and shirts. They don't ask is this blood of mine for white or black or yellow or brown. They give.

I am going over to the unit Xmas party. Don't feel like a party, but have to show up, for a few minutes, then I'll come back and write more. The EM have a better time without the officers around anyhow.

9:30 P.M.

A lot of noise, much drinking. Took some pictures and came back. This morning after rounds, Arne, Ed, Andy, and I came back to our tents and slept. All of us were exhausted after working at a fevered pitch for 9 hours without stopping. It was difficult to sleep. Noise. Trucks. People walking in and out. Telephone. But I slept anyhow. The air raid siren rang, but I just stayed put. The raid was over in about 5 minutes. Probably an unidentified plane. After 6 hours I got out of bed, still tired but feeling better. Took another 2-helmet sponge bath, shaved, clean clothes, and by then it was time for mail. It has slowed up. Letters from you from a week ago Sunday. Am awaiting the pictures you took with the folks. I try to write (them) cheerful but truthful letters, but having you, a part of me, makes them feel good.

Just had a call from Bob Brown wishing the fellows and me a Merry Xmas. Send him one of the slides with him on it. I meant to give him one but forgot.

Now to dream of you, to live again in a world devoid of loneliness. Your husband,   Melvin

THURSDAY, DECEMBER 25, 1952, 1:00 A.M.

My darling—

Am sitting at Bert's desk in the peace and quiet of Brooklyn. I like not hearing the bustle of 96th St. Just an occasional car passes. One feels that people inhabit these parts but have now gone to sleep. It seems natural for me to be here. Although of course nothing will be "natural" until we are doing it together, it is good to know that I can relax at 1299.

It is late, but I can go on writing and writing. Perhaps the knowledge that I am under no pressure to rush anywhere tomorrow morning. Above all it is that my heart is so full to overflowing with love for you that it has no place to go. I can't take it to bed with me because it would have me squirming about for half the night. So I write it down and you read my words and we make love through the mails. Hello, my darling. What are you thinking at this moment? What are you doing? What are you feeling? Across 9,000 miles our bodies feel the same longing, our minds have the same visions. Oh how I love you. Let me count the ways. I love thee more than the breadth and depth of every day living. If I had the poems here now, I would whisper each line to you across the miles. My own words are not adequate.

Martha wasn't there this morning. Robert Cohan, a member of her group, took her place. His analysis of movement is excellent. I don't know where Martha gets these boys, but they're all good-looking, clean cut, and move like Greek gods—but none like my Apollo. To see you stretched out on the bed, strong body in repose.

How far should a college professor bend to the will of the Trustees when they cry Red? This serious and timely theme is treated in a really funny play, "The Male Animal." We enjoyed Bud Epson's acting.

And now my love, I shall tiptoe into the bathroom hoping not to awaken the folks. And then under the quilt on Bert's bed, remembering the last time we slept under it, how we huddled together, pulling the quilt away from each other, giggling and loving behind a closed door. How much the folks enjoyed having us here, watching our love bloom under their very eyes. I love you. Your wife,   Dorothy

THURSDAY, DECEMBER 25, 11:00 P.M., XMAS

My Darling—

It has been quite a Christmas. Awoke to a cold frost. Even put on my long johns as I hoped to get to one of the USO shows that was in the vicinity. I was wrong. The Chinese and North Koreans pushed last night and this morning, not to get anywhere, but just for nuisance value. By 8:30 the admitting ward was filled. I kept going until 6:30 P.M. with ½ hour for lunch. A good turkey dinner, but we didn't have time to enjoy it. We had many seriously injured and more deaths today than we've had since we started. It is heartbreaking to work for hours knowing you're licked, but you hope for a miracle. Some, fortunately, you can put back together.

Finished late for supper and rather than wait around for them to cook up some eggs, I went back to the tent. Had just gotten comfortable when I was called back for some more cases. Made rounds and then a pleasant surprise. Some show people came by and gave a 25-minute performance.

My head aches. My eyes are tired. My body longs for sleep. My heart is heavy with the sorrows of the world. I miss you. I love you, my sweet.

Melvin

THURSDAY, DECEMBER 25, 1952, 9:00 P.M.

My beloved—

With this year ending, I feel that we are rounding the bend. The uncertainties at the back of our minds loom disproportionately large when we cannot talk them over in the security of each other's presence. How quickly time passes. Instead of wishing the days and nights away, we should be clinging to each moment together.

Awakening at 8:40 this morning, I opened the window, and went back to bed. I could almost smell you under the quilt and hoped that Mom hadn't washed the cover since we last slept here. Knowing her, I doubt it. Didn't get up until 11:00. Rubbed the sleep out of my eyes and walked into the kitchen to talk to Mom. She was hungry so I got Pop out of bed. She is evidently following your advice and taking some cognac before going to bed. She mentioned that she had also taken some this morning. We kidded her and I said that I was going to tell you to hurry back before she becomes a "shicker" [Yiddish, "drunkard"].

Brunch included herring in wine sauce. The folks said they were going to send you some, but I convinced them to wait, that your grocery store is well-stocked.

No more paper left and since the folks have gone to bed, I don't want to bother them for more. Still so much to say.   Dorothy

FRIDAY, DECEMBER 26, 1952, 10:00 A.M.

Good Morning My Love,

This morning on rounds, the fruit of yesterday's labor was more than I had realized. Our small ward (40 beds) was almost full. I wish the people responsible for making peace could come on rounds every morning for a week and stop at each bed, saying, he can go, he stays another day. When we say go, it means the patient goes to another hospital for weeks and months of waiting, discomfort, operations, and then what. Some go home—what a way to go home. Others go back, wondering when they might be hit again. Day after day we empty the ward—only one or two patients left—by morning the beds are full again. I don't think I'll ever forget this. One feels small and impatient attempting to fight death and pain from disease. Here one feels absolutely helpless in the fight against destruction. If each man who says war is the way—bomb the Chinese, use the atom bomb, etc.—could feel the bitter cold and know the fear of death close by and experience the shock of steel cutting a limb to ribbons, he might hesitate before he waved the flag and shouted, "Death to our enemies." Maybe I'm wrong. Maybe we should bomb the hell out of Manchuria and China. We could do it I'm sure and probably in the end more UN lives would be saved. But they too, even though their skins are darker and they don't know what modern plumbing is, they feel pain. Their wounds bleed. They die.

Read in one of the newspapers that a patient of mine—remember the boy back a few weeks that had a leg about to come off and abdominal injuries—was in Tokyo, apparently well, except for loss of a leg. He's lucky! I didn't think he would live.

The USO people came. They too were tired and cold and sympathizing with themselves and their hardships. They would give us a break with a few songs. We looked OK, taking pictures, joking with them, but then they saw the patients (those who were awake enough and well enough to enjoy the show) and saw how their faces brightened. They are show people and they joked with them because that is the way they train themselves to act. But there was a change in their demeanor. I felt warmer toward them because they knew that their discomfort was not so bad. They then wanted to sing and they felt more humble. They learned that war wasn't just Generals' dining tents, clubs, and ogling GI's. I walked briefly through the hospital with Walter Pigeon, Keenan Wynn, and one of the girls. And they felt the horror and frustration, seeing the sick ones—amputation stumps, plaster casts, yards of adhesive, tubes, oxygen tanks, patients lying immobile or gasping for breath. When they left, they were thanking them (the patients). Maybe when they get back they will tell others.

You know how I love to work. Yet I've come to hate this, along with the army, a machine of men where they lose sight of the fact that men

have souls, that there is something miraculous about the fact that man
lives. He breathes, walks, and he thinks. Yet to the army, he is a screw, a
bolt, a hinge to make the machine work. Maybe it is necessary, but it is
debasing. A man cannot be proud and content with himself because he
is a soldier. He can only feel that when he stops being a soldier and becomes a man, when he cries when a friend is killed, or when he is
afraid, or when he gives his life to save another, then he is a human
again. I hate the inhumanity of it and I hate my part in it. Yet I know
that mine is the better part. I should have been a musician. Then I
could only have loved what I did and finished the day filled with beauty,
not horror or depression. I would not be glad to see the day go by, as I
do now. I exist in a nightmare of war and injuries—stretchers and bottles of blood flowing into veins and running out onto the floor. I live in
it and tolerate it because one day it will be tomorrow and that tomorrow is you, my wife, my Dorothy. Tomorrow has sunlight, colors that
dance, wind that plays music, and skin and hair that excite. The numbers on the letters are getting larger. Where has the time gone? Where
will we ever find it again. You understand my half-expressed thoughts, I
know. Your husband   Melvin

SUNDAY, DECEMBER 28, 1952, 9:00 A.M.

My Darling—
    I would be in bed now trying to sleep but for two things. The
houseboy stripped my bed, supposedly to change the sheets, but since
there are no clean sheets, he is putting them back on again. And they
are cleaning the stoves. I am seated right next to one just lit and beginning to warm up.
    How quickly man can accomodate to most things. I am a creature
of habit. My routine of surviving here now is just that. Notice, I do not
say—living—I do not feel alive. I am numb. I have no real feeling except the ache of missing you. I was struck by this last night when I was
called at 2 A.M. Had just about gotten comfortable when the phone
rang and Rick and I had to go over. I got out of bed, shivering in the
cold, dressed hurriedly, and walked out into the night, aware only of the
beauty of the moon high in the sky shedding its cold light around me.
Down the path to the hospital, into the operating room. Took off my
shirt and jacket, wrapped the rubber apron around me (had on a clean
pair of wool trousers), washed my hands. The patient was ready. I had

glanced at the chart and knew what had to be done. Without examining the patient (the MD on call had examined him and seen the Xrays, and in this case, it was a straightforward bullet hole—no fractures), finished about 2½ hours later, washed up, dressed, went back to the tent, undressed, got into bed and slept. Had a mixed-up dream of you and me and a lot of people going places. No sooner had I fallen asleep, when the alarm rang. I was getting up, dressing in the cold near the stove, warming my clothes before putting them on, walking back to the hospital. I realized then that I was just moving, not feeling, but acting, as though I was somewhere apart, watching myself doing these things. I felt the emptiness of these movements, and I remembered back less than a year ago to Willimantic where I performed almost those very same actions of getting up in the cold—and the difference. The telephone stirring us into wakefulness, the feeling of your body rolling against mine as I turned and held you to me. Your sleepy smile as you handed me the phone. The excitement and anticipation of what I might find at the hospital. How different I felt working with Jim [Major] and Eddy [Ottenheimer, at Windham Hospital in Willimantic, Connecticut, part of the Yale residency program], enjoying it to its fullest, learning, knowing that in most cases, here was something unavoidable that we could help fix! Then best of all, saying goodnight, seeing that there were still hours left to the night, going back, undressing in the dark, knowing you were there, half-awake but awake, sliding in beside you, your arms around me, your legs around mine as you pressed your warm body against my cold one. How vivid those days are, as are all my memories compared to the haziness of yesterday and last week.

Dorothy, Dorothy, I love you so!!!

Rumors persist, but we received patients from the 45th Division last night, so now we don't know exactly what is in front of us, or what is going to happen. One minute we are north of the Yalu and the next back in San Francisco.

Have a good Sunday. Rest. Be careful of others on the road. I keep hearing of all the car accidents.

11:00 P.M.

I know now why I have no trouble writing, because I write of what I feel and think and of what happens. I don't have to make things up.

You wrote in the letter I got today that by living in our letters, we continue to grow and learn about each other. And we shall not be strangers when we are together again. Art and Rick were talking of just that while I was writing, saying that they fear they will be strangers to their wives when they get home. I make no comment.

Goodnight for now my love.   Melvin

SUNDAY, DECEMBER 28, 1952, 10:00 P.M.

My darling—

My husband, how thankful I am that we came to know each other, that your overcoat was so soft to my cheek, that we did arithmetic problems on the roof of New Haven Hospital [deciding when we could afford to get married], that our days and nights have been filled with unexpected pleasures. I love you Melvin.

I slept better tonight. Awakened at 9:30. Mom was already in the kitchen and I went into the bedroom to kid Pop about getting out of bed. He just snuggled closer under the covers and told me to "take a slow shower." This I did and Pop got up. However, Mom continued to rush him, so that he complained that he was "putting the right sock on the left foot."

We had a good-sized brunch and left for Patchogue [a Long Island, New York, town where some of Mel's mother's family had settled when they arrived from Russia]. Although I begged them to take our car, the folks insisted that they wanted to put mileage on theirs (now at 85,000). I told them that when I went to Japan, the car was theirs. They didn't say anything, so I hope that they'll comply.

Mom drove most of the way. Just before we got to Patch., Pop took over. Aunt Gitel was all ready for us with grapefruit, gefilte fish, pickled tomatoes, blintzes and sour cream—the works!

We left about 4:00 because we wanted to avoid the weekend rush back to the city and also to see a 60-minute television program about Korea by Edward Murrow called "See It Now"—actual films and recordings from Korea taken during and before the Xmas week. It was well done, but we decided that your movies compared favorably—really—I think better! Murrow took pictures of the fighting and included shots of nurses at the 8055. Only name I remember is Evans. I wonder how people who haven't seen as much as we have reacted to the program, which was intended as a public service. It must have been a real thrill for those relatives to see their boys, especially those who aren't as fortunate as we are to have a camera bug over there.

Had some of Mom's stuffed cabbage. After doing the dishes, we read the papers and watched the "Ed Sullivan Show" and "Break the Bank." The folks are now watching "What's My Line?"

Today was clear. Just as you are thankful for the snow which keeps the fighting to a minimum, we are thankful for roads free of snow. Today was the coldest we've had, about 15 degrees. It was cleansing and fresh. You and I would have bundled up and either gone ice skating or out into the country for a brisk walk, and then home for warmin' up and lovin'—the Sunday *Times* and music. Martha Graham said something I don't agree with. Perhaps I misunderstood her. Listening to music while doing other things such as housework or studying was bad. "It ruins your ear," she said. "You lose the rhythm."

My love, please don't "freeze your . . . off!" Don't risk all for a shower! I can send you some Chanel #5.

After leaving Valley Stream, I really would like to get to work on your letters, to type up a few copies of some material for publication, including your description of the people you work with, but of course not mentioning names. I would be doing it mostly for me, because I love to re-read your letters. Perhaps some of our friends and family would like to share your experiences. Cousin Martin [Abramson, the journalist who had suggested a series of M.A.S.H. features] might be able to make use of them. I could send you copies as I went along and you could edit them.

Oh my love, my love, the day will come. We shall laugh together until the tears come and cry together until the laughter comes. Goodnight, my sweet. The tomorrows without you will be long.   Dorothy

MONDAY, DECEMBER 29, 1952, 11:30 A.M.

My Love—

Spent a relatively quiet night—only one case of a drunken corporal who fell and broke his leg while posting the guard, which means waking the next one coming on duty. He had a bad fracture, but was so anesthetized with alcohol that after giving him some morphine, I was able to set it without any other anesthesia. Put him in a cast and went back to sleep.

TUESDAY, DECEMBER 30, 1952, 7:00 P.M.

My Darling—

I have found out that a path up the mountain across the river is perfectly safe. A lot of the enlisted men use it to cross over into the next
valley to go hunting. Gene and I exchanged movie cameras and took a
roll of film of each of us. We crossed over the river on the ice and then
up the river bed to the base of the path, then up to the top. I'm sure my
Mom will be worrying about the ice breaking. You can tell her the river
is only 2 feet deep.

The news on the radio is that the number of points necessary for
rotation, except in the front lines, is 40. That means staying almost to
the end of my tour in the army and makes me even more determined to
get out of Korea to Japan or Okinawa.

Neal Ryan is an easy-going 30-year-old from Chicago. Catholic (but
not a rabid one), married, 3 children. He is a mature person though he
has only had a high school education. He is supply officer and does a
competent and conscientious job. Has a good sense of humor and is
someone who likes and respects people. His feelings about many things
are different than mine, but about basic moral issues we are in agreement. He is a regular army aspirant, perhaps because he is not a pusher
and might get lost in the fierce competition of civilian life. Am not at all
sure about this. He drinks along with Rick and Art, but has never gotten drunk, and never would think of drinking if he had to be on duty.
(The others cut down, but not too much.) He enjoys the articles and
cartoons you send and comments how you back me up in my fight
against the Republican reactionaries in this tent by providing me with
documentation. He often sends the cartoons and articles to his wife.

It grows late and I'm OD again tonight. Another of the boys isn't
feeling well, and I'm covering. Goodnight darling. We "bide our time,"
as you say. Your husband,   Melvin

TUESDAY, DECEMBER 30, 1952, 11:55 P.M.

My beloved—

I finally finished *Came A Cavalier,* a beautiful love story and poignant account of conditions in France during World War II. Keyes,
writing about events of just a little over 10 yrs ago, depicts the separation of lovers and the horror and injustice of war. It seems the solution

is a selfish one, to get away from the horror ourselves and to live our own lives as best we can. As I write now, the first few minutes of the last day of this year have begun. In another few hours you shall be welcoming the New Year. Tomorrow, at noon, in the middle of a stretch, I shall think of you drinking a toast or saying a prayer to yourself. Happy New Year my beloved husband.

Strenuous class this morning. Martha went after us with a vengeance and we came off the floor panting but exhilirated.   Dorothy

January

Mom and I had more invitations than we had time or inclination to accept. Our intimates and indeed everyone who knew us and knew about Dad's death or Mel's absence were anxious to entertain us or provide us with distractions. My father's sister, Aunt Helen Newman, bought us Scrabble, the new game craze that was transforming solitary crossword puzzle addicts into competitive buffs. Her gambit worked. Mom and I became dedicated to a nightly game that in no way lessened our zeal for the *New York Times* puzzle, one of the few enthusiasms that Mel and I did not share. Although I complained to him that Scrabble was detracting from our reading, Mom and I welcomed any activity that absorbed our attention for an hour without depressing or boring us.

Almost 4,300 physicians had been inducted into the service so far during this "police action." This was a different breed of serviceman. They were not soldiers. They were not sailors. They were doctors. Doing the job they were assigned, most of them worked tirelessly. At the same time, among themselves, they mocked army procedures and criticized their superior officers.

In his letters to me, Mel lost no opportunity to chew out the generals. Inherently honest and stubbornly outspoken, he found it difficult to say what they wanted to hear. When asked for his opinion, he gave it candidly, sometimes shocking his colleagues and eliciting raised eyebrows among his regular army bosses. However, coming closer to the time of his application for transfer to Japan, he was particularly careful not to incur the wrath of anyone who might delay his transfer. He suggested that I start the new year by setting the passport process in motion.

For us, this New Years Eve was just one more night apart. For some, being mired in Korea was a valid excuse to drink themselves into oblivion. For others, the existential fact of being alive was inebriating enough. The peace talks were stalemated. The battles continued. Not even the inauguration of a general could change those stagnant conditions. Painfully alert to his personal responsibility, Mel worked at building patient morale as relentlessly as he lamented the waste of life and limb. His letters reflected the stress.

THURSDAY, JANUARY 1, 1953, 9:45 P.M.

Melvin, my beloved—

Mount Vernon, a comfortable living room beside a dying fire. The red coals crackle in the stillness of the country. Wherever I am it is always the same. You are away and I am incomplete.

Yesterday, dance as usual. Martha's latest: When criticizing movement that was egotistical rather than genuine she said, "I don't mind you being as VAIN as a peacock, but you've got to be as FUNCTIONAL too—otherwise you'll never get your tail up!" I was lousy in class. Guess I was just too tired to do it justice. Walked over to Madison Ave. to take the bus and realized the buses were on strike. Took a cab home and gave the guy a 35 cent tip for 65 cent fare—for New Years. On Madison Ave. a little girl was playing with the snow at the base of a telephone pole. She looked up at me and smiled as I passed. At that moment, an elderly man who was nearby reading his paper said, "Don't you dare touch anything! If I see you touching snow again I'll cut your hands off!" I looked at him with horror and then to the little girl who appeared more bewildered than frightened. All my sorrow welled up. How can we avert wars when there are people like that in the world? What will the little girl be like when she grows up?

Gerry and I are spending the night here in Mt. Vernon with the Newmans. After a good dinner of leg of lamb, Gerry went to the hospital with Dave and watched him do a lid operation. In the meantime, cousin Freddy, Aunt Helen, and I watched Burns and Allen and then played a fascinating new word game, "Scrabble." Aunt Helen is sending it to you.

I met a girl at the Graham school whose husband is in Korea. They were married a month before we were and he went into the service a few weeks later. I don't know where he was stationed, but at the time they decided it wasn't practical to pull up their N.Y. roots. They just saw each other weekends. Soon after, he was sent to Pusan. He's due to be discharged in June. Think of how much further ahead we are. We're almost at #200.   Dorothy

THURSDAY, JANUARY 1, 1953, 6:00 P.M.

My Darling—

New Year's Day has come and gone. I'm not really aware of it being one day or another. I'm tired physically and mentally and emotionally. Why celebrate a New Year? Is it that once a year one should stop to review the year and to look ahead—a time for introspection, for re-evaluating one's hopes and ideals? As I crawled into a cold bed this morning, I found it difficult to think of anything but the happiness we've had. It was with effort that I recalled the sorrow and despair and horror. I remember the fulfillment of living with the one I love. Although I can't ignore what's around me, I can do little but hope and look forward to OUR near future. I'll ignore the ominous warnings of atomic warfare and amphibious landings and just think of you.

On rounds this morning, most of the boys dragged, shaking off the effects of having drunk too much. Six seriously injured patients had come in. The ROK soldiers we're getting now reveal how badly this country is lacking in medical facilities. They have almost no doctors near the front. Even though plasma is provided, they don't use it. Life is cheap. The soldiers we get are semi-starved, compared to the ROK's assigned to U.S. divisions. The surgical problems are approached differently, since you always wonder what will happen to the patient. No excellent follow-up and rehabilitation programs, no unlimited hospital facilities and reconstruction surgery. So you try to do more, to make a limb that can be used with a simple prosthesis, to do things that will avoid complicated surgery later. It's a challenge, as the patients are not strong healthy males who can take almost anything. Abdominal operations have to be done quickly, amputations in minutes. One can be tempted to say, Why bother? What sort of life can this shell of a man have? He will only die. But you cannot succumb to such reasoning.

My surgery is continuing to improve. I can do things in a hurry and not be sloppy. My judgment is surer. At one time I felt I would have to get some residency training at a place where I could "do a lot." Well, this is it. Now I only want to finish the formal residency to learn how to handle more complicated problems. Then one day, my love, we shall go out and see what the world has to offer. But more important, what we can give to it. We ask only to be allowed to live together. We shall give much more than we ask.   Melvin

FRIDAY, JANUARY 2, 1952[3], 10:00 P.M.

My Darling—

I am now sure the Col. is a complete fool and an ass. By his watch I was late for rounds today by 3 minutes. So in true army fashion he wrote me a communication which I had to "reply to by endorsement." I was mildly annoyed by the pettiness of it, especially when he tolerates the gross inefficiency and drunkennes of Mr. Willard. Having a few moments I sat down with tongue in cheek and righteous indignation and wrote the enclosed note. (The Col. and I are having quite a correspondence.) I presented it to him with the endorsement. He took it and asked, "Are you sure you want me to read this? Is there anything disrespectful or insubordinate in it?" I sort of tsk tsked (holding back a smile) and said gently, "Why Col., you should know me better than that!" He failed to see the humor. He got deeper and deeper telling me he knew he couldn't offer anything but we had to have rounds because someone from higher headquarters told him that "Col. so-and-so of the 8076 MASH always had them." Those are his words. Well I then began to feel sorry for him so I got the conversation around to what we could do to make rounds interesting. He finally agreed that there was nothing we could do since they were for the sole purpose of deciding on the disposal of patients and we could not spend time discussing cases. (However I was nice to him and told him I would come on time.) Then I suggested that we form a Journal Club and meet once or twice a week to discuss cases and articles. He agreed it would be a good idea and it shall be broached from higher headquarters, i.e., from him at our next meeting. I was almost sorry I had written it. He is afraid of his shadow. General Atwater is coming in about 10 days and he fears one of us might say something to him—about anything. What a life he must have. He believes the officers should not associate with the EM and that a CO should not be too sociable with the junior officers. So he sits alone in his tent at night, drinking some, reading westerns. When I came in one night to give him some pictures of the practice move, he was hungry for company and for talk. I am going to buy something for him when I go to Pusan in a week or so. We'll call it— be kind to Cols week.

11 points are gone and the days go. We will be together when the earth begins to bloom again. I love you Dorothy my love.   Melvin

SATURDAY, JANUARY 3, 1952[3], 9:00 P.M.

My Love—

Attended a useless ½ hour class on map-reading. Guess they want us to have something to do, as all officers in Korea will have to pass an examination on it in a few weeks. I think I shall just read the manual. By the time it was finished, the admitting ward was full and I was on duty. I worked until 5:30 P.M. These Koreans are in a sad state. They are allowed to lie around for 24–72 hours before they are evacuated (compared to the 4–10 hours for our GI's) and there is no need for it. We've told them again and again.

Spent the evening finishing a novel by Jan De Hartog, *The Distant Shore*. Easy reading but the characters do not have depth. While reading I listened to a recorded concert Helen Traubel gave in Taegu. Her speaking voice and her laugh remind me of Kate Smith, but her singing voice—ahh—

I put your pictures on the wall next to my bed where I can see you whenever I look up—from my letters to you, when I go to sleep, when I awaken. I can look at you.

I had to smile at your comparison of me as Apollo and the Greek God dancers of Martha Graham. My body feels clumsy and heavy. I haven't done any exercise. Also I can afford to lose 10–15 lbs. That is why I do not want any more food. If I really want some I can get it at the PX.

Am covering for Ed Svetke who is watching the movie "The Greatest Show on Earth."

11:30 P.M.

This daily butchery is depressing and now, with Koreans who don't understand what is going on, it is like veterinary medicine. This is a bad dream. Men killing, destroying, sitting in cold and mud and filth. Do they really hate each other? I doubt it. What are the issues? And we spend a fortune on this, money that could be feeding and clothing people, teaching them. Look at this waste: Gasoline here costs $1.29 and oil $1 a gallon. In the past month, we've used in this unit alone (160 men and hospital) 7,000 gallons of gasoline and 25,000 gallons of oil. Can you imagine that? And we look for ways to balance the budget. Abolish military spending and we can be in the black. What? Military spending is the basis of our economy. Then our economy is false. Production and spending should be for living—not dying. Oh well. What can we do—everyone is so stupid!

Was happy to hear on the radio that Sen McCarthy was accused of speculating with funds (donated for his anti-communist fight) and even if it isn't true (which he claims) it is a taste of his own medicine, being accused and convicted before he is tried.

Sleep well my beloved. I am close to you as our day draws closer. Your husband   Melvin

SUNDAY, JANUARY 4, 1952[3], 11:15 P.M.

My darling—

I am always glad when you tell me of the visits of USO troupes, not only because of their morale building, but because they will be coming back here to relate to other Americans what they have seen—perhaps some of the horror will penetrate the minds of those who know nothing of what is going on over there.

As I drove Gerry to the station this afternoon, we turned on the radio. Madeleine Gray was singing "Songs of the Auvergne," the same arrangement we have—and I thought back to the first time I heard those recordings, one of my first weekends visiting you in New Haven. You were changing from whites to clothes and went in to shower. I sat on the bed in your room and listened. Everything, the records too, new and exciting. Although I was happy at the moment, little did I anticipate the great happiness which lay ahead of me—of us.

I hope that it will be possible for you to make the call next weekend. I shall be in at every moment after 7 P.M. on those nights. When I think of hearing your voice, your breath—oh my Melvin, I love you!

11:00 P.M.

For 25 minutes I did techniques since I don't want to lose all I've gained in these 2 wks. So I shall try to do them every night until I can begin to take classes every day. Mom wanted to know what I would do when I got to Japan. "Continue my techniques and take Japanese dancing lessons." Incidentally, I was surprised to learn how much of Graham's dance theory is based on oriental dance.

Goodnight my darling. I worship the passage of time.   Dorothy

SUNDAY, JANUARY 4, 1952[3], 11:00 P.M.

My Love—

I've just found out that the Surgeon General, the 8th Army Surgeon, and the FECOM Surgeon will be coming here next Saturday and spending the night. I had planned on leaving Saturday to be sure to be in Pusan by Mon morning. Now I am wondering if I shouldn't stay for Saturday night and talk with them to let them know me—especially the 8th Army Surgeon and the FECOM Surgeon (both Generals) since the FECOM transfer depends on these men. So if you don't get the call Sun night you will know why and can expect it the next night or soon after. I shall do what I can with these old bastards. Why they are going to spend so much time here I do not know, but this MASH, sans (regular) nurses, is one of their babies. We are going to have a party for them that night. The Col told me to start holding patients so our wards will look full and we will appear busy when they come. What a lot of crap. I told him he need not tell us why it was being done. We knew, but we would have some patients on the wards. What an organization this army is. I hate it more and more.

Irv asked me to take a small wart off his 5th finger. It was cracking and bothering him when he typed and had been getting larger. So I took it off and he was pleased that it didn't hurt but for the 1st stick of the novocaine needle. That started things. I worked from 3 P.M. until 10 P.M. on fractures, head injuries, bullet wounds—none too serious except a skull fracture that I patched up temporarily until he could be transferred to the 8209 MASH under the care of the neurosurgeons.

I haven't had to work with Rick, since he hasn't worked for 10 days now. He is perfectly well, walking about, staying up late drinking, but just a lazy bastard. Most of the other fellows are aware of it. He had been asking for a 3-week convalescent leave, but was shamed out of it.

Don't send the *Surgical Clinics* anymore as the unit library now gets them.

My eyes are closing, and my writing is getting illegible I'm sure. Hold my head in your lap and let your cool hands rest on my forehead and your lips brush mine. Your husband   Melvin

MONDAY, JANUARY 5, 1952[3], 9:00 P.M.

My Beloved—

The day started grey and dismal. Rounds went on without me since a Korean came in with a leg off, just about dead, cold, frostbitten. I spent the next 2 hours bringing him back into a condition where we could take him to Xray and then to the operating room. By the time we finished with him and another it was 1:30 and Horne (the anesthetist) and I ate lunch. It had cleared and the temperature was not too low, so Horne and I decided to finesse the map course (I can get all I need by reading the manual) and we went down to the river to ice skate. Borrowed skates from one of the corpsmen. Horne had never skated before. It was a howl to watch him crawl onto the ice on all fours. The snow covering the ice did not interfere at all. We took some movies which I'll send off tomorrow. A year ago we went ice skating, arm in arm, around the lake. I remember enjoying the feel of your cold cheeks against my lips.

Rick is cooking up some ravioli. A way to spend time. Finally got some clean sheets.

The other day, the boys were fantasizing. If we had plenty of money and didn't have to work for a living, would we have gone into medicine? I was the only one who said yes. Some said they didn't know. Art, I'm sure didn't want it, but his father is a physician. Rick is only interested in making $40,000 a year. Ed Svetke says it is a way to earn a living. Gosh, I've said this before: There are so many easier ways to earn a living. But everyone is different. N'importe.

I shall stop now. I can't sit still. I shall go outside and walk for a few moments in the quiet of the night.

Goodnight my dearest.   Melvin

JANUARY 7, 1953, 8:30 P.M.

My Love—

We are keeping patients now and there is more work keeping the wounds clean. The Col. tries to rationalize his position by saying, We want to find out what will happen if we keep patients. I've been too polite to tell him we know. That's what we go to medical school for. But, I've got my name tag and 8th Army patch sewn on so they (the brass) will know who I am.

I walked down by the river in the snow for a short while before lunch. I had just finished reading a selection from *Magic Mountain* where Hans Castorp is caught in the snowstorm out on the mountain. Mann has a command of language that comes across even in translation. I read each sentence slowly, savoring it like a tasty morsel. "The child of civilization, remote from birth from wild nature and all her ways, is more susceptible to her grandeur than her untutored son who has looked at her and lived close to her from childhood up, on terms of prosaic familiarity. . . ." Remember the waitress at Jasper Lake [Canada] complaining of Lake Louise? "Only one view," she said.

After lunch I worked on a corpsman with sinus trouble. Rather than send him south for 2 weeks of traveling and waiting for treatment, I turned ENT [Ear, Nose, and Throat] man for the day and irrigated his sinuses. It apparently worked.

Went to a map reading class because I was informed that we all had to appear and I didn't want to get Neal in trouble by either having to turn my name in or not turning it in. (He wouldn't)

With some difficulty I have finally gotten a journal club that will meet weekly. Art and Ed had no wish to attend. Art is lazy and uninterested in anything except doing nothing. Ed I think is playing a role, saying he didn't need a journal club to have people tell him what to read now that he is out of school. Actually he has not been reading any medical literature. You remember in Willimantic how much I enjoyed it, learning by talking—and listening. It is always worthwhile to exchange ideas. There are enough of the other fellows who feel as I do so that we shall start one next week.

I love you.   Melvin

THURSDAY, JANUARY 8, 1953, 11:00 P.M.

My darling—

The snow came down all day, turned to sleet, and now rain. Hope it doesn't freeze. Driving tomorrow will be impossible. Got to school on time this morning loaded down with books, lunch, boots, etc. I really must have looked like a high school student. Taught my first class in loafers before I had a chance to change my shoes—felt good!

My throat seems better and I helped it by sucking Pine Bros. cough drops. They were something to chew on anyway, and how I wanted that today! From the moment I got into the house this afternoon, I have done nothing but nosh [Yiddish, "eat snacks"] raisins, dates, candy, fruit, cheezits. You know, my love. Like you. Just another way of easing the frustration.

We ate dinner at 5:30. I spoke to your Mom, read the paper, *New Yorker* and *Lydia Bailey* for a while. Came across: "I truly believe that the most ignorant of all people are those who dare to express opinions on war when they've never had a hand in the fighting." You have said it so many times in different words.

Still don't know about my replacement at Valley Stream although they're working on it.　　D

THURSDAY, JANUARY 8, 1953, 8:00 P.M.

Dorothy My Love—

It is eye opening to see the effect of a lack of mail on the morale of the entire unit. The activity of the day is usually built around the arrival and dispersal of mail. When it is not forthcoming, a pall of gloom settles over the place. Maybe I imagine this because of my own spirits.

Spent the latter part of the morning doing dressings. We have a ward full of Koreans (now that we are keeping patients until the general has come and gone). They make quite an audience. First, they are not used to American ways, especially in a hospital. Korean hospitals are hell holes, filthy, no personnel. When a Korean family sends one of its members to the hospital, they all go to take care of him. This occasionally creates problems when one of the soldiers arrives with eight or ten of his buddies. It is difficult to explain to them that they can go back and we'll take care of the patient. Our relatively aseptic ritual of dressing change also opens their eyes. By the time I had worked on a few patients they were all pointing at their dressings, clean or not, wanting them changed—like children. So I spent an extra hour changing dressings. Most of them are aware that we are trying to help them and are grateful, if unable to express it verbally. They do it by the expression on their faces. One can become callous in treating Koreans and take out some of the frustration of being here by considering their lives cheaper than the GI. When one is tired and fights the dirt and language barrier, the temptation may be just to say "what the hell." But especially when I work hard, as I did this morning, and indeed at all times, I try to act and work according to the problem and not who the patient is.

The dressings done, and orders given for washing up the patients—

almost all needed a good scrubbing and back care to prevent bed sores, and liberal use of DDT powder. Then changed a dressing on Irv's finger. It is healing nicely and has given him no pain.

Goodnight my wife. I love you with everything that is me.

Melvin

FRIDAY, JANUARY 9, 1953, 11:00 P.M.

My Love—

The Col's scheme to keep a full ward backfired. We've had to evacuate patients tonight to make room for the new ones. There are a dozen amputees on the ward and several have died on us. As usual, the army way of doing things is the least efficient. Medical care has been difficult because of the unnecessary load. We shall get rid of some more in the morning.

It's good to sit down now and relax into our world.   Melvin

SATURDAY, JANUARY 10, 1953, 11:00 A.M.

Goodmorning, my love—

And a miserable morning it is—still raining and no sign of clearing. Many areas in New Jersey, Westchester and Conn. are without electricity because the ice on the trees has weighted them down causing power lines to fall to the ground.

11:15 P.M.

I spent the afternoon reading *Lydia Bailey*. Work and correspondence went to the dogs—an exciting story with fantastic characters. No "peace at any price" here. The novel favors minority groups and doesn't contain one kind word about the French. A small group of people control war and peace. One scene struck me particularly. When Albion meets Lydia after their 3-year separation: "I recall my breathless inability to do more than whisper her name, over and over. . . . all the unintelligible but necessary nothings that help two lovers, after long separation, to still the churning inner tumult that for a time makes coherent speech and thought impossible." How afraid I am to be too hopeful.

Since you sound as though you are anxious to lose weight I shall try to control the amount of food that is sent to you. But I know that the other boys get packages and it must be nice to reciprocate.

I imagine you on your lonely cot in that desolate spot and try to project myself into your arms. I think of days ahead—going to Japan—40 points in Korea—if the latter applied to you, I would come to Japan anyway and wait for weekend passes. Oh my darling, I just want to be with you.   Dorothy

SATURDAY, JANUARY 10, 1953, 10:00 A.M.

My love,

It is too cold to sit in our tent, so I am over at the supply tent and seeing a typewriter free decided to make one of my letters legible, though I don't know about that, especially since my fingers are sore from sewing the name and army patches on my shirts in preparation for the generals' visit this afternoon. What a surgeon. Can't even sew his own shirt.

Yesterday seems like a dream already. These Koreans are as dazed and surprised at being injured as the GI's, as though they are saying, "Could this have happened to me?" One after the other the patients passed through the OR. I didn't even go out to see them in the pre-op ward. To save time, as I was finishing one I would have the next one brought in and prepared for surgery, take a quick look at his X-Rays, wash my hands, and start in again. I wear the rubber apron to keep my clothes from getting too dirty from blood and from the irrigating fluid we use to wash out the wounds which oftimes squirts all over me.

Incidental note. Am glad to see you know how to use the heater. Do you also know how to use the defroster? As to my letters . . . if you think you want to. . . . I don't think I write well enough, but maybe if you rephrase some of them. . . . I am lazy and write in a stream of consciousness style . . . no punctuation or sentences. . . . Try it my love and see what it looks like. . . . I don't have to edit them. . . . leave out names and designations. . . . if you have the time and want to . . . go ahead.

My love, another parking ticket. If you get many more I'll have to come home and bail you out of the clink. How could you? I never park where I shouldn't. I told the boys about it and they had a good laugh. Then a few of them said: My wife would never tell me about that even if I were home. Again, the element of hiding something. Is it fear? I don't know.

Rochester Med School is a good one and in a large enough city where there is a selection of cases and adequate numbers. [A friend had asked Mel's advice.] In med school, the actual clinical material of ward cases is not as important as during the internship. It is the lack of personnel and money for teaching purposes that hampers them. Probably in the next 10–20 years the state schools will be the only ones that can continue the financial support necessary, except perhaps for the very wealthy schools.

Almost time to eat. Will stop and get this into the mail. Can look forward to some more mail today I hope. We love today. . . . from so far. . . . my wife . . .   Melvin

MONDAY, JANUARY 12, 1953, 10:00 P.M.

My darling—my beloved—

It was an ordinary school day. I accomplished some work the last period, gave an extra help class, and left a Cafeteria Supervision meeting early. I had had enough and walked out with authority so that people were bound to think I had permission. If they had questioned, I was going to explain that I was expecting a phone call from Korea. I got home at 4:30 and was surprised to see your Mom here. The overseas operator had phoned to say you would call at 8:15.

After dinner we sat around waiting waiting. Each time the phone rang your Mom and I dashed for separate phones. I told her to let me take the calls. I wanted a minute alone with you. But believe me, my darling, as soon as I heard your voice, I didn't care who was listening. To hear you say that we WILL get to Japan! Yes, you heard my cold, but it's just runny. Will probably start to dry up tomorrow.

I heard you. We spoke. And the words I want to say now do not come. Just to hear your voice—the strength, the surety, the love. I try to reproduce the individual sounds in my mind. It was almost as though we had made love. The desire, the tension, the call, then basking in the warmth of you.

From what I have been reading and hearing over the radio these past few days, there has been fighting in the eastern sector, which means that you will be busy when you get back from Pusan. There is about a 10-day interval before your letters reach me now.

The glow has worn off and I am faced with the coldness of the nights ahead. If we really can talk once a month, the time will go more quickly. I mourn these lost months apart.   Dorothy

"Stoves in tents burn Diesel oil."
(*Photographer unknown*)

"New haircut. Bald spot is optical illusion." (*Photographer unknown*)

Incoming patient. Corpsmen replace evacuation bag.

Seriously wounded patient being transfused during transfer to triage area.

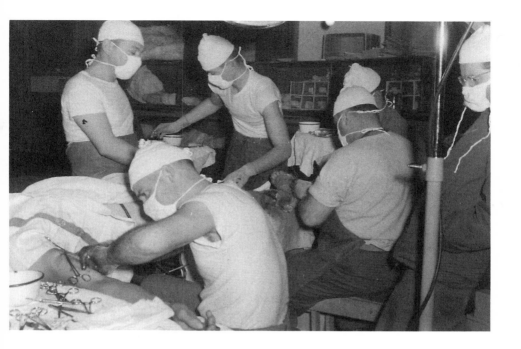

Three separate surgical teams debride wounds of right arm, trunk, and both lower legs.

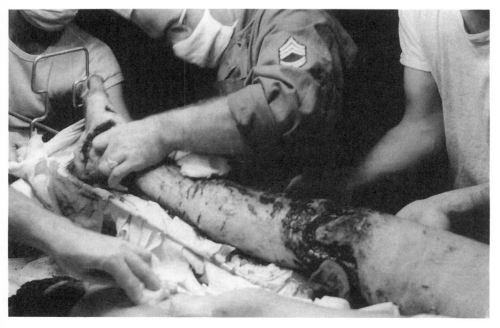

"His right leg had to be removed above the knee."

Helicopter evacuation

A30 Airfield. Jade is code name for Corps Headquarters.

"Only the seasons change."
(Photographer unknown)

Physician of the day. Hakata Army
Hospital, Fukuoka, Japan, 1953.
(Photographer unknown)

First Lieutenant Melvin (NMI) Horwitz. *(U.S. Army photo)*

Korean War Memorial, Washington, D.C., 1995. *(Photograph by Joyce Levy)*

TUESDAY, JANUARY 13, 1952, 8:00 A.M., 4:30 P.M.
PUSAN

My Love—My Darling—

At 9,000 miles I could sniffle with you, but couldn't give you the pills to cure it! It was so great to hear you, even though I did most of the talking. Actually it was about 10:30 before the call finally went through. How long before were you notified? Thanks my darling for thinking of Mom and letting her listen. You are so good. I wonder if I would have. I'm a bastard!

As good as it was to talk to you and to be so close to you for those few minutes (5=$20) it was just as bad to hang up. Bang. And a curtain of 9,000 miles came between us. I wanted to hold you close to me and burn your cold out. I went out, happy and sad. I looked at the ships in the harbor, wanted to get on one of them.   Melvin

TUESDAY, JANUARY 13, 1953, 10:30 P.M.

My darling—

Took a make-up class with Sophie Maslow, one of the originators of the New Dance Group, some years back a member of Graham's group. How much I have to learn. I still feel that the Graham school offers a more exacting and satisfying technique, and I was surprised not to find more professionals there, more of the devoted starving-for-art type. The atmosphere is friendly and wholesome. From what I had heard about Martha, I expected to see her sitting up high on a pedestal with all kneeling at her feet.

Fun to read about your ice skating. I'm sure the exercise feels good and gliding along must have given you a sense of freedom.

And now goodnight. Close your eyes to what is around you. Sleep well, dream well.   Dorothy

WEDNESDAY, JANUARY 14, 1953, 8:00 P.M.

My Darling,

Saturday seems far away. Yet the events are fresh in my mind. I made some notes as I flew up today. Washing and getting scrubbed for the generals' arrival. Wool uniforms with name tags and army patches,

my brass shined, me shaved, powdered, and my camera loaded. They
arrived. All of us rushed out, not so much to say hello as to get pictures.
It was a farce from beginning to end. Half-saluting we shook hands as
they looked at our name patches and said, "How do you do Horwitz,"
as though they had known us all our lives.

Genl Armstrong, Surg General US, a slight man, pleasant smile, and
politician's handshake and voice as well as mannerisms; Gen Shambura,
short, rotund, hearty voice full of insincere warmth; Genl Guinn, taller,
thinner, ascetic, somewhat cold, with roving hands on the nurses' back-
sides. Dr. Reinert, the AMA representative to the armed forces who is a
famous urologist. Made over $250,000 last year in a clinic he runs but
does no work in. A crude, lewd politician of the first order who keeps
telling everyone how much he gave up to take the job he got and how
much he sacrificed in the 1st world war. The worst sort of man to represent me, but the sort of man the AMA and the army want. He repre-
sents mainly the MD's who did not serve in the last war, now are well-
to-do and who do not want to be called up at all, would rather we
served longer. And who probably will not have to be called, though they
could just as well serve in the States (many of them in their 40's) and
relieve the younger men to go to the Far East; a Col from Ft Sam in
charge of the army residency program and the course at Ft Sam. This
procession wandered through the hospital, half-interested, somewhat
surprised at our nice layout and disappointed that most of the patients
were Koreans so they couldn't speak to them and make an impression.

AS YOU KNOW THIS IS BEING WRITTEN FROM A VERY PREJ-
UDICED VIEWPOINT. I HAD NO RESPECT FOR THESE MEN TO
BEGIN WITH AND JUST ABOUT CONTEMPT AFTER THEY LEFT.

We had been told that the Surg Genl wanted to speak to us, but that
was a mistake. That's just what he wanted everyone else to think. Actually he didn't want to talk to us since he would have to answer questions about replacements, policy, and why there was such a lack of
planning. So they retired to their tents to wash up and then we met
them at the club. They promptly got drunk, became noisy, told dirty
jokes, and attempted to be fatherly in sympathizing with our plight at
being in Korea. It was disgusting. All they see are the clubs. They go to
cocktail parties and speak to regular army officers (mainly CO's) who
are bucking for promotion. Genl Guinn kept trying to get Kay Phillips
into a corner to cop a quick feel. She resisted admirably and it was a
show in itself to see the maneuverings. The infantry should take note

and learn how to approach an objective. By this time, we had been joined by Genls White (they call him Blood and Guts) and Ruffner, the men in charge of the divisions we support. The genls aides, 2 for each, were there also, serving no function. Talking to this Dr. Reinert was a farce. He would not listen seriously to any complaints or suggestions or questions but would say, "I know, when I was in WWI. . . ." Genl Armstrong would not answer any questions but would refer you to one of the aides or Cols who knew nothing. The Col from Ft Sam asked me what I thought of the course at Ft. Sam. I told him it kept me out of Korea for 8 weeks and that I probably learned very little, got some introduction to the army, e.g., how to put on a uniform. True to your husband's pattern, I had the insignia on my collar reversed, rank on the left instead of the rt. One of the pilots came over and whispered to me inobtrusively of the mistake. I excused myself and went out and fixed it. I don't think anyone else noticed, or if the Col did, he kept quiet about it. I think that in itself made the evening worthwhile. I tried to take Shambura aside and get him to tell me he would transfer me to Japan soon, but no go. The only thing I could do was to get him to say I could request a specific service, and in that way I might be able to remind him of my desire for a transfer later on towards March. Well, by this time everyone was polluted, with the generals patting each other on the back verbally and physically, so we repaired to the dining room. In order to find out who sat where, the Col had to call up division and ended up by speaking to the Korean steward in charge of the genls' mess who told him of the protocol. Rank! So a visiting genl with 3 stars had the guest of honor's chair in the center while Genl Armstrong, the guest of honor, sat to the side. Logical, eh what. I prepared to sit down in my place when Kay came over to me and asked if I would mind changing since a Col had been placed by mistake down with the Lts. Heavens, what a blow! So I did, naturally. She thanked me later and said, "I asked you since I knew it wouldn't make any difference to you and you wouldn't raise a fuss," a small compliment over a minor detail.

After the dinner there were speeches. It made me think of a fraternity dinner or political convention, though I have attended neither. But the Col got up and introduced each one. He was so obvious in his TL-ing [Yiddish acronym, "ass-kissing"]. They occasionally threw a crumb to us poor peasants and told us we were doing a magnificent job by doing what they had told us to do. Armstrong had the temerity to say, (and I was tempted to send this to the *New Yorker*) "I like to be in Ko-

rea. It is RELAXING after the confusion of Washington." I was so mad I
had difficulty controlling myself. He should be lying in bed with one
leg off or having to butcher these poor kids and he would know how
relaxing it is. That SOB. My blood boils when I think of him. After that
they retired to the club for some more drinking and I went to work
with some of the other boys. The genls' aides were having a private party in their tent and raising cain. The boys (other people at the MASH)
were having a private bitch session in their tent. Well, between cases I
went out to the john where I met General Guinn puking his guts out. I
didn't feel a bit sorry. I was OD that night and worked all night.
Stopped in for a short while at the boys' bull session and heard them
express sentiments similar to mine.

I met the generals leaving. They were very friendly. While the Col
again was saluting and making sure the jeeps were warm, I'm afraid I
shook him up by shaking hands with all of them, when they offered
their hands. To each one I said, We do not have too difficult an existence here but after a while we can think of nothing except our families
and all we want is to go home. Efficiency and morale are nil when this
sentiment predominates, so please try to keep the replacements coming. They half-smiled and said, We'll try. But I'm afraid it made no impression. All they will report is that morale is high, everyone is comfortable, and all those wonderful boys are doing a magnificent job
taking care of the wounded. I'm afraid the administrators shall inherit
the earth. From what they seem to be doing to it, they can have it.

All I want is you my darling and the chance to live somewhere
where administrators and politicians care about people. I love you and
were it not for that I don't think this existence would be worth anything. I am with you always.   Melvin

THURSDAY, JANUARY 15, 1953, 7:00 P.M.

My Darling—
When the Generals left I went north to the airstrip (on my way to
Pusan). There I met one of the pilots who fly small evac planes for artillery spotting. They have been getting shot at with radar-directed anti-
aircraft guns and have many war stories to tell. Underneath their brava-
do is fear, which they freely admit to. They wear armored vests and sit
on sandbags. The flight was smooth, the mountains as picturesque as
ever, and the war seemed far away. While there have been many air acci-

dents I am not afraid to fly, since I feel fatalistic about it. These pilots are careful, more so than jeep drivers.

Pusan was never bombed. Some kids go to school, walking in 2's and 3's with small cases on their backs. I am used to seeing oriental features now, and the faces of these children are familiar. Men and women in western and native clothes walk about doing their business. There are many small shops. Were it not for the poverty and filth, it might look like any city. Except—interspersed amongst the "normalcy" of the city, and indeed almost crowding it out, are the refugees and orphans. Beggars and invalids sit and stand on corners, in alleys, usually in the sun (much the same as in the Bowery). Street vendors and pushcarts crowd the streets. There are hundreds of dirty children dressed in GI clothing and rags, noses running. (I have pictures of them.) Children of all ages approach me—"Shine Lt"—running alongside, looking hungrily at my warm clothes and gloves. I try to be hard-hearted and stern-faced. I glower to keep them away, but still more come and I want to stop and give them something to eat, but I can do nothing. (Later on in my story, you will see I couldn't help myself.) Want woman Lt. Nice clean. No whore house. (These kids are from 8–12.) Me pimpo Lt. Nice girl. Blow job Lt. Me show you town Lt. And on and on.

I walked down to the telephone exchange. The small anteroom was full. I got my call slip in and waited. A few calls went through, then the circuit broke. This went on through the day. I finally gave up and started back.

The hospital club has two pianos. I sat down at one and played what little my fingers could remember. Two Korean waitresses (14–16 years old) stood on the side watching and when I ran out of music, one of them brought me one of her books, short rondos of beginning piano music with instructions in Korean. I played some for her and then after much persuasion she played, quite nicely. After what I had seen during the day, it made me feel good. Don Oken and I played ping pong as we talked of the past, present, and future, and of his work. Pure psychiatry. He works with another officer. Don has had very little practical training—mainly psychosomatics—and this other fellow even less. It probably doesn't make much difference as no real psychotherapy can be done in the short time they have. The equivalent qualification in a surgeon would be disastrous. Don himself realizes the lack, but does the best he can.

It got very cold Mon night, and the water pipes froze at the hospital (real civilization—hot and cold running water and sinks).

I floated out of the telephone exchange, still hearing your voice. Wandered around taking pictures. Had a hamburger at the RTO (Railway Transportation Office) and a milkshake, a rarity in Korea. As I stood at this snack bar and ate, I looked across the street at two Korean shoe shine boys watching. I guess I felt guilty, because after I finished I bought two more hamburgers for them, brushing off their offers of "shoe shine for Lt, presento." I don't like the cities. I am too chicken-hearted to see these kids roaming the streets, huddling together for warmth. Two waifs came into the telephone exchange, 6 or 7 yrs old, one leading the other. They came close to the barely warm stove, noses dripping. One told the other to wipe his nose and took off his gloves and put his hands against the stove, as dirty as could be, shaven head to minimize the habitat of crawling creatures. $46 billion for war. How many stoves that could buy!

It was good to be back, away from the crowds, the dirt, the poverty. The snow-covered hills looked peaceful and clean. Here in the tent, the boys are talking, Rick cursing as usual, Art bitching and half-drunk, telling us about R & R, getting polluted and ending up with a Japanese prostitute, not having a guilty conscience because he was drunk.

I love you my darling. Your husband,   Melvin

FRIDAY, JANUARY 16, 1953, 10:45 A.M.

Good news! Today at Valley Stream there were 4 applicants for my job. We have been spreading the word—Adelphi, Teachers College, Columbia, etc. I am sure that this means they will hire somebody. Therefore, I shall be able to leave very soon. I began to tell some people who hadn't known. "Japan" was on my lips at every moment. Everyone shared my excitement, and telling them all seemed to bring us a few steps closer together.   D

FRIDAY, JANUARY 16, 1953, 8:30 P.M.

My Beloved—
   A story: The unit is short of anti-freeze. Ernie is the motor officer and also a pharmacist. So he went over to ordnance and spoke to someone. Heard he had sore feet. Came back, mixed up some god-awful concoction for his feet. In return got a 55 gal. drum of antifreeze—it was impossible to get it via normal requisition channels.

For the past 10 minutes a discussion has been going on, "How to end the war." "Use the atom bomb." I keep saying, War never solved a problem. The boys talk. Roosevelt sold us down the river. Democratic war, etc. I try to point out how in the 30's Hoover was blamed for the depression and now he is revered. They are just talking. I don't know the answer, but it isn't more killing.

I am depressed by the feelings of the people in the tent. I want you with me.   Melvin

SUNDAY, JANUARY 18, 1953, 2:00 A.M.

My darling—

Tonight we watched Sid Caesar. I literally held my sides laughing during his ridicule of national personalities and how the English and the French might do the play, "Zero Hour."

I had to fight with your Mom per usual to let me help with the dishes. She wanted to wait until I went home and then do them. She can't seem to accept the fact that it is pleasant for me to work with her in the kitchen and chat—like a daughter. I guess we'll come to it naturally eventually. Such troubles!

SUNDAY, JANUARY 18, 1953, 11:30 P.M.

My Darling—

The day is over and I am glad to see it end.

I had just finished reading your letters when the chopper came in and brought a young GI who had a grenade wound of his back and buttocks. He and another man had gone after a wounded soldier in no man's land. They saw 2 Chinese soldiers. This boy shot and killed one of them. The other threw a grenade, killed the fellow next to him, and wounded him. He said tonight, "Now I know what a chicken thief with a load of buckshot feels like." It took me several hours to clean him up. Lunch. Then a Korean soldier. One leg gone. An arm just about. Then some others. I don't even know what. One after the other. Finished off with an appendectomy. I still get a sense of accomplishment at doing a job well, but I am heartsick at it. I don't have the zest for it. I cannot shut my eyes to what is happening and look just at the job. These are people mangled and chewed up for naught. Oh hell, why burden you my love.

I am enclosing the withholding slip from the army. You should be getting one from New Haven. I made $40 a month for Jan. Feb. & March. Note that we are allowed $200 a month deduction from taxable income for each month in Korea—6 months, $1200 deduction. So all the army income we have to pay tax on is $637.93. But I leave it to you to figure out. If you want to, send a copy to me—for fun—but it isn't necessary. Most of my army salary is not taxable, or only half of it (base pay) and then with the $200 deduction we only pay tax on $159 a month or less. Money. Money. What does it mean——?

Gosh I'm tired—physically as well as spiritually. Before I sat down to write I made rounds and stood there on a quiet ward, surrounded by my day's work. Good night now. Sleep and dream well, Dorothy.

Melvin

MONDAY, JANUARY 19, 1953, 11:00 P.M.

My darling—

A fairly normal school day, except for the fact of my imminent departure hanging over me. Although they have many applicants, they don't know exactly when they want me to leave. I still haven't told the kids. I will really miss them more than anything. The contact with teenagers, stimulating their imagination, is what I really enjoy. But I shall have it again some day—with our own children—and in teaching, if we want it. Perhaps in Japan it will be possible to do some kind of teaching.

There was a meeting of language and grade school teachers about foreign language being introduced in the lower grades. I think it's wonderful. The younger a child is, the more quickly he picks up a language aurally. There won't be much writing—mostly conversation, culture, and games.

I look ahead. We're in our seventh month. Melvin, my beloved.

Dorothy

MONDAY, JANUARY 19, 1953, 11:30 P.M.

My Darling—

Well, I hope you realize that if you follow your husband's advice on income tax, you will save lots of money, but end up in jail. The W-2 withholding form I sent you last night already took into consideration the $1200 Korean tax deduction and the $1800 is the amount we have to pay tax on. Oh well, I tried. The govt isn't quite as stupid as I thought. I'm sure we would get away with it, but OK you win. We'll stay honest. After all, the govt is going broke anyhow.   M.

TUESDAY, JANUARY 20, 1953, 10:30 P.M.

My darling—

Taught three classes and then went to Clara's [a social science teacher at Valley Stream] home for lunch and to watch the inauguration. Truman looked good and marched with real dignity and a broad smile. I felt sorry for him because he has given so much of himself and taken such abuse. Eisenhower made a good speech. When he appeared on the screen, I cried and was embarrassed (because I cried). When Rabbi Silver delivered an eloquent prayer, Eisenhower also wiped away a tear. How hard we have to work to keep a genuine democracy going. For the first time, I feared personally what might happen if we didn't. Ike has so many who are depending on him. How much it means to us to have a sincere group of individuals in government trying to avoid war. I'm afraid to look in the newspapers. From day to day, there is always some new horror exposed.

How I long to be near you, to put my arms around you, to wipe away the memories of your work day. I am your wife. I love you.

Dorothy

WEDNESDAY, JANUARY 21, 1953, 1:00 P.M.

My Love,

You ask why the Koreans have more casualties than the GI's. For one thing, they are not as well-trained and do not have as many good officers, even though there are U.S. military advisers with the small units as well. They stick their heads up when they should be in a hole. They often do not wear their helmets because they find them uncomfortable, so their incidence of serious head injuries is high. They do not have the armored vests the GI's wear because there are not enough of them in Korea yet. This increases the number of serious chest and abdominal wounds. Lastly, they go in for more hand-to-hand combat. The GI prefers to let the armor (tanks, artillery, and planes) do most of the fighting and exposes himself only when necessary.

Tonight I'm jealous of Ed Svetke and at the same time happy for him. His replacement arrived and he will be leaving about the 1st of Feb. I'll ask him to call you when he gets to N.Y.

The anesthetist and surgeon who came are both Jewish. ½ the doctors here now are Jewish. They brought good news about replacements. The only disquieting rumor again was that there may be an invasion. If so, this MASH would follow it. Oh boy.

Our proposed name change has nothing to do with the invasion. Apparently, Gen. Guinn doesn't like the name MASH and is changing it to "Army Surgical Hospitals" with a sub-designation "Mobile."

Heard a re-broadcast of the inauguration ceremonies. Ike's speech was good, but every so often I heard a General speaking, although you couldn't argue with anything he said. Listening to the ceremonies brought a lump to my throat. Your husband is a sentimentalist—the idea of the people inaugurating one man to lead them, to represent them.

Goodnight, my love. Seeing the new doctors made me realize that the months have passed. Your husband,   Melvin

FRIDAY, JANUARY 23, 1953, 11:50 P.M.

My Darling Wife—

After the movie, the officers were invited to a pizza party by some of the EM. We contributed anchovies and cheese and brought the beer and cokes, and they made the stuff. It was fun to sit and eat, drink a beer and listen to music from an accordian. We sang songs, laughed and joked. Yet I felt hollow, with a frightening detachment from what was going on around me. Singing and beer—almost as though I was in college. What is this? I am not happy. The music makes me sad. I finally got up and walked out into the crystal clear night, having thanked everyone and said goodnight. The cold air was refreshing. I felt close to you under the stars. Behind me were 20 men sitting and singing and laughing. Over the hills there were 20 more men and 20 more and 20 more who were perhaps wondering if they would be alive, or in one piece, in the morning.

Where are you now, my beloved? Standing in front of a class of children? Do they know as they look at you that we are far from them? Or are you reading this in the living room at 96 Street, shoes off, feet curled under you. This letter in your hands as I try to project myself 9,000 miles, out from this paper, to express my love for you, to make you feel my arms around you, my lips close to your ear telling you that Dorothy is beautiful, she is soft and sweet, she tastes good, smells good. This is my wife, the person I wish to share my life with, the woman I love.

Took a flu shot today. Given to individuals, shots are not known to be too effective, but in large groups like the army, in the presence of an epidemic, they may do some good. Take care of yourself. I do hope you have V.S. all straightened out.

Goodnight Dorothy.   Melvin

SATURDAY, JANUARY 24, 1953, 11:45 P.M.

My darling—

I left the house at noon today in a teeming rain. I was to meet Joyce [Levy, my friend since junior high school] at Daniel's, a French restaurant on Madison. Found a parking space, but had to wait for 4 traffic lights worth of traffic to pass before I could pull in. After a delicious lunch of cream of water cress (le potage du jour), cheese souffle (first I have ever had), tossed salad, chocolate mousse (more like chocolate pudding) and coffee, we sat and chatted, then took a cab to the Little Carnegie. We saw a new French film, "Forbidden Games," a World War II story of a Parisian orphan and her peasant boy friend. Their "forbidden game" is playing cemetery, killing little animals, stealing crosses, and making their own graveyard. The pathos lies in the motivation of the game and the helplessness of the children. The two little ones are excellent actors. The movie is so natural—something which an American film just can't seem to equal. I was able to understand the French with little reference to the English titles. You will have to work on your French to increase your enjoyment of French films! It was a beautiful film, so sad, so human.

How much a part of you I am. I was searching and you were searching. Then we walked together, waltzed together, talked together. We came to know each other in all ways. Now, every once in a while, I stand up straight, my body taut. I smile and think, I love and I am loved. I can't imagine you having your arms around me only to release me. How will we eat? How will we sleep? You will be beside me tonight and tomorrow night and each morning when I wake up. Then, one day, it will be real again. Goodnight, my beloved.   Dorothy

MONDAY, JANUARY 26, 1953, 8:15 P.M.

My darling—

My ninth graders presented me with a lovely compact, my initials engraved on one side and "9A9" on the other. I was really touched and didn't know what to say. Part of the thrill was seeing "DH" on the compact. I've never before had anything with those initials engraved on it. I didn't tell them that.

In honor of my leaving, the 6 members of the foreign language department went to Helen's for cocktails. She had given me a book of Japanese prints. I gorged myself on cheese and olives, to the tune of 2 Manhattans, then cookies and coffee, which was a good ending since we were all driving. Gladys performed and was really funny, miming gestures and facial expressions to records of Betty Hutton and Beatrice Kay. When we broke up, I was sorry to leave.

Your detailed letter on the generals was enlightening. I could just feel you getting all the venom out of your system. Bitch away! my love. I liked your line letting me know that you were writing from a "prejudiced viewpoint." Why shouldn't we be prejudiced? War is not our business—they are primed for it. That story about your insignia made me laugh and want to kiss your neck right above the damned insignia. See? Ft. Sam was not worthwhile. You didn't learn your lessons!

There is still more to say, but I shall close now as it is getting late and I ache—but mostly for you.   Dorothy

WEDNESDAY, JANUARY 28, 1953, 11:00 P.M.

My Beloved—

The wind is howling and blowing the snow which fell today into a blizzard. I am sitting at my bedside in pajamas and am very tired. I went to sleep from 3–5 P.M. Supper, and then a batch of patients came in. Again I lose myself in the problem at hand, but in the last 3 days I alone have done 6 amputations, among other things, one after the other, washing my hands time after time, putting gloves on and working. XRays, blood flowing into veins. On one patient we used over $500 worth of blood. (The army pays close to $10 a pint and add to that the cost of transportation.) Our ward has been full every night and we send almost everyone out in the morning. Finally got into bed last night and was awakened a few hours later—to amputate another leg on a young Korean soldier. To look at his face tonight as we made rounds, and he was examining the XRays that had been placed at the foot of his bed. With the aid of a Korean interpreter, I tried to explain to him what we had done and why. I had just finished the case—had breakfast and walked through the snow to the latrine—when in the space of 15 minutes, 5 helicopters arrived, churning up the snow as they came. This time they were GI's—and they were sick. Abdominal cases, fractures, chest, neck wounds. One patient with a wound from a missile that entered on the left side of the bridge of his nose, exiting on the right side of his neck—practically through his head.

By 5 o'clock when I finished I was tired, very tired. Tonight I saw Mario Lanza in "Because You're Mine." A silly story but the music and singing were beautiful. Then I came back to the tent, turned up the stoves and took a bath, after 3 days. The Korean soldiers had come in crawling with animals. You should see the spray and powder fly. I'm physically and emotionally fatigued. I hope I can sleep tonight.

My wife, what life is this, so far from each other. Your husband,
Melvin

JANUARY 31

As of tomorrow the name of the hospital will be 47th MASH. The address is the same.

February

In Korea, the United States remained the "unofficial agent" of the United Nations. Russia, claiming neutrality, provided the North Korean Communists with most of their military equipment, while the Chinese supplied them with "volunteers." As negotiations dragged on, Mel's M.A.S.H. was finally assigned nurses. The attempt to run a mobile hospital without them proved to be unsuccessful, and the strategic maneuvers that instigated the experiment never happened. As far as Mel knew, the plans were canceled. For reasons that no one seemed to understand, the name of this unit was changed to the 47th M.A.S.H.

Hospitalized with a painful, infected finger, Mel was temporarily unable to work. Although he tried to underplay his concern, I knew that he was worried about the infection spreading. His letters took on a new complexion. Along with descriptions of his discomfort in the role of patient, came directives for me to take the necessary shots and to make inquiries about air travel to Japan.

SUNDAY, FEBRUARY 1, 1953, 11:50 P.M.

My Love—

We have a lot of sick patients. Now it shows how much we need nurses. The corpsmen just can't give the same care. We told the Col, as we have in the past, and of course not much will be done. It's not his fault as 8th Army insists on our working this way. We have been lucky and not had any dangerous accidents, but we have to put in much time on the wards supervising, where we wouldn't have to if we had the nurses. I feel sorry for the one nurse in charge of the ward. She tries.

Just about lunch time a chopper came in with a Negro soldier who had more bullet holes in him (from a rifle) than I've ever seen. We only knew part of the story. That he had been drinking was obvious. Apparently he got into an argument and someone shot him. This was not a battle casualty. He had holes in his chest, abdomen, hip, and arm, and a fractured leg. We gave him several pints of blood and took him right into the operating room where I spent the next 5 hours patching him up. He received, in all, 23 pints of blood. That is replacing his blood volume twice over. Surprisingly he survived.

Goodnight my sweet. Sleep and dream well.   Melvin

SUNDAY, FEBRUARY 1, 1953, 12:30 A.M.

My darling—

By the time you receive this letter almost seven months will have passed since we last reached out and found each other in the darkness. I remember clearly that last night at the Chancellor, you so close, neither of us able to imagine the nights ahead. I held you and couldn't believe that you would not be there beside me the next night.

10:20 P.M.

I have been forcing myself to read that Spanish novel. It gets a little easier as I go along. I'm anxious to get on to something else, but I have vowed that I will not give it up this time.   D

FEBRUARY 4, 1953, 11:50 A.M.

My Love—

The Negro fellow I had done wasn't doing too well. Got up and went over to see for myself. I had put in too much work to let him die. Well, I sat and did the equivalent of special nursing for 3 hours. Went over his record carefully trying to decide what would help as he lay there almost dead. With a lot of luck and some good decisions, by 7 A.M. he was in fair condition. I ordered a helicopter to take him to the hospital that has the artificial kidney and the laboratory to do the studies needed. Had breakfast, did 3 cases when one more came in. It was just the beginning. This was a seriously wounded GI with his shoulder blown open and chest and abdominal wounds. While I was working on him, the patients started arriving. They had a big fight north of us and in the space of several hours we received 60–80 patients. We only kept the serious ones and sent the others who could wait further south for their surgery. At that, we worked steadily until 11 P.M. doing 26 major operative cases in that time.

I stuck my finger with a needle while working on a dirty case yesterday. There is an early infection which I am trying to prevent becoming anything worse.

11:45 P.M.

Yesterday is a bad memory of case after case, being exhausted, knowing I wasn't working efficiently, finally making rounds at midnight on a full ward sending out those who could go, then collapsing into bed.

My finger is bothering me, but this afternoon I worked on some patients who needed attention. The finger is still infected, but is coming to a head and will open and be OK, perhaps by morning.

Since the ROK's have gone on the line, our casualty rate has been higher and we've been one of the busiest MASHes in Korea. It has been shown that our corpsmen cannot take care of the pts properly in post-op. We've had a series of unfortunate incidents because of their lack of training.

Sleep well. Our day is coming.   Melvin

WEDNESDAY, FEBRUARY 4, 1953, 9:30 P.M.

My love—

In tonight's news broadcast there was mention of a Chinese proposal for an immediate cease fire and then negotiation of the prisoner issue. I realized how foolish it was to even hope. And yet, WHY? Why won't we accept a cease fire and negotiations? What are we gaining? It seems to be an endless futile battle. Now it looks even worse. Will the Eisenhower administration buck the world and allow the war to spread by backing Chiang? We have a general in the White House. In yesterday's attack the radio said that the Chinese pushed up to within hand grenade throwing distance from the emplacement. I thought about some of the boys from San Antonio at the Aid Stations and again, I was thankful. As you so colorfully put it, I want your "ass to be in one piece"!

I'm looking forward to your R & R in Japan, first of all because we will have more definite news about the transfer, I hope. And then, it will be a good change for you. If there were no possibility of a transfer, I would meet you in Japan. Yet, if you couldn't get to Japan and would have to spend 40 pts. worth in Korea, perhaps I could get a job there. They do have some civilian employees. I hope and pray that we will be together soon—no matter how! I love you Melvin.   Dorothy

THURSDAY, FEBRUARY 5, 1953, 8:00 P.M.

My Love, My Wife—

I've just finished soaking my finger. It really was a walloping good infection. It shows what trouble you can get into. Working so rapidly and being tired I guess I wasn't on the ball. Well a tiny puncture wound, in 12 hours, was red and angry and I had a streak of inflammation up my arm to the elbow. I put my arm in a sling to rest it, got a tetanus shot and started taking Terramycin. I've been soaking it regularly and had a tiny abscess opened by Arne. Now much of the redness and soreness is gone.

The hospital hasn't been busy at all Wed & Thurs, but it is talked about all over Korea, how we worked on Tues. I have never been as tired in my whole life. Previously, (in civilian medicine) when I've been tired I never had major responsibility for the patient.

At the meeting, we all told the Col., in turn, that the patients were being endangered by lack of good nursing care. We wanted it a matter of record that we felt the lack and were asking for more and better nursing, just in case any question arose later. The Col was in trouble because we had case after case to show him. Since he feels (unconsciously, maybe) that his army career depends on the success of this venture, he just dodges us at every turn.

Map reading—a joke—I guessed well and got an excellent. The journal club has fallen by the wayside. No one is really interested, so I shall not keep trying. I'll just do my own reading.

Irv Graham got a salami from home. I suspect the Jews have even invaded North Carolina. Wonder if Southern style kosher salami tastes any different! As for me I don't need any food. There is plenty around and I'm still trying to lose weight.

My lips on yours say goodnight. Know and feel my love for you which bridges the thousands of miles between us. Your husband,   Melvin

SATURDAY, FEBRUARY 7, 1953, 11:00 P.M.

My darling—

Up at 8:15 and left in nasty rain for Juilliard. It felt good to wake up
my body out of all its aches and stiffness, but the class was just fair. A
new instructor tried to cram in too much and didn't know how to analyze movement. Home at 11:20, munched on some bread, cheese and a
peach and was on my way to Brooklyn, your letter in my pocketbook.

Parked near the folks' apartment house, opened my pocketbook,
and took out the airmail envelope. In the cozy confines of the car, with
the trees of Brooklyn College as a backdrop, the soft patter of rain on
the windshield, I read your words of love. When I finally got upstairs, I
wondered if the folks could see the glow as I casually mentioned that
there had been a letter from you.

We watched Columbia slaughter Army in basketball. Then put on
the opera (Cosi fan tutti in English) and chatted. We always seem to
find interesting things to talk about—you, religion, politics, families,
you.

I picked up Mom, and we came into the city to meet Bert. Since he
was taking the car tonight, I suggested he meet us for dinner at Peach-
tree. It was good to have a man with us.

Mom and I saw an English comedy, "Curtain Up," about a play in
rehearsal and the trials and tribulations of a zany director and zanier
lady author. We had a few belly laughs.

The letter I have in front of me was written just last Saturday night.
How close—how far. Your dream of love is so real that my breath
comes shorter and my insides tighten. I love you so. Goodnight my
man,   Dorothy

SATURDAY, FEBRUARY 7, 1953, 8:00 P.M.

Dorothy My Love—

Ed Svetke received the Bronze Star for his action as a Battalion Surgeon with a tank outfit. While not detracting one bit from the decora-
tion, the Bronze Star in many instances is known to be an officer's
Good Conduct Medal and officers have been known to get it merely for
doing their job well in rear units. However, Ed did do something to de-
serve it in his action supporting the tank outfit and I am glad to see
him get it. In addition he had just qualified for his captaincy (after 20

mos of service—you now need 24). He is leaving for home on Tuesday. The ceremony was brief and I got some good pictures. After that I bundled up in my parka and started out for the airport.

As we came over the crest of the hill and could see the airstrip, there was a band lined up—a chrome helmeted honor guard, and MP's galore. While I love my wife very much, don't smoke, drink moderately, and try to do my job, I really didn't think they had to go to so much trouble to see me off on this trip to Seoul. However when I arrived, much to my amazement, no one snapped to attention, the band remained quiet and the MP merely asked, "What is your business here?" After giving him a suitable reply, "I'm supposed to leave on the 2 o'clock courier," in my best Walter Mitty fashion, I quelled him with a look! I entered operations hut, found it filled with generals, colonels, and majors, and in one corner the operations officer, fuming because he had been pushed out of his office by the brass. From him I learned two things. One, that the flights had been canceled—the winds were too gusty. And two, this fanfare was for Genls Van Fleet and Taylor. So I called, had a jeep sent for me, and while I waited, the Genls arrived and I got some pictures that should show you the glitter of the show.

I'm back here and will try to leave tomorrow morning. My finger is OK except a little stiff and I would not work anyhow until it is in A-1 shape, as I do not want to risk stirring up the infection.

Dorothy, I can feel you so close to me. Your husband   Melvin

TUESDAY, FEBRUARY 10, 1953, 10:30 P.M.

My beloved—

The time is growing nearer and your letters are so optimistic. Both of us know what the Army is and anything "unexpected" will not be unexpected. In the meantime it's fun to plan, look ahead, and take every possible step.

Had a 12:45 class taught by Yuriko, the Japanese girl who did the solo dance in "The King and I." She has a persuasive yet humorous way of putting things across. Have another minor floor burn on my foot. When I got home, Mom had dinner waiting. I have really been eating— I guess because of all the energy I burn up. After dinner and dishes, I read the paper, called your Mom, and took a shower. Showers take longer now because it takes me 10 minutes to scrub my feet. I'll have to start using brillo.

Another cold, windy day. As I left school and walked to the bus on Riverside Drive the sun had set and the sky was a deep orange across the river. The lights of New Jersey and downtown Manhattan twinkled in the coming darkness. The bus was a long time in coming. By the time I walked towards 9 E., the stars were shining brightly. It is a night for us. We should be standing out in the cold, arms around each other, the wind whipping about us, feeling as one with the universe. Goodnight my beloved. I give all of myself to you, holding back nothing. To have you receive my love and to know that with equal intensity I am loved, that is to live life to the fullest.   Dorothy

WEDNESDAY, FEBRUARY 11, 1953, 11:00 P.M.

My darling—

I can feel your aching finger throbbing until it opens. I hope that the work has eased up and you have had a chance to get the rest that you need so badly. Oh my love, stay well. I know you do what you have to do and I wouldn't want it any other way. Get all the sleep you can. Forget about the books for a while. Take care of your own body while you are taking care of others.

Goodnight my beloved. Sleep well. Dream of the together days ahead for us.   Dorothy

THURSDAY, FEBRUARY 12, 1953, 10:00 P.M.

My darling—

Today is Lincoln's birthday. How much time have you had to think about it? I am stirred by his words—hearing them on the radio repeated by Carl Sandburg, seeing them in the paper and recalling how absorbed I was reading Sandburg's first volume, *The Prairie Years.* I would like to read the other two. It takes a poet to do justice to his life. From what I know of George Washington, the only aspects of his personality which come to mind are his determination and his dignity. He was not a "man of the people" as was Lincoln. Lincoln's words have so much meaning today. I remember when Dad was in the hospital, Sandburg was the only book I had the patience to read, that and *The Roosevelt Story.* Reading about men's lives and being convinced, in this sad world, that they are capable of good and great things is what makes biographies appealing to me. Oh yes, I'm still finishing my Spanish novel. I don't like the story, but I derive satisfaction when I can read a few pages without having to stop to translate individual phrases.

I do like the creative aspect of my dance composition course and feel that it will help if I ever do any teaching. Mom is still shrugging her shoulders, but she does accept it. Otherwise we couldn't get along. I've already had 2 composition courses and more dance experience since then. More important, I have matured emotionally since we have known each other. I have lost almost all self-consciousness about my body and am able to feel more deeply whatever I am trying to dance. You have made me (not by trying, but through your love) accept what is me. I dance what is me. Goodnight my darling.   Dorothy

FEBRUARY 13

I was interested to read in one of your last letters of a Chinese proposal for a cease fire. Not a word of that appeared in our newspapers here in Korea. I do not know what the answer is, but Ike seems to be short-sighted and merely following the Republican line—abandoning wage price controls, etc. A General in the White House may I am afraid rely on the business men to advise him on civilian problems and then go ahead and solve the international situation as a military man.

You ask about Doug Lindsey. He has been regular army for quite a while, even while he was at New Haven Hospital. His ambition is to be Surgeon General (an administrative post). He finished his surgical training, got his Boards, and has probably not done a case since. At present he is Chief of Medical Operations in Korea, which means, under Genl Guinn, he directs the operation of all medical units.   M

FEBRUARY 13

I filled in the Passport Renewal slip, got marriage certificate out and ready to go with me on Monday to the Bureau. I dread the place. It is always bedlam and the clerks are so rude, even on the phone.   D

FEBRUARY 14, 1953, 9:30 A.M.

My Darling—
One of the fellows here has a tape recorder and while in Seoul I bought some tapes for him and me. Since I may not get to call you for

several weeks, I shall record a few and hope you can find someone with a Revere Tape Recorder so you can listen to them. If not, then go into a dealer and use one of theirs, as the Revere people advertise that they will allow you to. I shall be discrete since you may have to listen to it with people around, but not that discrete that I won't say I love you. These recorders are interesting and have possibilities. I wish I had known of them sooner, then I could have sent you tapes. You can re-record right on the small reel I send.

As to the car, there are several possibilities. One is to drive it to Frisco and have it sent overseas to me in Japan as soon as I get located. The other is to sell it or give it to my folks and buy a car in Japan if we have to. Don't know about parts and repairs in Japan, but they have lots of cars there.

I love you, Dorothy. Your husband,   Melvin

P.S. Copies of orders may take a few days, so if necessary get them made at Army Hq when you bring in the forms.

Enclosed are immunization forms. Ask, when you go for shots, if they have special forms available there for army dependents. Have whatever forms you use filled out in duplicate.   M.

SUNDAY, FEBRUARY 15, 1953, 1:15 A.M.

My darling—

Valentine's Day. The corsage of roses. "To my wife. To my Valentine." I pinned them to my coat and all day their fragrance reminded me that you love me.

Watched the first 15 minutes of a ballet class given by Antony Tudor. He spoke in a clipped British accent and always with a twinkle in his eyes. One of the girls had come in late. "Karen," he said, "it's bad enough to miss the first stretches, but to come to class without lipstick? unforgivable!" So she put some on. I figured I had had my money's worth and left.

Today, I saw children, American children, playing in Central Park—carefree, gay, well-fed. Whenever I see groups of young children now, I think of Korean children.

Mom said, "I don't like the spring." I skipped over the remark and tried to cheer her up. I wonder how long it will be before she likes the spring again.

There is talk of extending the draft time from 2–3 years.

Deposited by mail in Savings Bank $2 dividend check from Barbizon and $26.65 from Valley Stream for two days' work. Mom gave me $40 net for my week's work. I returned $15 figuring I wasn't worth more than $2 per hr. for the work I was doing.

[Cousin] Clara Gluck called and said her nephew, Bob Schwartz, was now in a training area near the front in Korea. They had heard from him regularly until last Tuesday. The only good word I could give her was that I hadn't heard from you either during the past few days. Oh my love, my love. There will be a letter from you on Monday, and, if not, then on Tuesday. Thank god you are not at the front. He's a youngster, barely 20—Gerry's and Bert's age.

Spent a pleasant afternoon with the folks, talking and watching an excellent new television show, "Omnibus." It included a documentary film on the growth of wheat, a dramatization of Saroyan's "The Oyster and the Pearl," and a presentation of Cellini's gold work by a curator from the Metrop. Museum. An unusual program!   D.

MONDAY, FEBRUARY 16, 1953, 11:45 P.M.

Hello My Love—

Awoke this morning to find a fellow by the name of Don Stewart in the tent. He is a 3100 MD from Divisions down for 2 days to watch us work. Again I felt like a senior with a freshman. He was eager to see and learn and do. Made rounds with him and then as cases came through, let him help. He started one case, but unfortunately ran into some troublesome bleeding and the patient being my responsibility, I took over. We shall be getting 2 of those fellows a week, for 2 days at a time.

Rick finally left and in spite of feelings I've had, I felt sorry to see him go. Basically I like him. It was just his ideas on many things—his standards differ from mine. It wasn't long afterwards that Elliot Jacobson, the anesthetist, moved in. He is pleasant, from Brooklyn, obviously a New Yorker by mannerism and speech.

I did an interesting face case this morning, but even so I am tired of this. I just don't want to see any more of these young men coming in clobbered up. I work, but my heart is not in it, except to try and give some semblance of normality back to the lives I take in my hands. The tears I shed (inwardly, always) are bitter, and my heart grows so cold at the sight of the destruction, or as I take an arm or leg off, that I have to stop and say to myself, I love, I am loved. This is madness, but I know where truth and happiness are.

I long for you my love. Sleep and dream of tomorrow, for it won't be too many tomorrows before it will be today, for us.   Melvin

Went to the Passport Agency at Rockefeller Center and got a new application. I can no longer renew my passport since it expires after 2 yrs. Had passport photos taken. I shall await word from you about shots. Will call Army Hq tomorrow to find out about storing our stuff. It will probably be easier that way, then the Army will transport it for us when we get back to the States and settle. Mom could use the room.
D.

TUESDAY, FEBRUARY 17, 1953, 7:00 P.M.

My Love—
Korea is called "the land of the morning calm," I think not because it is so calm in the morning, but because it is so windy in the afternoon.

Started *Yankee From Olympus,* which I'm enjoying very much. It is stimulating to read of these men, thinking, writing, searching for new ideas, and communicating them. I haven't been able to read anything requiring any concentration these last few weeks. Yet as I read today, my imagination was fired and I read voraciously, devouring each page.

I have always had the desire to be creative, but I don't think I have a creative mind. I can "do" but I can't create. I try therefore to "do" the best I can.

11:30 P.M.

If you have never read *Yankee From Olympus,* I recommend it. There is so much history and insight in it.

"If there is any principle of the Constitution that more imperatively calls for attachment than any other, it is the principle of free thought— not just thought for those who agree with us but freedom for the thought that we hate.

"The ultimate good desired is better reached by free trade in ideas . . . the best of truth is the power of the thought to get itself accepted in the competition of the market."

These ideas he expressed 20 years ago. Too bad that they cannot be considered today when freedom of thought and expression are in such danger.

At every page I wanted to talk to you, share my thoughts and listen to yours. One thing emphasized was the necessity to be oneself, to express individuality—to work at what one feels one will be happiest. Our love helps me to be me. I know you accept me—good and bad. I am a better person because of it.   Melvin

TUESDAY, FEBRUARY 17, 1953, 11:30 P.M.

My beloved—

Met Desh Sikh for dinner at International House, where we ate in the cafeteria with some of his Indian friends. Among other things, Desh is now working for the Indian Delegation at the UN. I asked him what the general reaction to the new administration's policies is. He said, "At the Delegation it is said that all the errors Truman made in 8 years, were made in the first 5 days of Eisenhower's administration." He went on to criticize dollar diplomacy and said that one must look beneath people's skins to understand them, that the American Government does not seem to care about understanding people of other countries. Unfortunately, I had to agree.   D

WEDNESDAY, FEBRUARY 18, 1953, 10:30 P.M.

My Love—

Another good omen—points are back to 36 and we are finally getting some nurses. That they have been assigned here means that this unit will not be moving as part of an amphibious landing, at least not in the near future. Everything should stay quiet until my transfer goes through. I hope so, my love, I hope so. The possibility of R & R is also coming up sometime in March, and that too would enable me to pave the way for the transfer.

And thus a day ends. One more to be counted off. Goodnight. I love you   Melvin

My darling—

How quickly one adapts to a new routine. Valley Stream seems far away and I have no regrets. My uneven schedule makes the time less ponderous than when I had each semester broken down into marking periods, each m.p. into weeks, each week into 5 days and weekend, each day into periods, each period planned, etc.

Whatever I do, the only activity which will give me a real sense of living will be when I step onto that plane in San Francisco and off it in Tokyo.

Although I do enjoy the Composition class, it is disappointing because much of the material is a repetition of what I learned in Colorado with Hanya Holm. The teacher, Eve Gentry, is a former Holm student.

Goodnight my love. I want you so much. Your wife,   Dorothy

My Darling—

Another day without mail. I hope you've been getting my letters regularly. Elwin is lying on his bunk, tired, smoking a cigar. Art is talking to him, drinking as usual. Ernie is sitting behind me reading a pocket book with a lurid picture on the cover, advertised as "How girls live in Wash. D.C. and fight for their men—an ADULT story!" I won't kid him about the book. If I run out of mystery stories, I'll probably be reading it.

I want to be next to you. As tired as I am, I want the soothing gentleness of your touch to spark my restlessness into passion. Soon. Soon.

Awoke at 7:30 and went over to the hospital without shaving. The helicopters were coming in one after another. I've been working all day with barely a stop. We got a fair number of GI casualties, the first in a long time. I'm sure the report in the newspapers will be "light patrol action in the Punch Bowl area!" but 24 men are lying in the hospital because of it. When will we learn that war is not the answer? I do not say that we should not fight aggression, but is that what we are doing here? Are we gaining anything? Have we exhausted every other possibility? God I hate this business. Destruction. Waste of men, lives, money, time. I hate to work in a rubber apron as blood and dirt spills over me. The difficult cases are a challenge and because of that I cannot say I do not enjoy the work. Now, I'm ready to quit for a while. To do nothing or to practice simple dispensary medicine and devote all my thoughts to you. Hold me close, my love. I never want to let you go.

A good omen. We got a radiologist and another surgeon today. Now we are overstrength in doctors. I hope that will allow me to get out of here earlier. My schedule is to apply March 15 and leave, if they let me, on April 15. I will only have 18 points, but we shall see.

My body is tired. I'll lie down and relax for a while. I'm not really hungry, but I feel like noshing. You know that feeling. Goodnight my dearest. Your husband,   Melvin

SUNDAY, FEBRUARY 22, 1953, 7:00 P.M.

My Dearest—

We are being assigned 5 nurses. The experiment is over. They have decided they cannot run a MASH without trained personnel. A 40-yr-old anesthetist arrived today from the 8055. Another problem has come up. The Korean army wants to draft all our interpreters. One of the officers had to go to Wonju to arrange to keep some of them until we get replacements. I avoided that trip but did get roped into a medical meeting at the Division Clearing Co. about 5 miles north of us. It is hard for me to realize that for the first time I, as a doctor, am in a position of having more experience than most of the doctors around me. It is fun in a way. I like to talk and I did today on some of the questions raised.

One thing of interest I learned, tragic in a way. The Koreans, as I've written, who come into this hospital look emaciated and starved. The daily rations given them by their army are the equivalent of 6 bowlfuls of rice, uncooked. In addition each Division has a sum of money to buy extras such as fish and spices. Well, the new divisions have little money, so the only thing the men can eat is rice. That is a terrific amount of rice when cooked and swollen and is like subsisting on bread alone. No wonder they are scarecrows. The 12th Division, the one ahead of us, had only enough money last month to buy one radish per man PER MONTH. The Korean doctor telling us this was bitter at his govt. which he intimated is very crooked and diverts the money. Good old Syngman Rhee—another one like Chiang Kai Shek.

No mail except for letter 214 which had been missent somewhere. The mail is really fouled up, but we should be able to get some since we now know where it is going. It means sending a truck 40 miles every day to get it.

Wish I wasn't so tired.

Enclosed two slides of me with the new lens. Golly, I really have taken a lot, but they are for you, for us. We needn't bore our friends with them.   Melvin

MONDAY, FEBRUARY 23, 1953, 11:30 P.M.

My darling—

We may surely speak in terms of weeks now rather than months. I hope nothing happens to upset the plans. Every day is colored by the thought of spring. By the time you receive this letter, it will almost be time to send in your application for transfer.

Gladys, Helen, and Clara came for lunch. Then we went to see "John Brown's Body," a reading by Tyrone Power, Judith Anderson, and Raymond Massey, with chorus. It was a moving performance. War was horrible then too and Stephen Vincent Benet says it powerfully. For me, the wounded were the wounded in Korea. Man recognizes the futility of war, but when will he learn?

According to the papers, the action has not been heavy during these few days. That means that you've been able to get some sleep. I'm always thankful for that and for the misery which is avoided.

Goodnight my darling. Tomorrow is a work day and a mail day.

Dorothy

TUESDAY, FEBRUARY 24, 1953, 2:00 A.M.

My Darling—

Syngman Rhee has instituted a monetary reform destined to ruin and impoverish most Koreans. They are allowed to draw only $10 worth (of the new Korean currency). The rest remains as a deposit in a bank and can only be withdrawn if the person can show dire need or for business where bank drafts are used. Many of the banks will not exchange the money and hence the people suffer. Rhee is a tyrant and as fascistic as Chiang. You can imagine how the Koreans working here feel. Enclosed are samples of the new Korean money (worth about 16 cents), the MPC (Military Payment Certificates—scrip), and some Japanese yen.   M

My darling—

Mom and I worked on figures all morning to get things straightened out for the yearly Maiden Form report.

Had a good class with Bob Cohan. I could tell by the way he criticized me he didn't think I was completely hopeless. Later a rip-roaring session with Nona Shurman. She is lively and we move around a lot in her class. When we improvise, we have to have an image in mind so that our movements come more naturally. When we danced "tenderness," my image was you, stretched out naked on our bed in New Haven. You are limp from exhaustion. She said that my feeling of tenderness came across. I didn't tell her why!

The class ran overtime and I didn't get home until 10:40. Made myself an ice cream soda, glanced through the *Post,* now I'm ready for a good hot shower and bed.

Will you get a medal for all the warts you remove at the 47th?

It's exciting to read about the Colonel getting things moving for your transfer. Okinawa or Japan—wherever it will be, 2 things should be considered in the following order: Where will you be surer of getting to? Where will you be able to do surgery? It's a gamble in either case, but we can just do as much as possible and then hope.

Sleep well, my husband.   Dorothy

My Darling—

It is a spring-like afternoon. I miss you at this moment more than ever. The only way I can relax is to write to you. To think that it is possible to be with you in a few weeks or perhaps just a month or two is unbelievable. All I can think about is you and you.

Woman of mine! Your mother writes that you are skinny, only 114 lbs. If you feel well and eat plenty, then I won't worry, but make sure to eat!

That Negro soldier I wrote about with all the bullet holes in him died about 4 days later, even with the artificial kidney. Well, I tried.

There are a lot of brush fires around. The ground and shrubbery is dry and the air filled with smoke haze.

Had a haircut and look as though he took a bowl and used it to cut around my head, just missing my ears.

As to the money, I still get $100 a month and will keep the $350 going to you until you get over here—OK?

I love you my wife. Spring is on its way.   Melvin

THURSDAY, FEBRUARY 26, 1953, AFTER MIDNIGHT

My darling—

My knees are black and blue and red. The red usually turns to blue the second day, black the third, an ugly brown color, and then disappears. Is that all right, Dr. my love? Mom is worried because I'm hitting the same spot. Actually, when I get to be a better dancer, I will be taking the weight in the rest of my body instead of on my knees—clunk!

Are you tired yet or shall we stay up a little longer—no? All right, then let us crawl in together, cuddle close and whisper about this evening—a few kisses and giggles and lots of grunts about the luxurious feeling of each other's bodies—too tired for love making tonight—more stretches and rubs, then relaxation in each other's arms—a last goodnight.   Dorothy

FEBRUARY 27

Had a snack—gefilte fish, chopped liver, apple pie with butter pecan ice cream and an egg cream [soda, chocolate syrup, and a dash of milk]—just to show you that I'm not dieting. Don't follow my example! Actually, the last few pictures you have sent don't show you as heavy as previous ones. Does the bulky winter clothing dwarf you?   D

SATURDAY, FEBRUARY 28, 1953, 11:30 P.M.

My darling—

Each one of your letters contains more concrete news concerning the transfer. Today I waded through some Army papers about storage and I need 6 copies of your overseas orders. Send them as soon as possible so that we can get those things out of the way.

Had a talk with Joyce the other day—about careers. In spite of her degree in chemical engineering, she still can't get a job. There was an article in the *Times* about there being two positions available for every MALE graduate engineering and science and that the shortage is expected to increase. The Carnegie Institue of Technology said that wom-

en would "eventually have better opportunities." We still have a long
way to go. Although a career isn't my priority, I can still identify with
the thwarted efforts of someone like Joyce. She's so damn bright.
There's no doubt that her woman-status and maybe her name Levy has
held her back.

Mom mentioned that they're going to re-institute the twice-a-day
mail delivery. That will mean TWO high spots in each day.

Watched "Show of Shows" and the Knicks' game, last quarter. Have
you ever seen the Globetrotters? One of their former members, Clifton,
is on the Knicks and was a joy to watch.

It was exciting to read about the Holmes book. The words have a
courageous, true, and life-loving quality. I think that Stevenson's words
have the same appeal. I hope that the Democrats don't put a clamp on
his lips. At present, they are discouraging him from expressing opinions
on troublesome domestic problems. On foreign issues, he may speak,
because he happens to agree with them.   Dorothy

March

Stalin's death and Salk's new polio vaccine were peripheral to our insular universe. We focused on charting a course for Japan. Navigating the channels of bureaucracy, Mel used his R & R time to visit our probable destination in order to ready the transfer. His letters to me became travelogues heralding unfamiliar landscapes. I packed cartons and studied Japanese.

In spite of my elation, the sense of unreality and disbelief that had gripped me when we separated the previous July returned unbidden to load my mind with real and imagined doubts. Would the army foul up our itinerary? Could we count on a fixed departure date? Would my Japan-bound plane crash? Yet, in my most unruly fantasies, I couldn't invent a convincing image of how he would look when I got off that plane in Tokyo and spotted him in the crowd.

SUNDAY, MARCH 1, 1953, 10:00 P.M.

My Darling—

I'm sitting in the center of the tent in a blood-spattered T-shirt. My boots are covered with plaster and blood. My head aches. Soon I shall go to bed and, I hope, sleep off this fatigue, but first I must talk to you, my wife.

Friday night a POW came in, shot through the leg. He was a 21-yr-old, North Korean, big and healthy-looking compared to some of the South Koreans we've been seeing. The short haircut helps give them a cleaner look. This was our enemy—and yet I felt sorry for him—not that he was taken prisoner, but that this young kid was shot and now was scared stiff, in an American hospital, unable to understand what was going on. I am sure he had been told he would be killed or tortured. He went into the operating room, wide-eyed and shivering. He was done under spinal anesthesia so that the intelligence people could talk to him. When we were finished, his comment was, (via interpreter) "Very nice."

I fell into bed 2:30 A.M. Sat morning and was out again at 5:30 A.M. to see several ambulance loads of patients. While I was supposed to be off at 8 A.M. I was tied up with a case until 11. Then I let myself get talked into some exercise. Neal, Ernie, and I ran out to the main road and back (distance ¾ mile). We all just about collapsed. After a shower I finally stopped puffing and lay down to nap for a few hours. Several cases did come in late in the afternoon. At 8 A.M. I saw a patient with a belly ache who I thought should be left alone. Too many other people thought he had appendicitis, so we took out his normal appendix. However it is much better to take a "cold" one out than to leave a "hot" one in. I guess there is a new regiment on the line because the soldiers look better fed. Worked the rest of the day, took ½ hour out for our cocktail hour and to say hello to Genl Guinn and Col Lindsey who came on an inspection tour.

Now to bed. Your husband,   Melvin

SUNDAY, MARCH 1, 1953, 10:30 P.M.

My darling—

How I long to feel your eyes upon me from across a room and to answer your looks with all the fire of which I am capable. If I were teaching now, I might lose my temper while waiting for an answer. "The man I love sleeps on the other side of the world! What do I care for your laziness!" I might, my love. But now I stand on a gym floor and do plies and stretches and when my toe points, it points toward the east and each time I do a contraction my body tells me, I want him.

Dorothy

MARCH 2

When I got home I found my passport waiting. I'm all set—just say the word! The Japanese Consulate will give me a tourist visa for 2 months. Once I am over there, I can claim dependency rating and that entitles me to stay as long as you do. It takes just one day to get the visa so I will wait with that until we are more sure of the date. If the Army sends me, I won't need a visa. It seemed like years before we'd be writing in this way!   D

My Love—

A Korean full of holes in his back and a GI dead on arrival with I don't know what. I turned the case over to the night crew. I cannot wait to get out of here. Probably 3 weeks away from here, if I am not doing surgery, I'll be wanting to work, but never away from you. I am set to fly to Seoul on the 9th and will see about the application. I don't know if they will approve it within 30 days, but they certainly should within 60. If they do not send it through quickly, it won't be because I haven't tried.

Awoke this morning to go over and fix up one of the EM's ingrown toenails. While I was standing there I was approached by two other men to take off small tumors of their skin. I declined as this is not the place to do elective surgery except the most minor. The chance of infection is too great. The air is filled with dust. We never can get the floors really clean. One of the nurses also asked me to fix her toe. I could develop quite a practice.

With Neal ready for transfer, Ernie ready to rotate home, Art due to leave in a few weeks, and me, the conversation in the tent is as you can imagine. Elliot takes quite a ribbing, especially about the new nurses, being the only single man in our tent, in fact, in the outfit.

The moon is waning. The numbers on the letters get higher. The number of pictures I take gets bigger. Soon I shall be able to scrub your back or your bottom in the shower or just look at you in the morning and say, "Good morning my lovely wife!"

And now—oops—air raid siren, lights out. I'll finish later.   M

My darling—

Everything I do is more and more centered about the trip from here to your arms. Tomorrow I will buy stationery, the last I shall have to buy.

Ed Svetke called. Tomorrow he is to report to Killmer and to get out on the 26th. He and his wife came into NY tonight. He is in good spirits, of course. He asked me to send him the movie of his being decorated and reassured me that you were in safe territory, lest I worry. I tried to explain about our frank attitude, but it sounded silly.

In order for me to get a Japanese visa, you must write a letter (send it to me) confirming that you will be responsible for all my expenses while I am in Japan and in transit.

Thank god you are an individualist! I hate mustaches. If you do grow one, be sure that you don't send any pics—I might never get to Japan. Incidentally, I called the airlines about reservations and they said to call not later than 2 weeks before to get reservations for Japan. Pan-American has 3–4 flights weekly from San Francisco. I asked Ed if Rick's wife was going over, because he had spoken to her. He said, "Oh no, Rick will only be over there another 3 or 4 mos." My god! That's a lifetime. But then I remembered what Rick's plans were for Japan.

You mentioned that Art favors McCarthy. I hope that my articles have been of some help. I shall keep them coming, fast and furious.

I walk around with more air under my feet these days. I hope it isn't in vain.   Dorothy

WEDNESDAY, MARCH 4, 1953, 11:00 P.M.

My darling—

At the 5 & 10, I bought a large frame to fit some of your pictures. Do you mind, my love, being encased in Woolworth's best? Mom insists I bought it because Jimmy Stewart's picture was in it. Now, I have you in sand, in snow, on your bed, in fatigues, in parka, with bare chest, and with *Time* on your hands, and that look in your eye. Even though they are posed, they do catch your many moods.

I wondered today if you had heard the news about Stalin's death and what the general reaction to it was. I think Max Lerner's column says what can be said. I can't help feeling that there won't be any major changes in policy in the immediate future. One thing I did hear over the radio this A.M. which I did not read in the paper—There is a growing movement of South American countries in the UN to pressure Red China into accepting the Indian peace proposal. Lodge immediately tried to squelch it saying that the time isn't "right" yet.

And with these depressing thoughts I say goodnight my love. No mail today—perhaps tomorrow.   Dorothy

FRIDAY, MARCH 6, 1953, 11:00 P.M.

My Love—

I want to leave tomorrow and be with you the day after. I do not trust the army and will not trust them 40–60 days into the future.

I don't feel like working any more. I'm waiting and wanting you. When we are together again then will I live and want to do things.

Did I write you about the CO of the 8055? Stupidity in the army. He became engaged to a nurse and they were to be married as soon as his divorce came through, but Eighth Army frowned on the romance. Well, with the nurse having only 23 days left, they transferred her here, to separate them. There was talk of sending the Col. to Okinawa. He is a nice fellow and it is shame about this business. I can't imagine why they frown on it, except that they might be afraid of the publicity of nurses taking medical officers away from their wives back home. Are you worried, my love?

The hour grows late and again I am tired, longing to be with you. Dorothy, Dorothy, where are you now?   Melvin

SATURDAY, MARCH 7, 1953, 11:30 P.M.

My Beloved—

Spent ½ hour with the C.I.D (Criminal Investigation Dept) about that pt who was killed. They were trying to find a defense for the fellow who shot him. From my point I could not add anything to help though the man was very interesting to talk to.

Gene received a salami and about 10 of us sat around eating. At the same time we got to talking about what kosher means—even reading the Bible where it is described. Some of the boys had never heard the term and they were quite interested. We discussed it rationally, comparing the different religions' rituals. We really learned more about each other and understood each other better having exchanged this information. I don't think any of the fellows here will teach their children anti-semitism—and I don't think I am being over-idealistic.

Typical of most discussions, we went on to sex. Being a city boy, I found out tonight how chickens copulate. (Join the army & get an education.) As in a usual bull session—home, wives, children, travel, why we do not like the army, income tax and how to defraud the govt and land in jail!

Let the days pass. I shall not miss them now. When we are together will be the time to hold on to each day. Your husband,   Melvin

SUNDAY, MARCH 8, 1953, 2:45 A.M.

My darling—

I go ahead with passport, shots, storage, etc. and yet I feel it unrealistic to be optimistic. It's funny, people say—Oh Japan! Isn't that exciting! I start to explain and then I realize that it sounds trite when I say: Wherever we are, as long as we are together. So I say: Oh yes! It's very exciting! And it is. To be with you in a foreign land, getting to know a new people, another culture—having people get to know and like us—Americans—together. We MUST learn to speak the language! From now on you ought to turn from your occasional study of French to study Japanese. I mean it!   D.

SUNDAY, MARCH 8, 1953, 3:00 P.M.

My Darling—

The hills are greener—the rain has washed the snow off all but the highest mountain top and my heart sings as I dream of you. It is difficult to believe that the lazy droning of an airplane motor high in the sky may mean death for someone. Or the distant thunder is not the echo of a lightning bolt, but the sound of the madness of mankind. Try as I might to forget, this war intrudes here, as I stand to the side of the road to allow an ambulance to go by.

I've been reading Santayana's novel and enjoying his prose, a mild gentle exercise. I haven't read more than 200 pages, yet there is much in it that I mentally marked to talk over with you. Maybe I enjoy the book because his thoughts are similar to those we have expressed—being yourself, accepting yourself for what you are, living truthfully, allowing others to live their lives.

Will you send a few salamis. I can use them to feed the boys before I leave (so I can leave them with a good taste in their mouths).

Well, I hear a helicopter and though I am not on duty I go out and look. I love you.   Melvin

SUNDAY, MARCH 8, 1953, 10:30 P.M.

My darling—

Went into the junk room and started to unpack cartons. I'm making lists 1) things to store (Army gives us a special inventory) 2) things to send to Japan (my clothing, iron, linens, etc.) 3) things I may or may not need in Japan. Approximately how long shall we be there? The clothes of yours we don't send to Japan we'll leave here at 9 E. 96: underwear, sneakers, bathing suits, ski clothes, Army overcoat, slacks and sports shirts? phonograph records

After 8:00, Mom and I sat down to a game of Scrabble which lasted 1½ hr. This is taking me from my reading!

Soooon.   Dorothy

MONDAY, MARCH 9, 1953, 8:30 P.M.

My Love—

I am at the 121 Evac again, and if I do not write with jubilation, at least it is not with despair. My request for transfer will be sent in the next few days as I had planned—50–50 chance of getting something done by May 1st or sooner.

There is the gamble that I'll be sent to Northern Japan which is almost as bad as Korea regarding housing, but I think we must gamble or not try at all. When I get back to the MASH the final form goes in. I will then have to work on getting to Japan and the transfer.

While I was at EUSAK Headquarters I also saw Lindsey, who I now feel may be like a 2-edged sword, both potentially helpful and harmful. He again offered me a job at Hq in Seoul asking, "Melvin, why don't you give up surgery and take a staff job?" I parried him politely and held back my true feelings. It was difficult. He would like to see someone else, I guess, give up all the years of training.

He did make one request. He asked what the export house you work for sells. When I told him, he half-jokingly said, "Have them send a few samples. We'll give them to the house boys." Anyway, send one Maiden Form bra about a medium size and one generous size with "falsies." I'll give it to him as a joke. Am not sure about this at all. Let me know what you think.

Well I'm still hopeful of expediting things, my darling. If not, they know me and will, I think, at least not delay the transfer. I shall continue to fight to get to Japan and to be with you. Your husband,   Melvin

My darling—

Guion Rogers came at 8:30 and I played parts of a cantata for him, describing the sequence of voices and chorus. I also notated music that he played and dictated. He brought me two of his records.

On her way out to play canasta, Mom met him. "I got such a shock! You didn't tell me he was a Negro! I know it's terrible, but it makes me uneasy." At first I was annoyed, but then tried to reassure her by explaining that he has been coming to the Lighthouse for 15 yrs. and everyone there knows him. Funny, I thought that I had mentioned it to her.

Now to dream, to imagine the warmth of you beside me.   Dorothy

My darling—

I am sitting in the quiet of the Juilliard library. Somewhere in another room a piano is playing. On my right are shelves with "Collected Songs," on my left "Orchestra Scores." The people in this small, sunny room are all doing some kind of work in music. So am I, singing a song of love to my husband. They all look absorbed and happy. Why not? How unlike the atmosphere which surrounds you now. Light ground action on the Eastern front, today's paper says. So you are busy.

I saw Yuriko at the end of class and mentioned that I was going to Japan. She was very excited and said, "Oh, you'll have to meet some of my friends. One of them is the top dancer in Japan." She said that the fad now is Ballet and exclaimed, "Isn't that silly? with our short legs and long torsos—"

Mom has some dance lessons left over at Fred Astaire and asked me to go with her. It was fun, just the idea of dancing, but it certainly isn't worth $7 an hour. I didn't learn anything I didn't already know. I use up more energy in one minute of Modern Dance than in the whole hour of this stuff. I should hate to teach it—so cut and dried. I remember waltzing at the Ambassador, first becoming aware of each other. One of my camp friends saw me there and said that I looked as though I were in heaven. She wasn't far from wrong.

I spoke to Jean. Bill got the job! She said, about us, once you are together you will no longer be biding your time. That's what we're doing now, my love: biding our time.   Dorothy

WEDNESDAY, MARCH 11, 1953, 10:30 P.M.

My darling—

I am still just outside Seoul. Awoke this morning to the sound of a howling windy rainstorm. I lay there trying to decide whether to get up and check on the plane or assume the inevitable that it wouldn't fly. After a short while I arose and called across Korea to find that in the eastern area it was even worse—raining and snowing. So I went back to bed and slept until 11. Met some other doctors, all here for various reasons similar to mine—there was one Hurwitz who had been at New Haven Hospital for 3 weeks while we were on our honeymoon. Then he was called into the army. Another fellow and I wandered around Yong Dong Po, stopped into the PX and tried to arrange to buy another lens.

Lou Eisenberg (MASH medical officer) and I set out for Seoul, hitched in and went to the Air Force Officers' Club. It is equivalent to a swanky N.Y. cocktail lounge and restaurant. Mirrored walls, neon lights on the bar and youthful air force colonels and majors. It reminded me of the show "This is the Army" where they did a parody on the Air Force. At any rate we sat there feeling good in the luxurious atmosphere and had a few cocktails. We met 4 other doctors and had a delicious steak dinner for $1.75. The Air Force flies the stuff in. Finally called Eighth Army Headquarters for a jeep to take us back to the 121. It was difficult to believe that there was a war, except as we drove through darkened streets through a blacked out area over the bridge.

The weather cleared about noon, but still the wind kept the planes from flying. So here I sit in a BOQ, wishing I were back at the 47 MASH just because there is probably mail from you. Last night I dreamed we were together in our cheerful bedroom at 15 Howe St. in New Haven. I love you Dorothy.   Melvin

THURSDAY, MARCH 12, 1953, 11:30 P.M.

My darling—

Each time I read of another plane incident over Germany, and there have been two during the last three days, my insides tighten. First I think of how there might be a change in our plans, and then almost simultaneously, I think of the horror of what an all-out war would mean. In spite of what we think of the merits of the new administration, we know that they are going to try pretty damn hard to keep us out of a full-scale war. I think they would like to stay in Washington for a while.

It has been a rainy, raw day. I look as grey as the day without any lipstick because of my cold sore. I can imagine you kissing me all around the sore. That little spot would get better damn quickly, because it too would want to be kissed.

Had a workout with Bob this morning. Sometimes I think he is sadistic.

Mom said she needed me more at home than at the office, so I picked up shrimp and flowers, set the table, and helped make hors d'oeuvre. I went through your movies and slides deciding which ones to show to this evening's company. They have a nephew in Korea going to the front as an ammunitions repair man. I wanted to pick out the more cheerful pictures. Wound up showing some of the first reels (landing at Inchon, 618 Med. Clr. Co., Inf. Band, USO show) and from the slides: Dallas group (they wanted to see the family), series on helicopter going to pick up a patient, Thanksgiving, and some snow scenes. It really is an art to know when to stop, because I could go on forever.

Goodnight my sweet.   Dorothy

THURSDAY, MARCH 12, 1953, 11:00 P.M.

My Love—

Still in Seoul. The airstrips in the East were snowed in and a gale blowing. Made rounds in the hospital, then came back and read for the rest of the afternoon. Went over to K16 air base Air Force Club and sat around playing bridge. We heard they were to have a dance. The musumes (Japanese for "my sister"—Korean adaptation, young unmarried girl) would be coming later. The band made up of air force personnel arrived, then about 40 Korean girls. It was fascinating to see them, all dressed in Sears and Montgomery Ward clothes, attempting to be "western." I felt a little sad at this, as some of them were attractive in an oriental way. Of course all are prostitutes. But this is an army-sponsored affair. They come in a big bus and must all leave that way. The band was excellent. Many of the fellows, just as in a taxi dance, danced with the girls and bought them drinks. One thing was good to see—half a dozen Negro officers in the club sitting with the others and all friendly—no question of white or colored officers.

I enjoyed the music and watching people, but my heart was 9,000 miles away. Seeing all these girls and the fellows—single and married—with them just made me realize all the more how much I love you and miss you. Most of them were not just dancing, but later, followed the bus that takes the girls out of the compound and lets them off in the nearby village. You should have seen the line of jeeps following that bus!

Enclosed are two Polaroid pictures that an enlisted man was discarding because they were spoiled. It gives you some idea of the contrast of the Koreans on the street and those dressed up.

I miss you Dorothy, so very much. Melvin

P.S. I had finished writing my letter to you, was just folding it and putting in the pictures, when one of the fellows who was with me tonight said, "You're not sending those pictures to your wife, are you?" "Why?" I asked. "I couldn't even write I was at the dance tonight. She would be jealous and sure I had gone chasing one of the gals."

Well, I laughed, put the pictures in and started to close the letter when I just wanted to share this thought with you.

SATURDAY, MARCH 14, 1953, 11:45 P.M.

My beloved—

How important Saturday nights used to be before we loved. Then every night became important and Saturday was just one more night of love. So it is now. Saturday means one day, one week closer to you. I go for my first shots Monday.

This time of year is difficult. Whenever I breathe deeply of spring I think of Dad doing just that when he came out of the hospital. I remember going to the hospital with your Mom on a day like this last year at this time, seeing a few blossoms peeking through prematurely. She was wonderful to me and I shall never forget it.

Goodnight my sweet. Stay well.   Dorothy

SUNDAY, MARCH 15, 1953, 11:30 P.M.

My beloved—

I typed up the Income Tax, made an extra copy for our files and sent one to you. I guess I was in the mood for tedium because I checked off our bank vouchers and even got the balance to tally. Mom came home and we had a concoction type dinner. Didn't have the patience to go back to work on the "room" so I began to read the pocket book *New World Writing* which you sent me. The selections were absorbing and except for intermittent questions from Mom who was doing her Spanish homework, my attention was undivided. I read 2 short stories by Gore Vidal and Wright Morris and found in them what I expected, a morbid twist in the situations and characters. Then I read 2 literary criticisms—one on Simenon and Spillane, the other Carson McCullers. The former is witty and assigns detective stories to a proper place in literature without being arbitrary or pedantic. The latter brought back vivid memories of McCullers' weird, fascinating stories of lonely characters and an evening in New Haven when we read and discussed "Ballad of the Sad Cafe."

By this time I was in a reading mood, so I picked up Mann's *Joseph in Egypt,* read 2 pgs. and put it down. That was not what I wanted. I did find Eve Curie's biography *Madame Curie* and became so absorbed that I read 150 pages wishing you were across the room so I could have read you passages.

Goodnight my sweet, my husband.   Dorothy

MARCH 16, 1953, 11:00 P.M.

My Darling—

The Col signed the approval on my transfer today. It is on its way to Eighth Army and I hope soon to Japan.

Awoke early and went over to work on the boy with the ingrown toenails. Saw a few patients on the wards and had some coffee. Sat down to read when some patients came in. One of them was a "stateside" case—an incarcerated hernia (one that was stuck). It was fun to do something like this because, for once, you finish a procedure, remedy the situation and know the patient will not have to go off to a series of further procedures. It also gave me something to compare with my civilian surgery. I used to take 2 hours to do a simple hernia and today a complicated case took an hour & 10 minutes, only because I now know what I am doing and do not waste time.

We shall be in Japan approximately 1 year. Do not take too many household utensils as we can get them cheaply there. Also only essential linens. If you should come on your own, by plane, we shall have to wait and have the army (or we shall do it) send the heavier stuff over later. Phonograph records you might as well leave out for your Mom and Gerry. If we do buy a small victrola in Japan, we can get some sent or buy new ones. Travel as lightly as you can, unless we do get you sent by the army.

My wife, I am alive with the joy and excitement of you.   Melvin

MONDAY, MARCH 16, 1953, 11:40 P.M.

My beloved—

Sat down with Mme Curie. A sad part, the death of her husband. I continued reading until her courage returned so as not to leave the book on an unhappy note. With only a few more chapters to finish, I plan to read next another biography. For me now, they have more meaning than novels. In spite of all the hardship and suffering the subject endures, there is the underlying feeling: Life is worthwhile living. And even the trivialities of a person's life assume importance as they fit into the structure of a realistic portrait.

I love you Melvin. Even now, we are as close as others who have daily contact. How I long for that daily contact.   Dorothy

TUESDAY, MARCH 17, 1953, 9:45 P.M.

My beloved—

I got my first series of shots today! Typhus, cholera, and small pox vaccin. I have to come back in 2 days for an exam of the vaccin. and then on 2 or 3 other dates. The last should be about April 10. I only need a typhoid booster because I had the series in 1948 before going to Europe. I don't have any record of the tetanus shots, but I think I had them. Sent a Special Delivery letter to Bucknell to find out. The arm is a bit stiff. It serves as a reminder of what is ahead.

Because of the St. Patrick Day parade I couldn't use the car, so I took the 5th Ave bus along Madison. When it took me 25 minutes to go 10 blocks, I gave up and walked. Saw Bishop Sheehan's program the one everyone has been talking about and for which he won an award, along with Lucille Ball's "I Love Lucy." I also watched "Where Was I?" a new quiz type with a panel of celebrities. Its interest depends upon how clever the celebrities are.

In your discussion on comparative religion, did you mention that "Kashros" is based on biblical as well as sanitation reasons—"not boiling a kid in its mother's milk." The discussion on sex which followed sounds fascinating. How DO chickens copulate?

As far as being assigned to northern Japan, let us not worry about housing until the time arrives. As long as we find a bed and a roof over it, it will be sufficient. Will there be an opportunity to do surgery there?

Mom says that I am already in Japan. My mind wanders off in the middle of a conversation. Goodnight my darling.   Dorothy

THURSDAY, MARCH 19, 1953, MIDNIGHT

My darling—

Took a 9:00 class with Bob Cohan—without arm-falls. (The vaccination itches like hell.) I came directly home in a pouring rain. On the bus I sat near some Japanese students and listened to their conversation (in English). At one point they wondered what "those yellow flowers" were in Central Park. I turned around and told them "forsythia," looking forward to the time when you and I are riding in a bus in Japan and someone identifies flowers for us.

I had not received the tetanus in 1948. Took a subway down to the Dispensary and had my vaccin. examined, and received shots for typhoid and tetanus. Evidently, I don't need them for yellow fever. I shall ask them about a Schick Test [diphtheria immunity test].

The New York Buddhist Church, at 94th & Amsterdam, is in an old brownstone, in part, occupied by a Japanese family. Lots of activity—one group holding a conference, another rehearsing a play—all in Japanese.

My class was informal and enjoyable, with four of us including the teacher. I am the only woman and the only beginner. They have completed 20 lessons from *Japanese in Thirty Hours*. One of the students speaks well and is learning to write the characters. The other was in Japan (I guess in the Army) and wants to go back again. He has a working vocabulary. The first hour was spent learning conversation: greetings (review for the others), in the store, in the taxi. The teacher uses the repetitive method which is good, because you really get a feel for the accent. I shall have to study hard this week.

Goodnight my darling. Everything I do now is in preparation for "you," for "us." How many times I shall awaken to look at you, to touch you, to know you are there. I love you.   Dorothy

FRIDAY, MARCH 20, 1953, 11:00 A.M.

Good Morning My Love—

Had just gotten to sleep when the phone rang. The hospital calling. The pharmacy floor was flooded. So I told them to start digging drainage ditches. The rain stopped during the night. This morning it is misty. The area has drained fairly well, much better than our old area. The river is muddy and choppy and has risen about 2 feet. I guess with all this mud we won't have showers for a while as we take our water for them from the river.

Spent part of the morning talking to the boy who lost his legs. He took it quite well—sort of. "Well, I suspected as much last night—I guess I'll have to change some of my plans." I smiled and encouraged him, told him about the center in the States where they fix him up with artificial legs. Yet I kept asking myself, Why, why? What has been accomplished? What great ideal has been saved by this boy. What hill has been won? Just part of the day's activity. The headlines are filled with atomic explosions and airplanes being shot at—instead of attempts at peaceful settlement. Fighting should be a last resort. The more I read and hear about our congressmen, the less I respect most of them. They are clever, yes, but narrow and more interested in the effect of their words than the content.

Our life will soon begin again.   Melvin

MARCH 21

By doing vascular repairs we save not only limbs, but money. Every leg amputation costs the government $100,000 by the time the pt. lives to 50 yrs old.   M

SUNDAY, MARCH 21, 1953, AFTER MIDNIGHT

This is our spring and now we may begin to count the days. Tonight's paper had headlines about a DC-4 Transoceanic crash in California and I had a funny feeling in the pit of my stomach. Then there was an article about a turnpike crash in which 10 people were killed. But we don't leave anything to chance. We fight wars. This is a morbid way to begin a letter to you, my love.

Tonight Pop asked to see my Japanese textbook. For almost an hour he tested me on the lessons I had studied. We really had fun. I kidded him about being a "stiff teacher" because he really went at it with a vengeance. We were both surprised at how much I had absorbed. When we finished, he quickly memorized one sentence in Japanese and showed it off to the Moms. You can imagine the sensation.

At that point we decided to direct our intellectual prowess elsewhere and wound up in the dining room playing Scrabble. Pop won, in spite of the fact that Mom G. had set him off by telling him he couldn't spell socks "sox." According to the dictionary, "sox" is acceptable. Now Pop accuses Mom of cheating, and she will probably never hear the end of it.

McCarthy makes me angrier by the day and I wonder how long the Administration is going to take it. I am depressed tonight and the future seems so far away. We would be sleepily crawling into bed now, juicily chewing over the day's events and personalities, exchanging tasty morsels. I love you Melvin.   Dorothy

SUNDAY, MARCH 22, 1953, 11:00 P.M.

My Beloved—

The Col is off to the 43rd MASH for the Vascular Surgery course. Now I am the only one here who has done any of the blood vessel repair work. Since one never knows when it will be needed, it is good to have others available who can do it. This is one technique that will be valuable in helping me do cardiovascular surgery when I get back to New Haven.

All but one of the mustaches are off now, including Gene's. As to the question of less surgery in Japan—No place in the Far East does as much or as varied surgery as the MASH. There is also a tendency to send people with previous good surgical assignments in Korea to the less choice spots in Japan. However, as I've said, I am trying most of all, TO GET THERE, and then to get YOU THERE. Whatever happens next is secondary.   M

TUESDAY, MARCH 24, 1953, 10:15 P.M.

My darling—

I'm really glad I am not at Valley Stream now. I don't think I would have the patience. My present program keeps me occupied and interested and at the same time gives me the freedom to do the things I have to do without feeling the pressure of meeting deadlines. We are lucky that we are occupied in fields that interest us. Your experience will certainly be of value. And if mine does no more than satisfy a present need (I hope it does more than that) it will have been worthwhile.

Spoke with Yuriko again. When I mentioned that I was taking Japanese classes, she seemed mildly interested. She is not too communicative on anything but dance. She did say that the Graham group may be going to Japan on tour.

I have not had the chance to type up your letters. I am considering taking them to Japan. I suppose we will have access to a typewriter. Where is ours?

Tomorrow is soon.   Dorothy

TUESDAY, MARCH 24, 1953, 12:20 A.M.

My Love—

I was just walking through the admitting ward looking at a pt. brought in by helicopter. More horror. Both arms and legs gone—both eyes injured. I wonder if we are doing good by saving people like that. Well, we cannot be the ones to decide. An immediate contrast—a group of actors and actresses toured the hospital—2 actors, a few older women (40–50's), and two girls who looked about 18 (one, Audrey Dalton from Dublin, Ireland). All of them provided an interesting hour at the officers' club where we had a few cocktails before dinner. (I drank water, since I was to be working this evening.) Naturally we all—and I confess, me too—found the view of an attractive American girl very pleasant. They gave us pictures of themselves (the car they came in had a trunkful). Both actors, Don Taylor and Dick Shannon, had been in the army during the last war. They were a pleasant group who went out of their way to be friendly to everyone and later served dinner at the EM mess.

Movie tonight a remake of "Prisoner of Zenda"—much more Hollywoodish than the old Douglas Fairbanks Jr one, but in technicolor.

Then an ambulance came in and I helped Beveridge do some cases. Now here I am with you, my love. Another day ended.

Neal just asked whether I told you about the "girls" in the letter and I laughed and told him "I'm writing how I bravely fought them off today." Your husband.   Melvin

THURSDAY, MARCH 26, 1953, 11:30 P.M.

Melvin, my darling—

More vaccine and toxoid in my blood stream. More Japanese in my mind. Made it in time for the class and I knew, most of the time, what was being said. The 2 hrs flew and we stayed overtime. If I hadn't gotten up to go as well as saying in Japanese, "Excuse me, I am going home," we might still be there. It is a beautiful language and if the teacher is an example, I know that we will like the Japanese. I find it difficult to connect the friendly easy-going people I meet at the Buddhist Church with the "mad-men" we were fighting during the last war.

Now, my beloved, my head is full of the months ahead and how good it will feel to reach out and find you. April is less than a week away.   Dorothy

FRIDAY, MARCH 27, 1953, 10:15 P.M.

Oh my love!

My heart is beating so fast I cannot relax. I was concentrating so hard on listening to you. I am so happy that you did get the leave. Tokyo! If somebody told you a few years ago that you would be calling your wife from Tokyo and planning to live in Japan for a year, you would have laughed. And now we are laughing!

Immediately after your call, I called the folks. Pop was so funny. It was about 6:45. When I told him that I had spoken to you at 6:30, he said, "What? And you're not still talking? Tell him not to watch the time!"

Found my Teaching Certificate and sent it to Albany to have Spanish eligibility added and to have my name changed.

Gerry showed us slides from Canada and Harvard—good ones of him and his friends in Lab with their cats. We had an anatomy lesson from a vivid slide.

Goodnight my beloved. You'd better write as clearly as possible

from now on because I will be so dizzy I won't be able to focus properly. I love you, my husband. Sleep well in your comfortable bed tonight,
enjoy that hot shower, live in the luxury of our dreams for the near
future.   Dorothy

SATURDAY, MARCH 28, 1953, 10:30 P.M.

My darling—

Found Guion's studio without any trouble, your tape in my pocketbook. When we first put it on—at the wrong speed—you sounded like
Donald Duck. However, I was able to distinguish the first 2 words, "My
love." The voice doesn't sound like yours, but the rhythm and inflection
are familiarly dear. Guion is coming to the house some day this week
with the machine and I will record a tape. Since he insists that it be a
longer one, I shall write a script before then.

Watched "Of Mice and Men" on television, with Lon Chaney Jr.,
Betty Fields, and Burgess Meredith. It was very moving.

I was disappointed to learn that we weren't going to have a Seder at
your folks, just the traditional meal. I remember all the years of enjoying the rituals with the family all together, not necessarily religious but
rather adding warmth and color to our Jewishness.

TUESDAY, MARCH 31, 1953, 11:00 A.M.

My love, Good morning—

Dad passed away April 17th, the same date you were assigned to active duty. I think Mom would appreciate it very much if you wrote to
her on that date, as you had suggested. She has such a warm feeling for
you and I know whatever you write, my love, will be comforting. When
Pop said the Kiddush [blessing over the wine] last night, I saw her lip
quiver and her eyes fill up for a moment, but no one else saw it. She
doesn't remind people. Only sometimes she says to me: "Thank god for
children."

11:30 P.M.

After lunch Gerry and I drove out to Bayside Golf Links, hoping
to play. It was a beautiful beginning-of-spring day and the place was
jammed. The entire garment industry was closed for 2 days and must

have been on that golf course. We decided to forego it since we had to be in Bklyn for dinner. Went to a nearby driving range instead. Gerry suggested that I come down more slowly. I did that and it kept me from "moidering them." Went to Aunt Cookie's for a second dinner. It was delicious, but I'm glad I don't have to eat a third dinner. My poor little belly. I think I'm happier noshing all day than stuffing myself at one sitting.

Uncle Lou and Aunt Cookie are going to Europe for 10 wks. in May. They are going abroad to tour and I am going abroad to live. I haven't even looked at my clothes yet and Mom bothers me every day. Tomorrow. I guess it's because I know that we shall be spending more time out of clothes than in them!

I love you, my darling. Goodnight.   Dorothy

April

In the interests of peace, the United States expressed willingness to accept a divided Korea ninety miles north of the battle line. An exchange of ill captives was agreed upon, to begin no later than April 21.

At the M.A.S.H., the case load was low. Mel was in a state of euphoria bordering on incredulity. Still writing every day, he lost track of envelope numbers. It no longer mattered. His replacement arrived. One by one, Mel followed the precise steps mandated in order to leave Korea. There was a party for him. Mom gave one for me. Mel left the M.A.S.H. I headed for California. We would be together before the end of April.

APRIL 1

Most people want peace, but there are some on Wall Street who are afraid of it. Even the *Wall Street Journal* criticizes them. "War itself is a terrible thing, but we find more terrible yet the fact that there are men walking about who talk of peace as if it were terrible."   D.

THURSDAY, APRIL 2, 1953, AFTERNOON

My Love,

Me on R & R, a report for you from notes I jotted down in Tokyo: The officer who was to brief us gave a talk on Japan and said, "We give a VD lecture to the EM: All Japanese girls have it. That's all." It sounded as though anyone who was going to be exposed was going to in spite of what he said. I think that is true.

The plane had two decks and carried 140 men with ease. I met a fellow in his late 30's from Colorado and we decided to go to the Nikkatsu Hotel together. It was a clear day. We could see Mt Fujiyama's towering, snow-capped volcanic peak. Of course we took pictures. I believe there was not one man on that plane without a camera.

Couldn't help comparing the ride to Camp Drake this time with the one 10 months ago, and indeed with my first impressions of Japan. Then, Japan appeared dirty, primitive, and poverty-stricken. This time, it looked civilized and clean. I was excited because everything I saw and felt was pointed in one direction: Soon we would be enjoying this together.

The drive into Tokyo by cab was hair-raising. I was not used to autos traveling at 40 miles an hour. Add to that the madmen Japanese driving on the left side of the road. You will need a loud horn. They blow them all the time.

From the moment we arrived at the hotel I enjoyed the luxury— someone carrying my bags, a large comfortable room, good beds, and a modern tiled bathroom. You can imagine how it felt to use all the facilities and get into clean clothes. Called for room service and a cocktail, then tried to phone you, but the lines were busy.

We were there no longer than 20 minutes when a little boy in a white coat came in and said, "Can I serve you Lieutenants? Would you like to have a party tonight? I shall provide food, drink, and company . . . nice girls, yes?" Well, then and there, I realized that my companion was all for it. I dissuaded him for that night saying I wanted to walk about town, look around, and get some sleep. I had worked almost the entire night before leaving Wednesday and didn't get much sleep Wed night in Seoul. He agreed. About ½ hour passed and another boy came in. He had a "friendo" who worked at Mikimoto's, the pearl store, who got some bargains. He brought out 4 strands which he was going to sell us at a discount—for 80 dollars. They did not look like good pearls and were probably stolen, so we sent him on his way.

We had a drink at the hotel bar, something to eat, then started to walk about, stopped by people handing out slips of paper describing the clubs. We went to a beautiful night club where 50 or 60 attractive Japanese girls in evening gowns were sitting around waiting—a club for officers only, so they can charge higher prices and so officers can make fools of themselves in private.

We sat down and were immediately joined by two girls. They spoke a little English and tried very hard. It costs 500 yen to have them sit at your table, 2000 if they dance with you, and 8000 to spend the night. At 360 yen to the dollar, that was too expensive for me. They have to pay the club 500 yen for every night they work there, and only 300 if they do not get a customer to dance. They had a striptease show and did a few crude dance movements. They take off everything.

On our way back, my companion suggested that we get separate rooms so that we could have "privacy." There is a twelve o'clock curfew in the streets so most of the places close before midnight. You can travel later by cab.

Back to the hotel where we decided to change hotels in the morning, as we could not get single rooms.

I have so much to write, it will take me days to do it. Now, here are my lips and my heart, they are yours, my woman, my wife.

APRIL 2

Japanese class tonight. There is now another woman in the class. She has lived in Japan and was in Korea last May as a war correspondent.

Watakushi-wa anata-no tsuma-de imasu.—I am your wife.

You can answer: Anata-wa watakushi-no tsuma-de arimasu.—You are my wife. It's good in any language, and I want to hear you say it to me—with your eyes. I love you.   Dorothy

FRIDAY, APRIL 3, 1953, 11:00 P.M.

My Love—

I am afraid to write this letter for fear it will not come about! I am in Seoul now at the 121. Awoke at 6:30 A.M. to catch an ambulance down to corps hq. Then on a plane to Seoul with transfer papers in my pocket. I was going to place them on the desk of the personnel people myself. But when I got there and—I am still not sure whether to believe it—he said I don't have to apply, that FECOM Hq in Japan was sending a TWIX (telegram) on me and I COULD EXPECT TO LEAVE FOR JAPAN ON THE 15th OF APRIL. Is it possible? I don't know. I mistrust the army, but it looks good. So my darling get ready. I shall let you know by cable or phone as soon as I know where I am and when I can meet you.

I wonder if I shall sleep. Your husband,   Melvin

My darling—

I am growing impatient. The days pass quickly enough, but the weeks don't seem as though they'll ever end. I got up at 10:00 and found no mail. The sun was shining, but the day was gloomy. Called the Holm studio to find out about an extra class since Juilliard is on vacation this week. The cost was $2.25 for one class, given by a teacher I don't care for. So from 11:30–12:00, I gave myself a class, taking some fuzz off Mom's bedroom rug. It is more tiring alone, with no one to stop you for criticism. The group activity is lacking.

I sat down with your early letters and began to type up the sections for publication to give to Cousin Martin. I worked about an hour and got through 8 letters. I enjoyed it, because it is YOU all the time. It is interesting to compare your letters written 10 months ago to those I have received since. Your ideas and even literary style have changed—the ideas because you didn't know what to expect, and your style because of all the writing you have done since then and perhaps, your emotional experiences of the last months. Do you mind, my love, that I analyze? I love you Melvin—as a wife loves a husband, as a woman loves a man, as a lover loves a lover. How I want you now.

In another week or so you might be hearing some news. I'm ready to leave tonight. Hold me close. Let's not open our eyes until the day we can look into each other's.

Goodnight my love. Sleep well. Dream well.   Dorothy

11:00 P.M.

Your short stay in Tokyo sounds so full from the snatches you have written. It's a wonderful idea to jot down things as you go. I remember doing the same in Europe, but not so much because I wanted to share them—just to remember them. And soon we shall be sharing your notes within kissing distance.

This morning there were headlines and pictures of a shipload of Korean veterans returning to New York. I couldn't control the tears— whether it was because of those who didn't return or the expressions on the faces of wives and mothers, or us—I don't know. How I pray that there will be peace soon. At least there is more hope now than there was a month ago.

Goodnight my love. How many more times will we have to WRITE those words?   Dorothy

EASTER SUNDAY, APRIL 5, 1953, 9:00 A.M.

My Love,

I cannot wait to get out of here. There have been sporadic cases and for the moment I don't want to do anything. The boys are all anxious to work. They are restless and tense because of lack of work. So I sit on the sidelines and watch, help if it is needed—like an old popisan. They are sending another surgeon here in the next few days and he will be my replacement even though according to rules I don't need one. Perhaps by the 10th my orders will be in and a few days later I shall be on my way. I will be ready to go the moment they arrive. Every day away from you is one lost. When people say, Well, what is one day more or less, I don't even try to explain.

Russia is backing the peace talks. The prisoner exchange imminent. They moved one of the MASHes up to Panmunjom ready to receive them, screen them, and make them as transportable as possible. They will be sent back to the States as rapidly as it can be done safely. Wherever they are, they will be guarded and screened from visitors until they are back in the States. They want to let the families know and to question them and to try, I hope, not to make a political fumble of information. It looks good. I hope it doesn't fall through because if it does, we are almost certainly in for an all-out war.

I am so thankful you are you. I love youiloveyouiloveyouiloveyou. . . . Melvin. Boy the typing is awful—but probably better than if I tried to write—I am so excited.

SUNDAY, APRIL 5, 1953, 10:30 P.M.

My love—

According to the newspapers, the negotiation talks begin at 10:00 A.M. Dare we hope? Everything looks promising—at least for the immediate future. If only Russia continues to "speak softly" and enforces her words with deeds. How would peace affect our stay in Japan?

Drove Gerry to the station. Now the house is empty without him. He is very much like Dad in ways. I dreamed about Dad last night for

the first time in a long time. I guess the coming Yarzeit [yearly com-
memoration of the dead] and reading about research with atoms for
brain cancer. They can add 6 months to a patient's life. I dreamed that
he had an additional six months.

After dinner at the folks, we watched television—interesting inter-
view with McKay, Secy of the Interior and then Edward R. Murrow's
program—the latter included a large portion of a seder held in Western
Berlin by Jewish refugees. I hope we will have our own seders some day.

We thought April would never come. Nine months is a century. My
darling, Melvin, my husband.   Dorothy

SUNDAY, APRIL 5, 1953, 10:00 P.M.

There are many new people in the unit. Horne, Kay Phillips and I
are the only 3 left from the original outfit last fall. I am the surgeon who
has been here the longest.   M.

APRIL 7, 1953 1:00 A.M.

My Love,

Have almost finished listing my cases and they mount into the hundreds. As I go through the OR book I remember the days and nights we
were up doing them. It is not a happy recollection. While it is difficult
to predict the future, I have a feeling that this time the politicians will
get something done. In order to gain peace, we will, I think, at least
have to recognize Red China if not admit her to the UN. It seems ridic-
ulous to be dealing with and concluding a settlement with a nation
whose existence we still refuse to recognize.

After listing the cases I went over to a USO show. Dick Contino and
some other musicians. In spite of everyone commenting that Contino
had been a draft dodger, there was a good turn-out and he certainly
plays the accordion well.

Had been sitting in the tent about an hour when the telephone rang
and I have been working ever since. Not too many battle casualties,
mainly truck accidents. The fighting in this sector has been light. I
think and hope I shall have a quiet night now. I shall go out into the
night, walk the 20 yards to my tent, look up at the sky and think that
soon we can look up at the sky together.   Melvin

Good Morning My Love—

I sit now and count the days.

Some interesting facts: Up until this revival of the peace talks, the Reds have been allowing 20–30 letters from POW's a week to get out. Most of these were from Genl Dean. With the onset of the talks they released over 7,000 letters!

Quite an elaborate establishment is being readied for the reception of the prisoners. At Munsoni, an entire hospital is being built. We (the UN) have ready 81,000 blank medical forms for people who may be prisoners or missing. Many of them are no doubt dead. When a prisoner is exchanged all we will have to do is find out his name, pull out his card and jacket, tag him, and he is on his way to the hospital and home. No delay in paperwork. I was impressed with the figure of only 150 UN prisoners that the Chinese feel are sick enough to be exchanged. There is even an ROK hospital up there to care for the Koreans returned and to minimize any language difficulty.

In the event of a peace, we would remain here for at least 6–8 months. Then (or possibly sooner) many doctors would be returned to Japan and the States, but available for air return to Korea if the hostilities broke out again. So there is a gamble that if I stayed, I might be in the US say in 4–8 months. Will I take that gamble? Hell no. I'm on my way to kissing distance from you!!

I wonder if Gerry has to sign up for the last 2 years of ROTC. I am trying to get some information on it and will write to him. I'm afraid I haven't been a very good correspondent to either of the boys these last few weeks, but I'm sure they will understand.

The days ahead are too long, but fortunately there are only a few. Your husband,   Melvin

Good Morning My Love—

It is a windy, dusty morning of what I hope is to be my last weekend in Korea. Sam Poole is also awaiting orders, but his are for the US. It is strange that at the moment I have no wish for those orders. I just want to get to Japan, call you and say, "OK my love—on your way!"

I feel much better this morning. Was really tired last night and had the shots on top of that. Speaking of shots, I was wrong about yellow fever. They are no longer giving it to people coming to the Far East. But if you did get it, it will cause no harm.

You wrote of going over my letters and seeing the change in ideas and style. You ask do I mind your analyzing and you know the answer. We have been able to live together, even though so far apart only because we expressed in words everything that was us. We have changed, I am sure, though I am certain I would not be aware of it unless I had done what you have done, gone back over our first letters. Just think, my love, of us someday going over our letters together and remembering these days. I don't want to forget, to blot them out of my mind. These days apart from you here in Korea have made me realize more than ever the value of the more basic things, the importance of living life to the fullest, truthfully. How little the trivialities of our modern life mean. I love you. I am happy with that love and fulfilled by your love for me. My life is now us. To live together, working, creating—I pray helping our children learn the value of being themselves. I do not write well enough to put it all down. A life together is our only hope. Riches and finery and luxury are not part of that.

We will talk of all this. Your husband,   Melvin

SATURDAY, APRIL 11, 1953, 1:00 A.M.

My darling—

Today—preparing for this evening's crowd and naps and nose drops. Thirty-one people for a sit-down dinner! For me. They all brought little gifts—a kerchief, hosiery case, hankies, book, traveling iron, compact, movie film, traveling clock (we've got dozens) and a beautiful white cashmere sweater from the folks.

Now I shall stuff my nose with vaseline and try to sleep. Goodnight my sweet,   Dorothy

SATURDAY [SUNDAY], APRIL 12, 1953, 1:15 A.M.

My beloved—

I have re-read the long typed letters about Japan several times. So the Japanese women were no bargains! So you think your woman is a bargain! I think I'm a pretty expensive babe myself. I may not buy $40 hats, but I spend almost as much money on dance classes as you spend on cameras! It may be weeks before you receive this letter, but I must write, as I have for so many nights. I am so full of love for you.

Goodnight my darling. It is difficult to sleep. It is difficult to sit still. It is difficult to do ANYTHING but wait.   Dorothy

SUNDAY, APRIL 12, 1953, 5:00 P.M.

My Love—

This is it—PCS, Melvin Horwitz 01874640-Rel Assn 47 MASH to 8042 AU APO 613 Camp Drake for reassignment. Air Travel authorized. Oh boy. I was called on the phone and told that they were in. I let out a whoop and rushed over to headquarters to see for myself—and there they were. I should be able to leave tomorrow afternoon or the latest, Tues A.M. Oh my love it can't be true, but it is. By Wed or Thurs I'll be talking to you.

I've been waiting so long to write this letter and now here it is. I love you Dorothy. Here are my arms, soon to enfold you. Goodnight my darling   Melvin

MONDAY, APRIL 13, 1953, 11:45 P.M.

My beloved—

Today I went to work with Mom, not for the $5 but to keep from wandering around the house like a mad gazelle. I decided to stay away from dance until tomorrow because of my cold which is much better. While at the office I made some calls: 1) The Dispensary won't have any typhoid serum until Wednesday. 2) Public Health Svce. gives yellow fever inoc. and advised that I NOT take it. It is only necessary when going to and from or passing thru South America, Africa, India, and the tropics. If you feel strongly about it, my love, I shall get it when I get to Japan. 3) When I get my typhoid, I'll also get a chest X-Ray. 4) Japanese visa: I need plane ticket (new rule: one way) to get it and it can be obtained in one or 2 days.

Went to the Alvin Theatre to return dance tickets for Thurs. nite. I don't want to miss Japanese class. When I came home there were two letters from you which matched my manic state. Spent ½ hr. on the phone getting information about air trip to Japan:

Pan American: New York, San Francisco, Honolulu, Wake, Tokyo— 41 hrs. Northwestern: New York, Detroit, Minneapolis, Seattle, Anchorage, Tokyo—32 hrs. Amt: same.

Wrote to Albany asking them to return my Certificate. I want to take it with me.

Just helped Mom with Spanish hw. And now to bed, if I can sleep. Goodnight my love. It can't be too soon. Open your arms. Hear I come!   Dorothy

MONDAY, APRIL 13, 1953, 11:30 P.M.

My Love,

This is my last letter from Korea. I am now sitting at the airstrip in Seoul waiting for the plane which will carry me to Japan and to you.

After supper and rounds I came back to the tent and finished packing, everything but my camera equipment and toilet articles, for which I was sure I would need a 2-ton truck to haul. I wanted to be all ready to go, since the boys were giving me a farewell party and I didn't want to have anything left to do that evening. It was a good thing. Before we could do anything we heard the air raid siren, so off went the lights like so many times before. We sat in the darkness talking and quite unconcerned until we heard an explosion in the next valley. Then your husband could not be seen. He had his steel helmet on and was in the bunker before you could say Jack Robinson. That is all we heard. We knew nothing about it until the next morning. The alert lasted 30 min. Apparently an enemy plane dropped a few light bombs attempting to knock out the airstrip and a bridge. Now there is more anti-aircraft around than you can imagine.

With that over, we started a party, eating shrimp, anchovies, pate de fois gras with truffles, salami, drinking Manhattans, martinis, sparkling burgundy, and champagne. And they really poured the champagne. I had gotten 3 bottles to start the party, then every so often someone would go out and get another one. At about 3 A.M. I finally got to bed, very woozy and still disbelieving that this party was for me. I had been to so many for other people.

At 8:30 I had the switchboard awaken me so I could go around to clear the post. Laundry, library, mail room, tailor, club account, supply. All had to initial a sheet. Picked up my orders, papers, and records. Even then as I looked at the orders it didn't register. At lunch met some civilians from Walt Disney's studio who were going around the hospitals drawing cartoons and caricatures for the patients as well as for the EM staff. I said good-bye to everyone, shook hands, sent off a package to myself in Japan (through the replacement depot at Camp Drake—it should catch up with me some day) and got into the jeep with my duffle bag, handbag, and camera case. I had made the trip to the airstrip and Seoul so many times. It still was unreal, the same sort of unreality as when I arrived last July. I picked up my pay record across from the airstrip and boarded the plane.

This was the roughest trip I've ever had. The plane bounced all over and I kept thinking, this is my last trip and by God I don't want anything to happen. You can imagine, my love. We arrived in Seoul at 4:30.

My last night in Korea. It was very strange, difficult to describe feelings as I looked across the dark valley at the hills that are so familiar to me. I was glad to be leaving. Yet the feeling was more one of relief. The first prisoner exchange has been signed. Peace is imminent. I hope that we shall not have to live with the shadow of war over us ever again. This will not really be possible, I fear, but I hope for it. I have had my taste of war and the uncertainty and horror of not knowing what tomorrow will bring. The despair and ache of being apart. I love you my darling. Now to snooze for a few hrs more, then to board a plane and be on my way. I could fly myself I am so excited.

Sleep well. Dream well, my love. I shan't let you sleep very much when I have you next to me.   Melvin

TUESDAY, APRIL 14, 1953, 11:45 P.M.

My darling—

Since the mail came this morning, I have been in a whirl. You are definitely leaving on the 15th. You will call me and let me know when. I read all that business about San Francisco and finally calmed down to make sense of it. I think it is a good idea to try for govt. shipment, but if there is too much delay then off I shall fly. I called the airlines and they need 24–48 hrs. notice to cancel and refund. The guy who answered the phone asked me if I liked rice and wished me an enjoyable stay in Japan—very un-commercially. All the world loves a lover!

Got rid of tonight's Martha Graham tickets, in case you called. Called Crossworld Air Cargo, Post Office, Railway Express to find about shipping your things. Air Cargo is 4–5 days and cheapest—2.25 per lb.

Mom received your letter today and we both cried. But it made her happy. Because it is this time of year and I am leaving soon, I must continually remind myself to be patient—I don't always do a good job. Tonight she said that you know her better than I do. It was good to hear her say that, knowing that she feels close to you.

How can I wait, when I have been ready for so long.   Dorothy

———————

Mel scribbled a brief note to me on April 16. It was marked "return to sender."

I continued to write every day until April 21, the day I left for Tokyo on Pan American Airways.

AFTERWORD

He was there to meet me. Squinting up into the sun, smiling, army cap at a jaunty angle, he wore a khaki dress uniform. As always, my tears gushed unbidden. Even now, that photo-image of him at the Tokyo airport, opening his arms to enfold me, can be called up in the album of my mind.

The war was almost over, but there was still enough damage left to keep Mel busy at the Hakata Army Hospital in Fukuoka. I taught English conversation to Japanese students and professors at Kyushu University and Remedial Reading to GI's in army classrooms. Turning down the offer of housing on the base, we chose to live on our own in a Japanese residence in town—to become part of our neighborhood, to get to know the neighbors. We learned enough Japanese to converse and to bargain downtown. Later, when Mel had a two-week leave, we flew to Hong Kong and Bangkok.

It was a romantic year, an ideal time in our marriage to be thrust into the heart of an alien culture. As lovers, detached by distance from home and by nationality overseas, we had the gift of privacy. As nascent Japanophiles, we reached out to make friends and to explore a new country. The Japanese we met welcomed our open curiosity and youthful enthusiasm. A few have remained close friends.

Of course it's all recorded. On a dusty shelf in the storage room of our house in Connecticut, there's a bulging cardboard box of letters from Fukuoka. From April 1953 through March 1954, we wrote to our folks. We asked that they save our letters for us—"our journal." Maybe one day when we have time we'll read them, or our children will put them in a pile marked: to be read. Now, it is our children's envelopes that arrive, sometimes with postmarks we can't pronounce or stamps we've never seen—

from Ruapehu or Haifa, Vanuatu or Sydney, Pendeli or Enumclaw. Foreign and domestic, exotic or familiar, the trails of their curricula vitae encircle the globe. Continuing the family ritual, they send us the narration and description of their lives. When my mom died, I found among her belongings all the letters and cards she had ever received from her grandchildren. I returned them to senders.

In late March 1954, Mel's assignment was over. It was time to come home. We left Japan for California in a troop transport ship. The long no-frills cruise gave us a chance to reflect. We made plans—at least for the immediate future. When we arrived in New York, his folks were waiting, along with my mother and the man she would marry the following year.

Mel finished his surgical residency at Columbia–Presbyterian Medical Center in New York City, where our first two children were born. I completed my master's degree in French at Columbia, just in time for the move to a small town in Connecticut where we raised four strong, independent children. For thirty years, Mel practiced general surgery, also working as a research consultant in cancer immunology at the University of Connecticut. Seeking a new challenge, he earned a degree at Yale Law School, passed the Connecticut Bar, and now acts as a consultant in health law and policy. I taught for twenty years at a community college, intermittently doing graduate work in French and history at the University of Connecticut. Several years ago I retired to devote more time to writing. Dancing has remained my most compelling avocation.

My mother and Mel's parents lived into their nineties. Our brothers both got M.D. degrees. Bert practices orthopedic surgery and Gerry is Associate Dean of a medical school.

During the first years of our marriage, when I was deferring to Mel in the interests of harmony, we thought we had invented togetherness. Later, we discovered that not only did we need less of it, but that functioning independently helped to ease the tensions in this union of two strong-minded individuals. Mel learned sooner than I that he required intervals of solitude. The women's movement helped validate my own need for a measure of autonomy.

Did we live happily ever after? We've been lucky. Except for the aches and pains that accompany aging and the realization of the imperfectability of marriage that accompanies maturing, we've enjoyed the whole bloomin' process. We always did and still do talk to each other about deep and sundry miscellany. We laugh a lot—more and more at ourselves. We hang out with friends, old and new. We hike, play tennis, read paragraphs aloud, play chess, and edit each other's writing. In recent years, travel has meant chasing our itinerant children and grandchildren, which suits us just fine.

What role did the letters play in shaping our marriage? Did they free up and expand our modes of communication? Was the tell-all medium new to our relationship? I suspect that they forged a process of verbal intimacy and rapport that was already in place when Mel left. No dramatic transformation took place during this letter-writing stint. Even in the early stages of courtship, our relationship had been predicated on candor. Perhaps that was one of our mutual attractions. What prodded us into new levels of awareness was not the writing of the letters in and of itself, but rather the effect of being trapped in a war that we didn't believe in. Although the letters unconsciously became a means of self-discovery, we were concerned only with the particular, not the universal. Our knowledge of what was going on was limited to what we read in the newspapers. Our understanding of why the North Korean and the Chinese enemy were dying was defined by editorials written by liberal editors who themselves were struggling to make sense of this "police action." The letters were but reflections of our painful attempt to find a substitute for proximity. There was no epiphany along the way, but they did provide the continuity we sought in temporarily establishing separate lives.

E. B. White wrote, "Ideally, a book of letters should be published posthumously." Since we might still be around by the time this book goes to press, we had to make a conscious decision to publish without embarrassment or fear of libel. Some name changes took care of the latter and the book's happy ending took care of the former. We were not strangers when we met again after our separation. And we're still getting to know each other, even after forty-five years of marriage.

What I have left out is not with the intent of hiding any profound truths. I didn't have to sweep my brain for memories, wondering if I'd find some hard crumbs in the dark corners of my mind. All I had to do was copy what was there and cut, cut, cut—to maintain authenticity, to keep the reader interested, and to satisfy the publisher. Now I ask if enough content remains for the principals to emerge as real human beings. Let the reader decide.

Although the Korean tragedy confirmed our anti-war bias, it did not turn us into pacifists. We were too close to the just causes of World War

II for that to happen. But the memory of those who suffered and died, having reluctantly participated in the Korean disaster, remains with us. We don't want to forget. In this world without peace, the Korean "police action," our war, was yet one more war that shouldn't have happened.

POSTSCRIPT

Dear Aaron,

Good to hear from you as always and that you are back to work for a while before you leave, unless Mt. Ruapehu explodes again. I'm sure you have an even harder time than we do realizing that your sojourn in New Zealand is almost over. To me, it seems that you just left and also that you have been away for a long time. Perception is often a matter of mindset. We view an event, thought, or memory through the prism of being at a precise instant in time, and that instant is always changing. I can picture you now in my mind's eye with a volcano smoldering out your window, putting on your skis and going off to work. From what you've written, we'll have a good slide show when you return to New England at Thanksgiving.

Mom is in her study putting the finishing touches on the manuscript. She has spent a lot of time and energy on this book. Now she looks forward to pursuing other projects that have been on her desk for a long time. If her tennis elbow subsides, we can start playing again. Perhaps the long hours at the computer have prevented the tendon and muscle injury from healing completely.

Reading the letters I wrote is a humbling experience. I wonder who this person was. Not nearly as perceptive or analytical as I would have liked—self-righteous, hyper-critical, self-involved. Why? I realize now that I was frightened and apprehensive. I was young and had little travel experience. I was facing professional demands early in my career in a wartime environment. I am a devout coward when it comes to guns and bullets. A fearful memory of basic training, when I had to crawl on my belly for 50 yards (it seemed like miles) under machine gun fire, with tracers overhead, has stayed with me to this day, even though the machine guns were fixed in cement bases. The country was strange, the people different. My image of the Far East was based on early Alan Ladd movies where terrorists lurked in dark shadowed alleys. On the way to Korea, during our unit's brief stopover in Japan, we were allowed out for an evening to explore Yokohama. I'm sure, that night, my pulse rate was at the upper limits of tolerance. Months later, on leave from Korea, I returned to Japan for a week. The ominous streets had been transformed into a safe, comfortable, welcoming environment with friendly, helpful people in abundance. During those first months, my critical posture was probably a defense against insecurity. However, as time went on, I accumulated experience and gained confidence. My criticism of others became more realistic, less self-protective.

As a newlywed, I was separated from your Mom, my beautiful, vital young wife whom I loved with all my being (and 44 years later still do). I was angered by our imposed separation. Our only outlet was to pour out our hearts to each other. My prose was awful. My punctuation consisted of dashes, dots, spaces, and lots of exclamation points! All that combined with my illegible handwriting made the letters a whitewater stream of consciousness. Mom used to spend hours deciphering them.

I do think that the editing of these letters has been a worthwhile undertaking. Readers tend to gloss over accounts of lives and events expressed statistically. The personal has greater impact. One of my law school professors, Guido Calabrese (later Dean), illustrated this concept with examples of a nation being mesmerized when a fool drowns trying to row across the Atlantic, or when a whale is trapped in an estuary, while that same public ignores the 500 weekly deaths from auto accidents or coal mine disasters resulting from unsafe conditions. Perhaps individuals who read our personal story will be reminded of those who never returned or those who were irreparably damaged in this tragic war.

Professionally my experience at the MASH and at the Army hospital in Japan was invaluable. I learned how to deal with the unexpected and to manage complicated problems quickly and efficiently. When Dr. Frank Lahey was asked why he didn't perspire during prolonged procedures, he answered, "I used to, until I learned my anatomy." Even though I knew my anatomy, I sweated plenty. Working at the MASH meant dealing with, as I wrote in a letter, "anatomy knocked to pieces."

Looking back, I've survived the usual and unusual trials and tribulations of living this long. I have a wonderful family, good friends, and relatively good health. My surgical practice was satisfying and my current work is challenging. Life has been good to me, to us.

We have an exceptionally busy week coming up. Tonight we go to Laurie's and Ronnie's for dinner in their beautiful Succah, tomorrow to Trinity College to see "Belle de Jour," Thursday Mom has her book club. I'll stay home and try to clean up my study—your room—or you'll have to sleep on file boxes. Friday we go to a concert at UConn, Sat to NY for theatre with Paul and Bernice Merson. In between I have to get both cars into the shop. A recall. How did we ever get anything done before our present, more flexible schedule? My work with the Institutional Review Board keeps me stimulated and allows time for consulting and writing.

Laurie and Ronnie are busy seeing patients and writing briefs. Rose is being "chased by a monster" at her new nursery school. Laurie had a tag sale that netted her $53. Wendy and Tim have started their fall semester of teaching and are cleaning up their garden. Abbie has some new deals going and John loves kindergarten. He AND Abbie enjoy their karate classes. They all miss you and look forward to seeing you in November.

WARNING. I plan to take pictures of all of you individually and collectively. We have an empty space on the kitchen wall that we want to cover with your mug shots. If you don't cooperate, I'll disinherit you. So be prepared.

Enjoy the rest of your stay in NZ. I know you'll have fun in Fiji (sounds like a movie title) and the warm weather will be a welcome break before you head into winter on Mt. Rainier. Be well. Call. We love to hear your voice.

Love from both of us.   Dad

ABBREVIATIONS

3100	General Medical Officer
C3150	General Surgeon
AMA	American Medical Association
APO	Army Post Office
AU	Army Unit
BOQ	Bachelor Officers' Quarters
CID	Counter-Intelligence Division
CID	Criminal Investigation Department
Cl Co	Clearing Company
CO	Commanding Officer
EM	Enlisted Man
ENT	Ear, Nose, and Throat
ER	Emergency Room
EUSAK	Eighth United States Army Korea
Evac	Evacuation
FECOM	Far East Command
FEPC	Fair Employment Practices Committee
GP	General Practitioner
Hq	Headquarters
KSC	Korean Service Corps
MASH	Mobile Army Surgical Hospital
Med Bn	Medical Battalion
MLR	Main Line of Resistance
MP	Military Police
MPC	Military Payment Certificates
OD	On Duty

OR	Operating Room
PCS	Permanent Change of Station
PM	Postmaster
POW	Prisoner of War
PX	Post Exchange
R&R	Rest & Recreation/Rest & Recuperation
RA	Regular Army
Rel Assn	Relocation Assignment
ROK	Republic of Korea
ROTC	Reserve Officers Training Corps
SIW	Self-Inflicted Wound
USO	United Services Organization
VD	Venereal Disease

ACKNOWLEDGMENTS

Martin Abramson first suggested that the letters would make good reading, and Joyce Levy reminded me that they were part of history. Early encouragement for the proposal came from Ann Godoff, Jackie Farber, Ethel Longstreet, and Ellie Munro. Janet Warren and Jean Toddie provided motivation and good counsel all along the way. Arlene Norman, Helen Nix, Gladys Nussenbaum, and my book group furnished affectionate support. Thank you all for your continuing friendship. And with fond memories of the late E. J. Kahn, who, endorsing the project, said, "Maybe Mel, you, and I are among the few who believe the Korean War actually happened."

For their helpful advice, thanks to historians Thomas Paterson and Gary Clifford of the University of Connecticut, John Sutherland and Mary Ann Handley of Manchester Community College, and Jack Chadfield of Trinity College in Hartford. For Korean War Stats, I am indebted to Mary Haynes of the Center for Military History, John Slonaker and Louise Arnold of the Institute of Military History, Don Smith of the Center for Electronic Records of the National Archives, and Bob Hansen of the Korean War Memorial Advisory Board. The library staffs of the Mary Cheney Library of Manchester, the University of Connecticut, the Hartford Public Library, and Manchester Community College assisted me in my initial research.

Special thanks to my upbeat editor, Karen Hewitt, whose patience, wit, and enthusiasm kept the process moving. Above all I am grateful to my children, Abbie, Laurie, Wendy, and Aaron, suitably irreverent and gently reassuring, whose candid criticism was and is always welcome. And to Dear Mel, who continues to be my beloved correspondent and computer guru.